# The Handbook of
# Equity
# Style
# Management

# The Handbook of
# Equity
# Style
# Management

## Edited By
## T. DANIEL COGGIN
## And
## FRANK J. FABOZZI, CFA

Published by Frank J. Fabozzi Associates

Designer and Managing Editor: Stephen Arbour
Consulting Editor: Patricia Peat
Distribution Manager: Scott Chambers Riether

© 1995 BY FRANK J. FABOZZI ASSOCIATES

NEW HOPE, PENNSYLVANIA

This publication is designed to provide accurate and authoritative information in regard to the subject matter covered. It is sold with the understanding that the publisher is not engaged in rendering legal, accounting, investment advisory, or other professional services.

ISBN 1-883249-05-8

Printed in the United States of America.
1 2 3 4 5 6 7 8 9 0

*T. Daniel Coggin*

———

*To my wife Joan*

————————

*Frank J. Fabozzi*

———

*To the families
of the contributors
to this book*

# TABLE OF CONTENTS

# PREFACE

This is the first book to explicitly and singularly focus on the topic of equity style management. The time for such a book has clearly arrived. The topic of equity style management is not new to investment practitioners. Discussions of large capitalization "value" stocks versus small capitalization "growth" stocks have been taking place in investment meetings for decades. Equity style indexes were first introduced by The Frank Russell Company and Wilshire Associates in 1987, and by S&P/BARRA in 1992.

Starting with the work of Nobel Laureate William Sharpe in 1988, the world of investment management was introduced to a new methodology for the *systematic* assessment of equity style.[*] This methodology has now become known as "return-based" equity style assessment. Using a statistical methodology called correlation analysis, portfolios are characterized into equity style categories based on how well they correlate with a set of predefined equity style indexes. This set includes "value," "growth," "small cap," "medium cap," "foreign stocks," and several other indexes.

Once return-based style assessment was defined, those who prefer the alternative methodology called "portfolio-based" equity style assessment began to more explicitly define their approach. Portfolio-based style assessment is based on and consistent with what practitioners have been doing for years. That is, portfolio-based style assessment focuses on *specific characteristics of the equity portfolio* to arrive at a verdict as to the equity style of that portfolio. These characteristics include such individual style indicators as beta, P/E, P/Book, dividend yield, earnings growth rate, and market capitalization.

The growth and expansion of equity style management now includes such topics as equity style betas, equity style benchmark portfolios, equity completion funds, tactical style management and foreign equity style management. As a consequence, equity style management is much too broad to be adequately covered by one writer. This book covers the major topics in this field with contributions from leading experts in each subfield.

---

[*] William F. Sharpe, "Determining a Fund's Effective Asset Mix," *Investment Management Review* (November/December 1988), pp. 59-69. See also his "Asset Allocation: Management Style and Performance Measurement," *Journal of Portfolio Management* (Winter 1992), pp. 7-19.

# OVERVIEW OF THE BOOK

Chapter 1 by Christopherson and Williams sets the stage by defining equity style management and explaining why it matters (or should matter) to investors. Chapter 2 by Brown and Mott provides an exhaustive overview of the major equity style indexes, including the S&P/BARRA, the Russell, the Wilshire, and the Prudential Securities indexes.

Building on the work of William Sharpe, Chapter 3 by Hardy discusses and demonstrates the use of return-based style analysis. Chapter 4 by Christopherson and Trittin discusses and illustrates the use of portfolio-based style analysis.

Chapter 5 by Roll shows that three major equity style categories (size, E/P, and Book/Market) have different risk profiles, but that the CAPM and APT risk models cannot fully explain differential performance among the styles. Chapter 6 by Dorian and Arnott discusses a model for forecasting differential performance between equity styles. Chapter 7 by Quinton presents the notion of value-growth betas as a means of clarifying differential equity performance on the value-growth dimension. Chapter 8 by Campisano and Nederlof describes and discusses the role of the completion fund as a tool in the style management of equity pension funds.

Chapter 9 by Bagnoli presents evidence on the style dimension in foreign (non-U.S.) stocks. Chapter 10 by Leinweber, Krider, and Swank discusses the genetic algorithm as a promising model for the style management of international equity portfolios.

Chapter 11 by Compton and Chapter 12 by Allen discuss equity style management from the plan sponsor perspective. Chapter 13 by Trzcinka discusses equity style management from the perspective of academic finance.

# ACKNOWLEDGEMENTS

We thank Stephen Arbour and Scott Riether for cheerful, tireless and very thorough production assistance. We thank Patricia Peat for expert editing. Finally, we congratulate ourselves for having the idea to produce this book and for getting the best people in the field to contribute to it.

*T. Daniel Coggin*
*Frank J. Fabozzi*

*April 1995*

# ABOUT THE EDITORS

*T. Daniel Coggin* is President of T. Daniel Coggin Associates, an investment advisory and consulting firm based in Charlotte, North Carolina. Dr. Coggin has 17 years of experience in investment analysis and portfolio management. Before forming T. Daniel Coggin Associates, he was Director of Research at the Virginia Retirement System. Dr. Coggin has authored and coauthored a number of articles and book chapters on quantitative investment management, and serves on the editorial boards of several journals including the *Journal of Portfolio Management*. He has a Ph. D. in political economy from Michigan State University.

*Frank J. Fabozzi* is an Adjunct Professor of Finance at Yale University's School of Management and the editor of the *Journal of Portfolio Management*. From 1986 to 1992, he was a full-time professor of finance at MIT's Sloan School of Management. He is on the board of directors of the BlackRock complex of closed-end funds and the board of directors of the family of open-end funds sponsored by The Guardian Life. Dr. Fabozzi is a Chartered Financial Analyst and Certified Public Accountant who has authored and edited many books on investment management.

# LIST OF CONTRIBUTORS

Garry M. Allen  Virtus Capital Management

Robert D. Arnott  First Quadrant

Paul Bagnoli  Sanford C. Bernstein & Company

Melissa R. Brown  Prudential Securities

Christopher J. Campisano  Ameritech

Jon A. Christopherson  Frank Russell Company

Mary Ida Compton  The Common Fund

John L. Dorian  First Quadrant

Steve Hardy  Zephyr Associates

David Krider  First Quadrant

David J. Leinweber  First Quadrant

Claudia E. Mott  Prudential Securities

Maarten L. Nederlof  TSA Capital Management

Keith Quinton  Falconwood Securities

Richard Roll  University of California, Los Angeles
Roll &Ross Asset Management

Peter Swank  First Quadrant

Dennis J. Trittin  Frank Russell Company

Charles Trzcinka  State University of New York at Buffalo

C. Nola Williams  Frank Russell Company

# LIST OF ADVERTISERS

Acadian Asset Management, Inc.

BARRA

Boston International Advisors, Inc.

Paradigm Asset Management Co.

Virtus Capital Management, Inc.

# CHAPTER 1

## EQUITY STYLE: WHAT IT IS AND WHY IT MATTERS

*JON A. CHRISTOPHERSON, PH.D.*
*SENIOR RESEARCH ANALYST*
*FRANK RUSSELL COMPANY*

*C. NOLA WILLIAMS, CFA*
*SENIOR INVESTMENT STRATEGIST*
*FRANK RUSSELL COMPANY*

## INTRODUCTION

Today the concept of equity styles permeates the way investors think about the U.S. equity market and investment managers. What was once an arcane idea promoted by consultants and embraced only by their large corporate clients has expanded so that the popular press promotes it to the small investor. The public at large now has access to the same measurement tools as the large investor and is, like the large client, able to invest in style index mutual funds as an alternative to active management. Further, the concept of equity investment style has resulted in a veritable explosion of indexes designed to measure different segments of the equity market. No longer can a manager count on being successful by beating the broad market averages; the manager is highly likely to be accountable for exceeding the appropriate style proxy.

This introductory chapter covers a broad range of topics concerning equity styles, from basic style definitions to potential applications of style analysis. Our intent is to define the term "style," provide some historical perspective, discuss style-related tools, and apply the concept practically to asset deployment.

## DEFINING EQUITY STYLE

The notion of differing equity styles began in the 1970s as members of the investment industry began more actively gathering and analyzing data on market averages and investment managers (the advent of computerization doubtless did much to facilitate this effort). Although style descriptions weren't as well defined as they are today, analysts noted clusters of portfolios with similar characteristics and performance patterns. Groups of managers shared certain ideas about the best way to approach investing — the data were merely a manifestation of philosophical views about key determinants of stock price movements.

To see this point, consider two investors who are evaluating the same statistic from two opposing perspectives. They assess a stock's prospects using a ratio commonly applied in the industry, the price/earnings ratio. The "growth" investor is primarily concerned with the earnings component of the ratio. If the investor believes the company will deliver a particular future growth rate, and if the price component of the ratio remains constant, then the stock price will increase as earnings materialize, and the investor will be rewarded. The key risks for the growth investor are that the future growth does not occur as expected and that the P/E multiple declines for some unanticipated reason.

The "value" investor, on the other hand, is concerned primarily with the price component of the ratio and cares much less, if at all, about the future earnings growth of the company. For this stock to be of interest, the value investor must deem the P/E ratio "cheap" by some comparison. The value investor's assumption is that the ratio is too low (perhaps due to an overly pessimistic assessment of the company's future) and that the P/E multiple will revert to normal or market levels when others realize that prospects are not as bad as thought. If so, the stock price will rise. In this analysis, the investor is relying on movement in price, rather than earnings, to be the reward. The investor anticipates that the price/earnings multiple will rise, with little or no increase in the earnings portion of the ratio. The value investor's primary risks are that the stock's cheapness is misread, and that investor concerns about the company are indeed correct.

These two investors may assess the same stock at different points in its price and earnings pattern and from the opposing perspectives as shown in Exhibit 1. Often the value investor is the earlier buyer of a stock. If investor predictions are right, the price increases. This may be accompanied by earnings increases, although that is not the investor's primary motivation to buy the stock. As the price increases, the investor becomes uncomfortable with what seem to be expensive multiple levels and sells.

## Exhibit 1: Change in Price Versus Earnings

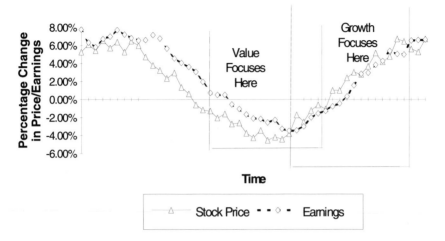

By now the growth investor has noticed the improving fundamentals of the company, which prompt interest in its future growth potential. The growth investor will purchase the same stock the value investor viewed as too expensive, and retain it for as long as the growth pattern emerges as anticipated.

Both investors are following logical courses, and empirical evidence can be found to support the profitability of both approaches. Their views of what is important to investing are diametrically opposed, however; and at the exact same time they reach opposite conclusions about the same stock. They buy and sell the same stock at different points along the price and earnings curves, both of which offer investment potential so long as the stock follows its typical pattern.

Note, however, in Exhibit 1 that there is a period of overlap when both the value and the growth investor may hold the same stock. An analysis of industry group performance also shows that stock groups often migrate from one group of investors to the other as equities experience a full business cycle.

To constitute a style, these investment philosophies must be held in common by a group of investors. While exact implementation of the shared philosophy may differ, the group agrees upon the factors that determine stock prices. If a philosophy is unique to a single manager, it is more appropriately called an investment "insight" that belongs to that firm alone. Such a firm would not rely on a certain factor, like growth or value, to add value and would have a set of portfolio characteristics different from a style group.

## Exhibit 2: Overview of Styles

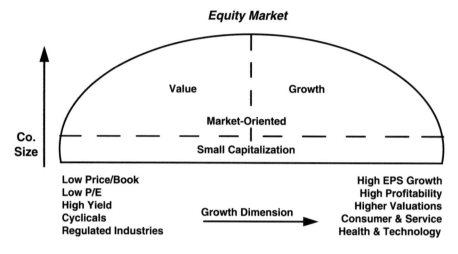

# TYPES OF EQUITY STYLES

While industry terminology for U.S. equity styles varies somewhat, the style descriptions developed by the consulting firm, Frank Russell Company, typify those used today. Russell identifies four broad style categories:

- · Value.
- · Growth.
- · Market-oriented.
- · Small-capitalization.

Exhibit 2 depicts how these styles relate to different segments of the equity market.

## Value

While value managers differ in how they define "value," they consider the stock's current price critical. Some organizations focus on companies with low absolute or relative P/E ratios (price in the numerator), while others stress issues with above-market yields (price in the denominator). Additional valuation measures these investors often consider are price-to-book value and price/sales ratios. A stock whose price has declined because of adverse investor sentiment (i.e., price behavior) may also attract some of these managers. Their portfolios frequently have historical growth and profitability characteristics well below market averages, contrasting sharply with the characteristics of growth managers.

The value style can be viewed as consisting of three substyles:

- Low P/E.
- Contrarian.
- Yield.

*Low P/E* managers focus on companies selling at low prices relative to current, normalized, or discounted future earnings. These companies typically fall into defensive, cyclical, or out-of-favor industries.

*Contrarian* managers emphasize companies selling at low valuations relative to their tangible book value. They often favor depressed cyclicals or firms with virtually no current earnings or dividend yield. Contrarian investors purchase stocks in hope that a cyclical rebound or company-specific earnings turnaround will result in substantial price appreciation. The quality of companies owned is frequently below average, largely because corporate earnings are depressed and financial leverage is relatively high.

*Yield* managers are the most conservative value managers, focusing on companies with above-average yields that are able to maintain or increase their dividend payments.

## Growth

Growth managers attempt to identify companies with above-average growth prospects. They frequently pay above-market multiples for the superior growth rate/profitability they anticipate. Other typical characteristics of growth managers include selection of higher-quality companies; an emphasis on consumer, service, health care, and technology stocks; and lighter weightings in deep cyclicals and defensive stocks. Regardless of the source of expected future growth or the level of the current multiple, growth not reflected in the current price is the key focus.

There tends to be two substyles of growth managers:

- Consistent growth.
- Earnings momentum.

*Consistent growth* managers emphasize high-quality, consistently growing companies. Because such businesses have very predictable earnings and extensive records of superior profitability, valuation multiples are frequently well above the market. These managers typically underweight cyclicals, as they tend to purchase market leaders in consumer-oriented industries.

*Earnings momentum* managers, by contrast, prefer companies with more volatile, above-average growth. They attempt to purchase companies in anticipation of earnings acceleration. They are usually willing to purchase companies in any economic sector, as long as the equities offer the best potential earnings growth.

## Market-Oriented

Market-oriented managers do not have a strong or persistent preference for the types of stocks emphasized in either value or growth portfolios; consequently, their portfolio characteristics are closer to market averages over a business cycle. A wide variety of managers with different philosophies fall into this category. Some may find a more "pure" growth or value orientation overly restrictive, and prefer selecting stocks wherever they might fall on the growth/value spectrum; others may purchase securities embodying both growth and value characteristics; or some wish to control nonmarket risk by reducing growth or value biases from their portfolio structures.

The managers in this group tend to follow four substyles:

- Value bias.
- Growth bias.
- Market-normal.
- Growth at a price.

*Value-biased* managers or *growth-biased* managers have portfolios with a tilt toward either value or growth. The tilts are not sufficiently distinct to put them in either the value or growth styles.

Many *market-normal* managers construct portfolios with growth and valuation characteristics that are similar to the broad market over time. Also included are those willing to make meaningful bets in growth or value stocks across time, but with no continued preference toward either.

*Growth at a price* managers seek companies with above-average growth prospects selling at moderate valuation multiples. Unlike managers in other market-oriented substyles, growth at a price managers generally do not offer wide diversification in portfolio structure or capitalization breadth.

## Small-Capitalization

The major distinguishing feature of small-capitalization managers is a focus on small companies. Many investors are drawn to this market segment because they find more opportunities to add value through research, since the companies are less widely followed by institutional investors.

Typical characteristics of small-capitalization portfolios include below-market dividend yields, above-market betas, high residual risk relative to broad market indexes, and a thin following by Wall Street analysts. Just as in the large- and medium-capitalization segments of the market, managers in the small-cap arena focus on different stock characteristics. As a result, the substyles within small-cap closely resemble the broad categories of large-cap styles:

- Value.
- Growth.
- Market-oriented.

Small-cap *value* managers seek underresearched small companies that sell at low valuations relative to assets, earnings, or revenues. They correspond to large-cap value managers.

Small-cap *growth* managers focus on less seasoned companies with above-average growth prospects. They primarily invest in the technology, health care, and consumer sectors, and their portfolios exhibit high growth and valuation characteristics.

Small-cap *market-oriented* managers focus on small companies that, over time, exhibit growth and value characteristics similar to the broad small-cap marketplace.

## EVIDENCE OF STYLES

### Portfolio Characteristics

Different management styles produce different portfolio characteristics and performance patterns. Exhibit 3 gives a profile of fundamental data for representative value, growth, market-oriented, and small cap managers. Also shown for comparison is the Russell 3000® Index, a broad market benchmark. Note that all statistics shown are dollar weighted, so that they accurately reflect where the managers are investing their funds.

*Capitalization Distribution.* The capitalization categories presented are determined by the rank ordering of companies within the Russell 3000 Index by market value, rather than by arbitrary capitalization cutoffs. The "large" category refers to the 50 largest companies in the market, the "medium/large" to companies 51 to 200, and so on. The Russell 3000 Index covers over 97% of the entire equity market.

As expected, the large-cap managers have the vast majority of their funds invested in the top 1,000 stocks in the market, which account for over 90% of the equity market's capitalization. The small-cap manager, by contrast, has the bulk of its money invested in the bottom 2,000 stocks in the market, which account for only 9% of the broad market.

## Exhibit 3: Comparison of Equity Manager Style Characteristics as of December 31, 1993

| Characteristic | Value | Growth | Market-Oriented | Small Cap | Russell 3000® Index |
|---|---|---|---|---|---|
| *Capitalization Distribution* | | | | | |
| % Large (Top 50 stocks) | 16.2 | 30.9 | 26.6 | 0.0 | 34.4 |
| % Medium/Large (51 to 200) | 25.4 | 25.0 | 38.9 | 1.4 | 26.3 |
| % Medium (201 to 500) | 22.9 | 37.3 | 21.0 | 3.7 | 19.3 |
| % Medium/Small (501 to 1,000) | 24.3 | 5.9 | 11.0 | 33.6 | 11.2 |
| % Small (1,000+) | 11.2 | 0.9 | 2.5 | 61.4 | 8.8 |
| *Valuation Characteristics* | | | | | |
| P/E on Normalized EPS | 12.9 | 22.8 | 17.3 | 28.6 | 18.1 |
| Price/Book | 1.43 | 5.32 | 2.54 | 3.44 | 2.60 |
| Dividend Yield | 2.70 | 0.62 | 2.09 | 0.35 | 2.51 |
| *Growth Characteristics* | | | | | |
| Long-Term Forecast I/B/E/S Growth | 9.8 | 20.6 | 12.9 | 19.3 | 11.9 |
| Return on Equity | 12.7 | 25.5 | 17.2 | 12.7 | 16.3 |
| Earnings Variability | 88.8 | 62.4 | 56.5 | 84.5 | 48.5 |
| *Economic Sectors* | | | | | |
| % Technology | 6.2 | 25.8 | 13.7 | 18.3 | 11.6 |
| % Health Care | 8.2 | 9.8 | 6.1 | 11.2 | 8.8 |
| % Consumer Discretionary | 7.2 | 29.2 | 19.9 | 23.4 | 14.2 |
| % Consumer Staples | 3.5 | 0.0 | 7.3 | 0.0 | 9.0 |
| % Integrated Oils | 4.9 | 0.0 | 6.5 | 1.0 | 5.3 |
| % Other Energy | 6.2 | 3.6 | 3.8 | 2.7 | 2.7 |
| % Materials and Processing | 21.8 | 6.5 | 7.6 | 4.7 | 8.3 |
| % Producer Durables | 2.3 | 0.0 | 6.1 | 9.9 | 4.2 |
| % Autos and Transportation | 1.5 | 3.4 | 3.5 | 4.4 | 5.8 |
| % Financial Services | 29.6 | 15.6 | 18.7 | 16.1 | 14.8 |
| % Utilities | 7.5 | 6.1 | 6.7 | 6.4 | 14.8 |
| % Sector Deviation | 24 | 25 | 12 | 19 | 0 |

*Valuation Characteristics.* Styles divide on valuation characteristics as expected according to our descriptions of investment philosophy. The value manager demonstrates below-market P/E and price-to-book ratios, and an above-market yield. The growth manager's characteristics are the opposite of those in the market. The market-oriented manager is close to market levels on these ratios. The small-cap manager shown here happens to have a growth substyle, so its valuation ratios are above-market; as discussed earlier, there is a full range of equity substyles in small-cap, so these characteristics are not necessarily representative of all small-cap managers.

*Growth Characteristics.* Earnings growth characteristics (here noted as those forecasted by institutional investment analysts and historical return on equity) conform to expectations, given the differing investment philosophies. The earnings variability statistic refers to the historical behavior of quarterly earnings relative to long-term trend-line growth; the higher the number, the greater the cyclicality of earnings. We noted earlier that the value manager tends to have higher earnings variability relative to other large-cap managers, and that is evident here; this usually occurs because of the value manager's greater willingness to purchase companies with cyclical earnings. The small-cap manager also has a higher earnings variability number, but in this case it is due to the less seasoned nature of the companies held, rather than due to ownership of cyclicals.

*Economic Sectors.* Economic sector exposure supports the other statistics shown in Exhibit 3 and confirms our sense of manager style. The value manager is overweighted relative to the Russell 3000 Index in financial services (typically a lower-multiple sector) and materials and processing, which in this case includes many manufacturing companies. The growth manager is overweighted in two traditional growth sectors, technology and consumer discretionary. The market-oriented manager has spread its bets the most among the sectors, as indicated by the sector deviation score. This score measures in aggregate the difference between the manager's overall sector allocations and those for the Russell 3000 Index; the higher the number, the more the manager's economic sector exposure differs from the market. Interestingly, the small-cap manager's bets relative to the broad market are smaller than those for all but the market-oriented manager. Often small-cap manager sector bets are larger since a small stock universe has different industry composition from a large-cap universe.

## Performance Patterns
Differing portfolio characteristics result in different performance patterns, particularly over short time horizons. Exhibit 4 shows performance for manager universes for the four different styles. In this example, we have plotted excess returns net of the Russell 3000 Index for rolling five-year periods that shift quarterly; the Russell 3000 Index is represented by the horizontal line.

Note the rotation of style performance over time, and the difference that style can make in shorter-term results. Growth lagged large-cap styles throughout much of the 1980s, but became the most dominant style in 1989, 1990, and 1991, ebbing somewhat thereafter. Value managers behaved in an inverse fashion from growth managers. Throughout all periods, the market-oriented group tracked market returns most closely, which would be expected, given their tighter factor bets relative to the market. The most prominent cycle is that of the small-cap style, which lagged significantly relative to large-cap styles in the 1980s, outperforming only recently.

## HISTORICAL PERSPECTIVE ON STYLES

Interestingly, while the style definitions we describe are commonly used today, they have changed fairly significantly over the years. Exhibit 5 shows the growth and percentage of change in manager style universes over a fourteen-year period.

- In the 1970s (not shown in this exhibit), the vast majority of large-cap institutional managers used a growth investment approach; value managers were far fewer in number, and the term was much less frequently used. Value became more universally recognized as a style as more investors embraced it during the 1980s. Exhibit 5 shows the large increase in the number of value and price bias investors during that decade.

- Small-cap investing did not emerge as a separate style until the early to mid-1980s; instead, a more nebulous notion of style prevailed that was more aggressive in its use of high-growth and smaller-cap stocks. The idea that small-cap investing could encompass a full spectrum of investment styles did not fully emerge until a few years ago, and in fact, many investors still equate small-cap with high-growth investing. Exhibit 5 shows the large increase in small-cap managers in the early 1990s.

More recently, a new "style" has emerged in the marketplace called "mid-cap" investing. The argument for this style is that medium-cap stocks have different performance patterns from their large- and small-cap counterparts.

While statistical analysis supports the case for medium-cap stocks as a differentiated segment of the *market*, it is debatable whether it is an actual investment *style* according to the criteria set forth in this chapter. Recall we have said: (1) managers adopt a style because they have a guiding philosophical belief that it will add value, and (2) many investors need to share a belief in order for adherence to it to constitute a style. Finally, a style should result in a clustering of factor tilts or portfolio characteristics between portfolios that share that style.

## Exhibit 4: Five-Year Rolling Excess Returns
### Growth/Market-Oriented/Small-Cap, and Value Accounts Universe Means Versus Russell 3000 Index
#### Periods Through December 31, 1993

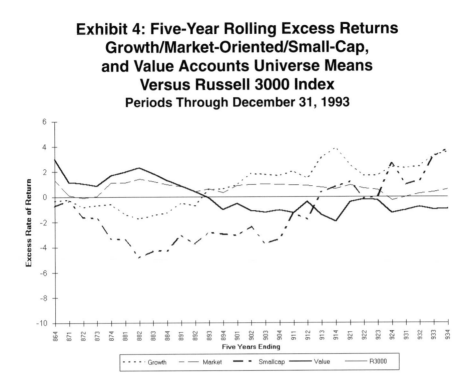

## Exhibit 5: Growth in U.S. Equity Manager Style Membership

| Style/Substyle | 1980 | 1988 | 1990 | 1993 | % Change 1980 to 1993 |
|---|---|---|---|---|---|
| Growth | 45 | 61 | 48 | 53 | 18% |
| | | | | | |
| Market-Oriented | | | | | |
| Earnings Bias | 13 | 16 | 15 | 18 | 38% |
| Market Normal and Growth at a Price | 58 | 50 | 51 | 42 | -28% |
| Price Bias | 5 | 17 | 17 | 18 | 260% |
| | | | | | |
| Value | 18 | 58 | 70 | 67 | 272% |
| | | | | | |
| Small-Cap | NA | 48 | 70 | 99 | NA |
| | | | | | |
| Growth + Earnings Bias | 58 | 77 | 63 | 71 | 22% |
| Value + Price Bias | 23 | 75 | 87 | 85 | 270% |

The mid-cap example is the first time that a style concept may have been introduced *before* broad adoption among investment managers. The differing behavior of medium-cap stocks in the equity market was noted in research and press articles, yet few investment managers had produced portfolios with a mid-cap profile. While they have typically owned a broad array of medium-cap securities (and many certainly have a medium-cap bias relative to cap-weighted benchmarks), managers had not adopted this concept separately as an investment philosophy.

A simple screen for mid-cap portfolios (defined as 70% exposure or more to stocks in the Russell Midcap Index) resulted in only 28 managers when this style started appearing in the press. This contrasted with 89 small-cap managers and 183 large-cap managers.

Whether mid-cap investing is truly a style or not, history and its appearance demonstrate that style concepts evolve over time, and undergo refinement in the process.

## CAPM, FACTOR MODELS, AND STYLE INDEXES

One might sensibly ask how styles and style indexes behave in light of capital asset pricing model (CAPM) theory and the assumption of efficient markets. If the equity market is efficient, then all stocks are correctly priced, given all available information. By extension, any choice of a market subset will yield a market return subject to variation due to sample size and the random character of specific risk. Yet this is true only if the CAPM determines the prices of assets, that is, if all stocks are driven by the same single factor, the market. As a consequence, all stocks will move up or down depending on their beta, and all other return will be specific return.

In such a world, no stock characteristic would lead to differential return. The implication of the one-factor CAPM is that stocks are not differentially sensitive to changes in interest rates or industrial production or any other economic variable. It is just this limitation of the CAPM that lead Barr Rosenberg and associates to develop their fundamental factor model and Stephen Ross to develop the APT factor model. Multifactor models accept stock differential sensitivity to forces that can change stock prices above and beyond the effect of the market.

A few points follow from this discussion. If styles exist, then certain other things must also exist. First, the returns to style portfolios and style indexes must be significantly different for the market. Second, the style portfolios and index style returns must be significantly different from each other. Third, style portfolios and style indexes should have on average different factor exposure patterns from the market as a whole and from each other.

The existence of universes of managers created according to style characteristics suggest that it is possible to create indexes based on the types of stocks the managers typically select. The virtues of an index are that (1) it is unbiased and not subject to the vagaries or fads of managers implicit in universes, and (2) it offers a passive alternative to purchasing managers when active management is not perceived as productive.

Chapter 2 will review the growing number of indexes that have been created over the years since Russell introduced its first indexes in 1988-1989. The variety and diversity of style index definitions are covered there, and we do not review all style indexes here. We do use the Russell 1000 Growth and Value Indexes to demonstrate the presence of style cycles that are somewhat independent from manager portfolios.

Briefly, the Russell Growth and Value indexes are created by rank ordering all stocks in the Russell 1000 by price/book. The capitalization-weighted median is computed. All stocks above the median breakpoint are placed in the Russell 1000 Growth Index, and all stock below the median are placed in the Russell 1000 Value Index. The choice of price/book is the result of extensive research.[1] While it is a simple rule, it is not simplistic and is supported by subsequent academic research[2].

The returns of these indexes begin in 1979. As shown in Exhibit 6, the spread in quarterly returns between the Russell 1000 Growth and Value indexes and the spread between the Russell 1000 and 2000 is often different from zero. Over the period, large-cap stocks outperformed small-cap stocks much of the time. The same can be said for value stocks, which outperformed growth stocks about twice as often.

Exhibit 7 shows the cumulative return differences from 1979 through first quarter 1994. Returns will look different depending on the beginning date, but over this period the advantage of value over growth has been about 2%. At the end of the fourth quarter of 1991, however, the cumulative return differential since first quarter 1979 was essentially zero. From second quarter 1989 through fourth quarter 1991, growth recovered all the return differential it had lost from 1983 through 1989.

[1] For a discussion of the research paths explored see Kelly Haughton and Jon A. Christopherson, "Equity Style Indexes: Tools for Better Performance Evaluation and Plan Management," *Russell White Paper* (Frank Russell Company, Tacoma WA 1989).

[2] Eugene F. Fama and Kenneth R. French. 1993. "Common Risk Factors in the Returns on Stocks and Bonds." *Journal of Financial Economics* (February 1993), pp. 3-56.

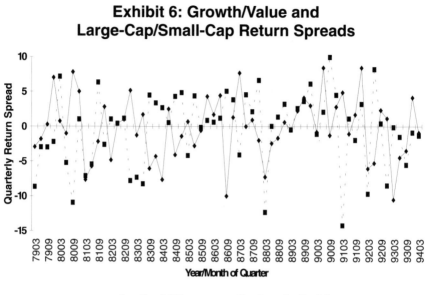

**Exhibit 6: Growth/Value and
Large-Cap/Small-Cap Return Spreads**

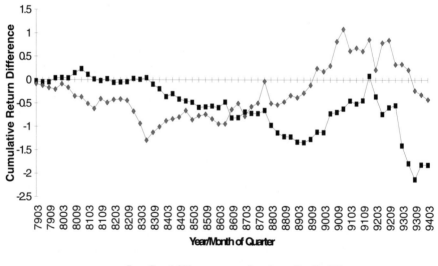

**Exhibit 7: Cumulative Growth/Value
and Large-Cap/Small-Cap Returns**

This raises the issue of whether we can expect any one style to underperform consistently for a long period of time. If one believes that value outperforms growth in the long run (as has been suggested by Fama and French and others), then the recovery of growth is an anomaly. If, on the other hand, one believes in efficient markets, then no market segment such as growth should be consistently underpriced. Hence, we would expect to see the type of recovery seen in the 1989 to 1991 period to happen again. Being able to time when growth becomes undervalued provides an obvious investment opportunity.[3] In any case, the index returns demonstrate that the style segments of the market behave differently from the market as a whole and do so consistently.

Style indexes are useful for performance evaluation of individual managers and combined manager mixes. In this sense, they can be used as normal portfolios.[4] If the style indexes accurately measure manager style, we would expect that the mean returns of universes of managers would behave more like the style indexes than broad market measures.

Exhibit 8 shows the regression statistics of the means of Russell Style Universe returns against the appropriate Russell style indexes. A benchmark that matches the universe of stocks from which the managers choose (i.e., its normal portfolio) will have a beta close to 1.0 (risk that is the same), an alpha close to zero (no abnormal excess return), and an $R^2$ close to 1.0 (a tight fit in return space).

For each style universe except market-oriented, the Russell style index has a beta closer to 1.0 than the alternative broad market benchmarks, the Russell 3000 and the S&P500.[5] The alphas of the style indexes are also closer to zero, except for market-oriented. For the market-oriented managers, the Russell 3000 and 1000 are all alternative broad market measures. The market-oriented betas are all less than 1.0, which is due to cash holdings.

---

[3] For a discussion of the valuation compressions between growth and value stocks that suggested in 1989 that growth was undervalued, see Jon A. Christopherson, Natalie LaBerge, and Dennis Trittin, "Has Growth Become Value?" *Russell Research Commentary* (Frank Russell Co.: Tacoma, WA, September 1989).

[4] For a discussion of normal portfolio construction and the role of style indexes in providing more precise manager benchmarks than broad market benchmarks, see Jon A. Christopherson, "Normal Portfolios and Their Construction." in *Portfolio and Investment Management,* Frank Fabozzi (ed.) (Probus Publishing: Chicago, 1989). pp. 381-397.

[5] While recognizing that the S&P 500 has serious drawbacks as a broad market benchmark because of its sector biases and capitalization biases, we include it in these analyses because of its familiarness.

**Exhibit 8: Benchmark Comparisons**
**Manager Universe Means versus Style Indexes**
**10 Years Ending December 31, 1993**

| | Beta | Quarterly Alpha | Annualized Standard Error | $R^2$ |
|---|---|---|---|---|
| **Growth:** | | | | |
| Versus Russell 1000® Growth Index | 0.992 | 0.368 | 3.210 | 0.970 |
| Versus S&P 500 | 1.136 | -0.043 | 5.208 | 0.922 |
| **Market-Oriented:** | | | | |
| Versus Russell 1000® Index | 0.962 | 0.158 | 1.308 | 0.993 |
| Versus Russell 3000® Index | 0.945 | 0.256 | 1.178 | 0.994 |
| Versus S&P 500 | 0.975 | 0.113 | 1.982 | 0.984 |
| **Value:** | | | | |
| Versus Russell 1000® Value Index | 0.969 | -0.110 | 2.474 | 0.970 |
| Versus S&P 500 | 0.882 | 0.145 | 3.690 | 0.934 |
| **Small Capitalization:** | | | | |
| Versus Russell 2500™ Index | 1.033 | 0.249 | 3.586 | 0.971 |
| Versus Russell 2000® Index | 0.924 | 0.769 | 4.462 | 0.955 |
| Versus S&P 500 | 1.211 | -0.418 | 8.958 | 0.819 |

We conclude from Exhibit 8 that using style indexes allows us to separate out style effects from manager universe group behavior, manager skill, and manager risk. Knowing the riskiness of small-capitalization versus the market as a whole, we can manage the plan to take this into account.

Style indexes by their nature also provide a passive alternative when hiring one or more active managers is problematical. Small pension plans may not have sufficient funds to hire a diversified set of active small-cap managers to manage their plan. Rather than hire one manager with a style bias, they may wish to simplify management and hire a passive fund manager or manage the money in-house. Alternatively, some large funds have so much money that to place all their funds they would have to hire an extremely large group of managers. Rather than deal with the headaches of managing all these managers, they often choose to index part of their money.

## STYLE MANAGEMENT: PRACTICAL APPLICATIONS

### Performance Measurement

It should be apparent what a difference taking style into account can make in evaluating manager results. Look at Manager X's performance compared to a broad market index like the S&P 500:

| | Annual Periods | | | | | Annualized Periods Ending December 31, 1990 | | |
|---|---|---|---|---|---|---|---|---|
| | 1986 | 1987 | 1988 | 1989 | 1990 | 3 Years | 4 Years | 5 years |
| Manager X | 11.2 | 1.4 | 24.6 | 16.4 | -11.5 | 8.7 | 6.8 | 7.6 |
| S&P 500 | 18.2 | 5.2 | 16.5 | 31.4 | -3.2 | 14.0 | 11.7 | 13.0 |

Given only this information, one would conclude that Manager X had not performed well. Yet when the manager's performance is compared to an appropriate benchmark (verified first by an analysis that the portfolio has small-capitalization characteristics), the conclusion regarding results changes markedly:

| | Annual Periods | | | | | Annualized Periods Ending December 31, 1990 | | |
|---|---|---|---|---|---|---|---|---|
| | 1986 | 1987 | 1988 | 1989 | 1990 | 3 Years | 4 Years | 5 years |
| Manager X | 11.2 | 1.4 | 24.6 | 16.4 | -11.5 | 8.7 | 6.8 | 7.6 |
| Russell 2000® | 5.7 | -8.8 | 24.9 | 16.2 | -19.5 | 5.3 | 1.6 | 2.4 |

Applying a benchmark that more closely embodies the stock universe in which the manager invests yields more information about manager skill.

One might ask (and many do) why comparisons that take investment style into account should be of such importance. The thinking is if investors cannot hire managers to outperform the broad market, then what is the point?

Over the very long term, managers should be able to beat the market regardless of style biases, or else they are not earning their fees. But in defining "long term," it is necessary to go beyond the typical five-year time horizon many investors choose. Style cycles can last, and have lasted, that long and longer.

One of the longest style cycles in recent years was the underperformance of small-capitalization stocks in the 1980s, which was shown in Exhibit 4. Small stocks grossly underperformed their large-cap counterparts for the better part of seven years, beginning in 1984 and ending in 1990 (there was one short-lived period of outperformance in 1988, but this quickly reversed). Managers who invested in that sector of the market were clearly swimming upstream.

In a much broader context, the cycle of underperformance in the 1980s is not unheard of. While this period is certainly at the higher end of the range for small-stock underperformance cycles, similarly long cycles have occurred before.

Exhibits 9 and 10 show long-term data for the Ibbotson-Sinquefield Small Stock Index versus the S&P 500 from 1926 to 1993. These data demonstrate how much longer-term one needs to think in evaluating performance.

## Exhibit 9: Performance of Small Stocks versus Large Stocks
### Ibbotson and Sinquefield Index Relative to the S&P Index
### Annual Rates of Return from 1926 to 1959

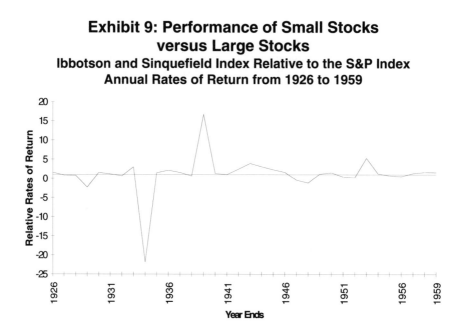

## Exhibit 10: Performance of Small Stocks versus Large Stocks
### Ibbotson and Sinquefield Index Relative to the S&P Index
### Annual Rates of Return from 1960 to 1993

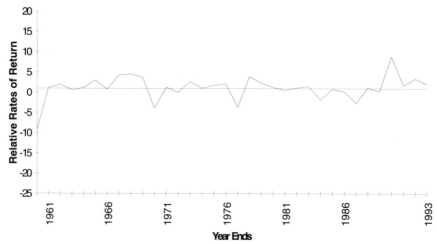

But the normal temptation is to use shorter time horizons. Also, it is unusual to find managers with sufficiently long track records where style effects would diminish in importance. This is why style analysis is so important. If investors select managers on the basis of historical performance versus a broad market benchmark, they may unknowingly hire a manager at a peak in performance that may be due solely to a style cycle. Conversely, they will be sorely tempted to fire a manager who has experienced underperformance solely because the manager's style category has lagged. These decisions can translate into a "buy high/sell low" pattern, which can be extremely damaging to performance. Of course, this analysis assumes that the managers being evaluated perform the way they do solely for style reasons and that other factors are not also at work.

## Achieving Target Equity Returns

The ramifications of style analysis go beyond merely selecting individual managers. Style orientation can play a critical role in the performance of an entire equity plan.

The first step in constructing a coherent equity strategy is to determine not only the investor's goals, but, more importantly, also how the investor defines risk. While this sounds like an obvious statement, this step is often overlooked. Most investors prefer to think of themselves as having long-term investment horizons and a fairly high tolerance for risk. But not many have examined equity performance patterns in detail and considered what their response would be to potentially long periods of underperformance due to style biases. As we noted above, style cycles may not fit the general notion that "long-term" is five years.

Risk is often also misdiagnosed. In the investment industry, risk is still often referred to as volatility of total return (i.e., standard deviation), when the investor really may be most concerned with a result that falls short of the overall equity market return (i.e., downside semivariance and/or probability of shortfall). Increasingly, the alternative investment is some passive instrument, so investor focus is appropriately on how an equity plan performs versus an index. For volatility reduction, the investor looks to other asset classes, with allocations according to long-term goals. Thus, investors may not rely on individual equity managers as the primary source of risk reduction, but instead, to deliver a better than equity market return.

Once an investor's risk tolerance has been defined, the second step is to diagnose the aggregate equity investments already held for potential structural biases versus the overall market. This step is important in determining whether there are *unintended* biases in overall structure. For example, an investor may have unknowingly built in a bias toward a certain capitalization segment of the market or a tilt toward growth or value. This may be particularly true if current manager selection has been made primarily on the basis of short-term historical performance without regard to style. Such a structure will subject the entire plan to underperformance from *unintended* style bets. An appropriate discussion for the investor in this case is whether these biases are appropriate for the risk tolerance level, and whether they should be modified.

Note these biases are separate from *intended* bets taken because of a conviction that they will pay off or a belief that the investor has hired the best possible managers regardless of style. But in either of these cases, presumably the investor knows the consequences of these choices and will not be alarmed at short-term underperformance because of this style structure.

Assuming investors have no preconceived ideas about style structure and are concerned with shorter-term risk, they can construct a style-neutral portfolio from managers with offsetting biases. The goal then becomes to produce outperformance from stock selection, rather than relying on a style bias to win over time. Style analysis plays a critical role in forming an accurate sense of manager portfolio structures and whether they indeed have diversifying performance patterns.

Regardless of the type of equity strategy selected, style analysis delivers, at a minimum, a key benefit in enhancing investor understanding of their investments. This should lead to better implementation of any change to an overall equity portfolio, as the reasons for the change and its potential performance impact will be better understood.

## BEYOND STYLE DIVERSIFICATION

A style-diversified approach is best for investors who do not spend much time studying the equity markets, have multiple parties to whom they must explain performance results, have shorter time horizons, or have low risk tolerance. But such a choice does not answer the question of whether one style is "best." All styles have their proponents, as anyone who has met investment managers will testify. But should any one style consistently perform better than the others over time?

The answer is "maybe." There are many studies that support the concept of value investing, and a recent article in particular provides some support for this approach.[6] Presented with such evidence, one feels compelled to consider it as "proof" that value and/or small

---

[6] Fama and French, "Common Risk Factors in the Returns on Stocks and Bonds," op. cit.

cap must be the best style. Whenever one is confronted with such data, however, several issues need to be settled in order to structure an equity strategy around it.

- What sort of portfolios result from the criteria used to define "value"? How would the investor involved react to their structure? If the style definition used results in concentrated economic sector exposure (e.g., a heavy tilt toward value sectors like financials or utilities), would the investor feel comfortable holding that portfolio through potentially significant short-term performance volatility?

- Does the performance derive from the factor being studied? Or are there other effects that need to be "disentangled" in order to determine that value is really what is driving the study results? Could some other effect be a factor?

- How many investors employ the approach today compared to the time the study was performed? The number of value investors has increased dramatically over the last decade, for instance, which may have increased efficiency in that market segment, making it more difficult to find mispriced assets. A similar trend has begun to emerge in the small-cap sector, although indications are that there is still far less institutional research available in that arena.

- Finally, why should history necessarily repeat itself? What is the relevance of the test period to the current market? While this type of analysis poses some risk of rationalizing whether markets are truly "different this time," some attention to the economic and market backdrop of the historical analysis is appropriate. Otherwise, there is a risk for assuming parallels exist where there are none.

Beyond obtaining the highest absolute return, risk adjustment can also influence the answer for investors for whom risk reduction is important. Over its history, the Russell 1000® Value Index has outperformed the other style indexes. Perhaps more importantly, it has superior risk characteristics relative to the other indexes. To those concerned with volatility of absolute returns (rather than performance deviations from the broad market), this risk adjustment is worth something. Even if value had underperformed the other styles, to some degree an investor might be willing to give up superior performance for a superior risk position.

In summary, even though there are no clear answers to the question of which style is best, the numbers alone point toward value as the superior style. These numbers, however, beg a host of qualitative considerations.

# CHAPTER 2

## UNDERSTANDING THE DIFFERENCES AND SIMILARITIES OF EQUITY STYLE INDEXES

*MELISSA R. BROWN, CFA*
*FIRST VICE PRESIDENT*
*DIRECTOR OF QUANTITATIVE RESEARCH*
*PRUDENTIAL SECURITIES INC.*

*CLAUDIA E. MOTT*
*FIRST VICE PRESIDENT*
*DIRECTOR OF SMALL-CAP RESEARCH*
*PRUDENTIAL SECURITIES INC.*

The authors gratefully acknowledge the help of Dan Coker,
Kevin Condon, Michele Eschert, Susan Levine, and Tara Stergis.

## INTRODUCTION

Over the past few years, the need to measure the performance of equity investment styles (such as growth and value) has preoccupied many consultants and plan sponsors. At the same time, fund managers have had to keep pace with these new benchmarks. It has become increasingly important to understand the characteristics of the various equity style benchmarks commonly used, especially since the style characteristics differ not only from growth to value, but also among indexes that are presumably benchmarks for the same style.

For investment managers being measured against a style benchmark, it is critical to know the characteristics of that index. If a portfolio's sector or size distribution is very different from the benchmark against which it is being measured, performance may be better or worse than the index largely because of those differences, rather than because of the manager's capability. A value manager, for instance, may be compared against a value index that is very heavily weighted in financial services and utility stocks. If those stocks have done well during the time period in which the manager is being measured, and the portfolio is underweighted relative to the style index (but perhaps not relative to the "market"), the short-fall may be attributable not to poor stock selection but rather to the manager's relative weighting decision. Many managers are reluctant to position portfolios with weightings that are as extreme as in many of the indexes.

Fund sponsors using style indexes either to judge outside managers or to make asset allocation decisions need to be aware of these characteristics as well. To be able to judge outside managers fairly, plan sponsors should know the biases of the respective style indexes and how their managers' portfolios deviate. This knowledge should lead to the choice of the most appropriate style benchmark for the manager. Thus, subsequent performance reviews need not dwell on benchmark misfit, but on stock selection success or failure.

Making asset allocation decisions on the basis of historical performance patterns of styles also assumes a knowledge and understanding of the various benchmarks. Different construction practices yield different characteristics. Hence what looks like a performance shift from growth to value may turn out to be a surge in performance by the interest rate-sensitive stocks. An asset allo-cation program built on incorrect assumptions may cause the plan to fall short of its investment targets.

In this chapter, we describe many of the style benchmarks developed to measure the performance of growth and value across the large-, mid-, and small-cap equity classes. We start with a simple explanation of the construction methodologies and then compare the resulting indexes. Our comparisons examine the indexes from two angles — how indexes differ across a single style, and how the two styles themselves differ.

## DATA

In all our discussions of size, we depend on similar sets of exhibits. Because exhibits are not referenced specifically, we describe their con-tents here. The characteristics described are as of December 31, 1993, except for the S&P MidCap indexes, which were launched in April 1994. The appendix to this chapter describes the methodology used to calculate fundamental characteristics.

## Descriptive Characteristics
Separate exhibits for each size category describe the number of companies, rebalancing frequency, exchange distribution, average size, and largest and smallest holdings.

## Size Distribution
Understanding how diverse or concentrated an index is can aid in understanding performance. Size distribution exhibits divide the companies into size categories by percentage of market capitalization. We take this approach because mean and median market-cap statistics do not enable a thorough understanding of the size distribution of companies within the indexes.

## Macroeconomic Sector Distribution
Differences in performance are frequently attributable to an index's macroeconomic sector weightings. These exhibits break down the indexes into twelve sectors according to percentage of market capitalization.

## Fundamental Characteristics
We calculate weighted-average values for trailing price/earnings ratio (both with and without negative earnings), forecast P/E using I/B/E/S, price-to-book, price-to-sales, debt-to-capital, and P/E to growth ratios, historical five-year earnings and sales growth, return on equity, return on assets, and average daily volume. We also include the average yield and the percentage of stocks that are dividend-paying.

## Performance Statistics
We look at the annual returns of the indexes for the ten years 1984-1993, and provide annualized averages for the entire period (if available) and the standard deviation of the returns.

## DEFINING THE MAJOR STYLE INDEXES

There are currently (at least) four services that provide widely used style indexes divided into size categories. Standard & Poor's (in conjunction with BARRA) publishes large-cap growth and value indexes based on the S&P Composite, and mid-cap indexes constructed from the MidCap 400. Frank Russell produces large-cap and small-cap indexes. Wilshire Associates and Prudential Securities divide their style worlds into three size categories: large-, mid-, and small-cap.

There are two schools of thought in the creation of these benchmarks: to sort by price/book, or to screen based on a set of criteria. S&P and Russell use the price/book sort method, while Wilshire and PSI use screening criteria to generate their portfolios. The method of construction, as well as the universe of companies from which the index is formed, can lead to substantial differences in the style index characteristics.

Although the indexes are constructed using different methodologies and universes, indexes of the same style tend to move in the same direction. The relative performance is generally very similar for the various pairs of indexes as well (Exhibits 1-3, 9-11, and 17-19).

It is worth mentioning some of the issues related to the different construction methodologies.

## The Value of Book Equity

The simplest and most popular method of discriminating between value and growth stocks is to divide stocks into two mutually exclusive portfolios based on price-to-book equity ratios. Recent deterioration of book equity as a result of the vagaries of accrual accounting, FAS (Financial Accounting Statement) 106 and 109, other accounting changes, and corporate restructurings calls into question the viability of this number as a way to distinguish between styles. Index providers try to place all companies on a comparable basis using various amortization methods to spread out some of the charges.

## Mutual Exclusivity

The indexes that rely on sorting a universe by price-to-book ratio require that every company from the main universe fall into one or the other style index. The argument can be made that some companies probably don't belong in either index. In addition, value is often in the eyes of the beholder, so some companies may fit both styles.

## Lack of Diversification

The standard style indexes tend to be overwhelmed by one or two sectors. Current value indexes, for example, tend to overweight financial services and utility sectors to a degree that is unacceptable to most managers. The three sections that detail the style indexes by economic sector will discuss this further.

## DESCRIPTION OF THE INDEXES

*The Prudential Securities* Large-Cap Growth and Value Indexes are selected by screening stocks in the top 15 percentiles of market capitalization in the Compustat universe (excluding REITs, ADRs, and Limited Partnerships) for companies with growth or value characteristics.

Mid-cap encompasses percentiles 8 through 25, and the small-cap style indexes include the 20th through 45th percentiles.

- *Growth* stocks have historical sales growth greater than 10%, rank in the top half of their size universe on the I/B/E/S forecast growth rate, and have low dividend payouts and debt-to-capital ratios.

- *Value* names rank in the bottom 50% of the universe on the basis of a normalized P/E (where the average of the five-year peak earnings and the current year forecast according to I/B/E/S is used for earnings). Additionally, companies that are dividend-paying must have sustainable dividend rates; that is, they have covered their four-quarter dividend for the past three years.

As of this writing, the *Russell Large-Cap Growth and Value Indexes* are constructed in the same way as the S&P/BARRA indexes, although the stocks are selected from the *Russell 1000* universe, which represents the largest 1,000 companies (based on total float, not total capitalization) in the *Russell 3000* Index. The Russell 3000 Index includes 3,000 large U.S. companies, which together represent 98% of the U.S. equity market by market capitalization. Only common stocks of U.S. companies are included in the index; in the case of multiple classes of stock, generally only one is allowed. Combined, the style indexes are all-inclusive and mutually exclusive. In June 1994, Russell launched growth and value indexes based on the Russell Midcap index using this construction methodology, but no data were available at the time of this writing.

The *Russell Small-Cap Style* indexes are created in a slightly different fashion from the large-cap indexes. First, the *Russell 2000* is sorted by book-to-price ratio, and quartiles are created on the basis of capitalization. The 25% of the universe with the lowest book-to-price is put in the growth portfolio, while the 25% with the highest book-to-price is classified as value. The middle 50% is placed in both universes, with each stock's weight depending on Russell's determination of the stock's exposure to growth or value, which depends on its rank in the overall sort.

The *Russell 2000* represents the bottom two-thirds of the largest 3,000 publicly traded companies domiciled in the United States. Russell recently dropped its Compustat rule (companies were allowed into the index only if they had two years of data available), which had the effect of significantly raising the financial services industry weighting.

The *S&P/BARRA Growth and Value Indexes* are constructed by sorting the S&P 500 companies based on their price-to-book ratios, with the low price-to-book companies constituting the value index and high price-to-book making up the growth index. Each S&P 500 company is included in either the growth or the value index, and the two indexes are constructed so that they each have approximately the same market value at the semiannual rebalancing. When new companies are added to the S&P Composite index, they are placed into the appropriate style index based on the price-to-book cutoff. Companies in the growth index tend to be bigger, so it includes roughly two-fifths of the S&P 500 companies. The same methodology is used on the S&P MidCap index.

The *S&P 500* (also known as the S&P Composite) is constructed so that, in aggregate, it represents a broad distribution by industry group comparable to that of stocks traded on the New York Stock Exchange. Decisions about stocks to be included and deleted are made by the S&P Index Committee. The *S&P MidCap 400* index includes companies chosen by committee at Standard & Poor's for their size and industry characteristics. None of the companies in the MidCap index overlaps with those in the S&P Composite. Some companies in the S&P MidCap, however, are larger than those in the S&P Composite, which is a function of the normal drift that takes place in any index as some companies' stock prices appreciate and others depreciate.

Wilshire chooses the stocks for the *Wilshire Growth Indexes* and the *Wilshire Value Indexes* by using a set of criteria to eliminate names from its (large-cap) Top 750, Mid Cap 750, and (small-cap) Next 1750 indexes. Elimination criteria for the Growth Index include history of less than five years, high dividend payout, low growth, low price-to-book, and low ROE. Companies with high relative P/E, low relative dividend yield, and high relative price-to-book are eliminated from the Value index.

The *Wilshire Top 750* index represents the largest 750 companies in the *Wilshire 5000*, which in turn consists of all securities traded in the United States for which price data are available. The Wilshire 5000 actually includes far more than 5,000 companies — over 6,400 as of year-end 1993. The *Wilshire Next 1750* is derived by taking the next 1,750 stocks (after the top 750) from the top half of the Wilshire 5000. The *Wilshire Mid Cap*, which is quite a bit smaller than either Russell's or Standard & Poor's mid-cap index, uses the smallest 250 names in the Top 750 and the largest 500 names in the Next 1750.

# THE LARGE-CAP STYLE BENCHMARKS

Style indexes for large-cap stocks have been around longer than the mid- and small-cap categories, but they were created much more recently than most of the other major benchmarks. The Wilshire and Russell indexes have been around for a number of years, while S&P, jointly with BARRA, released its indexes in 1992. Prudential Securities (PSI) released its own versions of style indexes in 1993 to address some problems it sees in some of the other style indexes. Exhibits 1-8 display the price performance, descriptive characteristics, and size and sector distributions of large-cap growth and value indexes. Although not available for use then, most indexes are cast back to the late 1970s.

## Growth Indexes Are Not Created Equal

The four large-cap growth indexes covered in our analysis show a variety of differences that result from not only the construction method, but also the selection universe. The S&P/BARRA index (which is selected from the index with the fewest stocks) has the heaviest large-company profile, with a weighted average capitalization of $25.9 billion and 67.3% of the market value in companies over $10.0 billion in size. The PSI growth index has the smallest size profile, with a weighted average market cap of $14.3 billion and only 38.3% of the capitalization in the largest-company size category. Much of this difference at year-end 1993 is attributable to the placement of one stock — General Electric, which fell into growth in three of the four indexes, but landed in PSI's value index.

The macroeconomic sector distribution points out a number of variations across the four growth indexes as well. The indexes created using a price-to-book sort (S&P and Russell) show heavier weightings in basic industry and utilities, although both have relatively small weightings. Consumer services and technology are two sectors whose weightings are quite a bit lighter than both Wilshire and PSI. Consumer staples is a heavy component of all the growth indexes, although PSI has the lowest weighting, at 10.5%.

In most cases, the fundamental characteristics of the four growth indexes are comparable, but the construction methodology and selection universe do lead to some differences. Using a definitive screen for growth as PSI does generates the most "growth-oriented" index. This index has the highest I/B/E/S forecast growth rate, as well as the highest historical growth in sales and earnings. The valuation for this index is also higher on both a P/E and price-to-sales basis.

## Exhibit 1: Large-Cap Growth Indexes

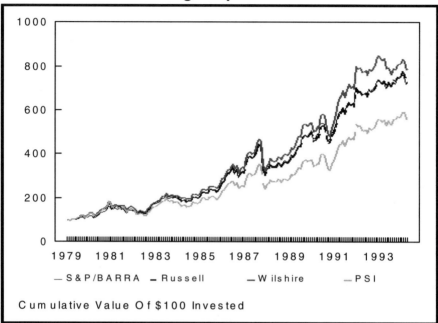

## Exhibit 2: Large-Cap Value Indexes

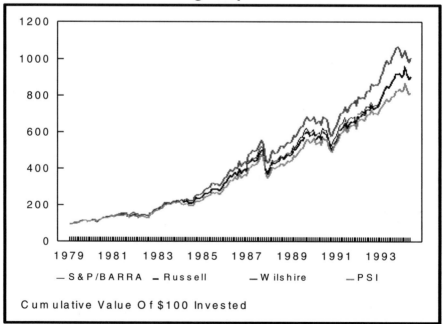

## Exhibit 3: Large-Cap Growth Relative to Value

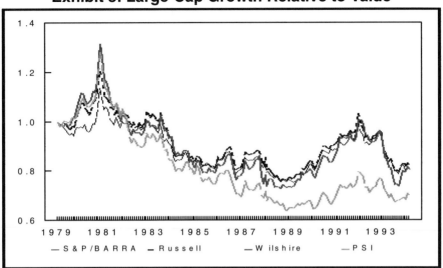

Yield is another distinguishing feature of the indexes. In both the S&P and Wilshire indexes, about 85% of the companies pay a dividend. Recall that these indexes are built from the overall universes with the fewest companies and are heavily focused on the biggest of the big-cap names, most of which pay a dividend.

## Value Should Be Looked at Closely

The value indexes also show a wide variation in size characteristics. The Russell index has the lowest weighted average capitalization at $13.5 billion, while the PSI index (with the inclusion of General Electric) has the highest at $19.0 billion. The concentration of companies in the various size categories is a bit more homogeneous in the value indexes. All have at least 75.0% of the capitalization of the index in names over $3.0 billion in size. The value indexes have at a minimum 95.0% of the companies listed on the NYSE as well.

From a sector perspective, large-cap value is heavily concentrated in financial services, utilities, and energy, and the index construction process determines which takes on the biggest proportion. By requiring companies to pay a dividend, Wilshire has the heaviest utility weighting at 33.9%, while S&P/BARRA has the lightest at 14.9%. Financial services ranges from 23.8% to 20.3%, suggesting that, regardless of definition, value means financials. The energy weighting varies from over 20.0% for S&P/BARRA and Wilshire, to the low teens for Russell and PSI. It remains one of the three heaviest sectors in all of the indexes, however. These large differences obviously highlight the importance of knowing your index.

## Exhibit 4: Descriptive Characteristics of Large-Cap Style Benchmarks

| | Large-Cap Growth | | | | Large-Cap Value | | | |
|---|---|---|---|---|---|---|---|---|
| | PSI | Russell | S&P/BARRA | Wilshire | PSI | Russell | S&P/BARRA | Wilshire |
| Number of Companies | 330 | 461 | 190 | 206 | 462 | 536 | 310 | 161 |
| First Full Year of Return | 1976 | 1979 | 1977 | 1978 | 1976 | 1979 | 1977 | 1978 |
| Index Rebalancing | Semiannually | Annually | Semiannually/As Needed | Quarterly | Semiannually | Annually | Semiannually/As Needed | Quarterly |
| Return Calculation | With Income | Principal and with Income | With Income | With Income | With Income | Principal and with Income | With Income | With Income |
| Exchange Distribution | | | | | | | | |
| Nasdaq | 23.4% | 12.3% | 7.5% | 10.8% | 4.6% | 4.2% | 1.6% | 3.1% |
| NYSE | 74.3% | 86.8% | 92.2% | 88.7% | 94.7% | 95.3% | 98.1% | 96.7% |
| AMEX | 2.3% | 0.9% | 0.3% | 0.5% | 0.7% | 0.5% | 0.3% | 0.2% |
| Total Capitalization | $1.1 Tril | $1.8 Tril | $1.6 Tril | $1.4 Tril | $2.1 Tril | $1.9 Tril | $1.6 Tril | $802 Bil |
| Average Size | | | | | | | | |
| Weighted Mean | $14.3 Bil | $21.1 Bil | $25.9 Bil | $23.5 Bil | $19.0 Bil | $13.5 Bil | $17.0 Bil | $17.3 Bil |
| Mean | $3.4 Bil | $4.0 Bil | $8.6 Bil | $6.7 Bil | $4.6 Bil | $3.5 Bil | $5.3 Bil | $5.0 Bil |
| Median | $1.6 Bil | $1.6 Bil | $4.4 Bil | $3.3 Bil | $2.1 Bil | $1.5 Bil | $3.0 Bil | $2.7 Bil |
| Size Range | | | | | | | | |
| Largest | $58.0 Bil | $89.5 Bil | $89.5 Bil | $89.5 Bil | $89.5 Bil | $78.4 Bil | $78.4 Bil | $78.4 Bil |
| Smallest | 725.1 Mil | 75.5 Mil | 128.9 Mil | 782.6 Mil | 725.1 Mil | 124.0 Mil | 127.0 Mil | 912.9 Mil |

Note: Data are as of December 31, 1993.

Source: Prudential Securities.

## Exhibit 5: Size Distribution of Large-Cap Style Benchmarks (Market-Cap-Weighted)

| | Large-Cap Growth (%) | | | | Large-Cap Value (%) | | | |
|---|---|---|---|---|---|---|---|---|
| | PSI | Russell | S&P/BARRA | Wilshire | PSI | Russell | S&P/BARRA | Wilshire |
| Very Large | $10.0B and Over | 38.3 | 52.4 | 67.3 | 56.5 | 46.7 | 38.1 | 44.4 | 42.5 |
| Large | $3.0B - $10.0B | 32.4 | 25.9 | 25.8 | 31.5 | 33.1 | 36.6 | 41.7 | 39.1 |
| Medium-Large | $1.5B - $3.0B | 15.1 | 11.7 | 5.1 | 8.5 | 11.7 | 13.2 | 9.8 | 11.6 |
| Medium | $750M - $1.5B | 13.2 | 7.2 | 1.6 | 3.5 | 8.3 | 9.0 | 3.0 | 6.8 |
| Medium-Small | $750M or Less | 0.9 | 2.7 | 0.3 | — | 0.2 | 3.1 | 1.1 | — |

Note: Data are as of December 31, 1993.

Source: Prudential Securities.

# Exhibit 6: Macroeconomic Sector Distribution of Large-Cap Style (Market-Cap-Weighted)

| | Large-Cap Growth (%) | | | | Large-Cap Value (%) | | | |
|---|---|---|---|---|---|---|---|---|
| | PSI | Russell | S&P/BARRA | Wilshire | PSI | Russell | S&P/BARRA | Wilshire |
| Basic Industry | 5.2 | 9.1 | 9.5 | 4.0 | 7.8 | 11.6 | 12.7 | 4.5 |
| Business Services | 5.2 | 9.0 | 8.6 | 2.2 | 1.8 | 1.3 | 2.5 | 0.3 |
| Capital Spending | 3.8 | 9.3 | 8.7 | 10.5 | 6.7 | 2.0 | 2.5 | 1.3 |
| Conglomerates | 0.1 | 0.2 | 0.3 | 0.6 | 1.3 | 1.2 | 1.2 | 0.2 |
| Consumer Cyclical | 2.1 | 1.5 | 1.6 | 1.9 | 5.3 | 7.1 | 6.5 | 0.2 |
| Consumer Services | 27.0 | 15.0 | 16.6 | 19.2 | 4.1 | 6.8 | 5.0 | 3.1 |
| Consumer Staples | 10.5 | 18.8 | 21.8 | 23.2 | 7.6 | 1.8 | 2.2 | 1.1 |
| Energy | 3.1 | 3.6 | 2.4 | 0.5 | 12.8 | 13.6 | 20.6 | 26.7 |
| Financial Services | 7.6 | 4.9 | 2.4 | 11.1 | 21.5 | 23.8 | 20.3 | 22.9 |
| Health Care | 11.8 | 15.1 | 14.5 | 14.4 | 6.1 | 1.5 | 1.4 | 0.8 |
| Technology | 22.1 | 10.6 | 7.0 | 11.6 | 7.5 | 7.7 | 10.2 | 5.0 |
| Utilities | 1.4 | 2.9 | 6.5 | 0.8 | 17.5 | 21.7 | 14.9 | 33.9 |

Note: Data are as of December 31, 1993.

Source: Prudential Securities Inc.

# Exhibit 7: Fundamental Characteristics of Large-Cap Style Benchmarks

| | Large-Cap Growth | | | | Large-Cap Value | | | |
|---|---|---|---|---|---|---|---|---|
| | PSI | Russell | S&P/BARRA | Wilshire | PSI | Russell | S&P/BARRA | Wilshire |
| LTM* P/E | 23.4 | 21.8 | 21.0 | 19.6 | 16.2 | 17.7 | 18.8 | 13.1 |
| LTM* P/E - W/O Negative Earnings | 25.7 | 23.0 | 21.7 | 21.7 | 16.5 | 17.5 | 17.9 | 13.5 |
| P/E - I/B/E/S Forecast EPS | 19.4 | 17.6 | 16.8 | 16.7 | 13.4 | 13.9 | 14.2 | 13.1 |
| Price-to-Book | 4.3 | 4.4 | 4.5 | 4.3 | 2.6 | 2.1 | 2.1 | 1.8 |
| Price-to-Sales | 2.2 | 1.9 | 1.9 | 1.9 | 1.2 | 1.1 | 1.0 | 1.1 |
| Debt-to-Capital | 32.1 | 42.8 | 45.2 | 37.4 | 51.5 | 52.9 | 50.0 | 51.6 |
| Yield | | | | | | | | |
| % Of Companies | 56.4 | 67.7 | 84.9 | 85.4 | 88.7 | 89.7 | 87.9 | 100.0 |
| Mean | 0.6 | 1.3 | 1.8 | 1.5 | 3.2 | 3.0 | 2.8 | 4.6 |
| P/E To Growth | 1.5 | 1.5 | 1.4 | 1.2 | 1.8 | 4.9 | 5.5 | 2.2 |
| I/B/E/S Forecast Growth | 18.6 | 15.1 | 13.6 | 14.9 | 9.7 | 9.4 | 9.4 | 7.6 |
| Historical 5-Year EPS Growth | 18.8 | 12.5 | 11.2 | 16.2 | 6.3 | 1.3 | 1.3 | 3.6 |
| Historical 5-Year Sales Growth | 18.4 | 12.7 | 11.0 | 14.8 | 7.7 | 6.3 | 6.3 | 6.2 |
| Return On Equity | 21.9 | 21.5 | 22.1 | 22.8 | 14.7 | 10.7 | 10.1 | 12.8 |
| Return On Assets | 9.9 | 8.9 | 8.9 | 9.3 | 4.6 | 2.9 | 2.7 | 4.0 |
| Average Daily Trading Volume (Thou.) | 938 | 916 | 1045 | 1014 | 716 | 546 | 629 | 475 |

Note: Data are as of December 31, 1993. Averages are weighted by capitalization.
* Latest 12 Months.

Source: Prudential Securities Inc., IBES Inc., and Compustat.

## Exhibit 8: Performance Statistics — Annual Returns of Large-Cap Style Benchmarks (Percent Returns)

| | Large-Cap Growth (%) | | | | Large-Cap Value (%) | | | |
|---|---|---|---|---|---|---|---|---|
| | PSI | Russell | S&P/BARRA | Wilshire | PSI | Russell | S&P/BARRA | Wilshire |
| 1984 | -1.2 | -1.0 | 2.3 | 3.0 | 5.6 | 10.1 | 10.5 | 19.1 |
| 1985 | 28.6 | 32.9 | 33.3 | 32.9 | 30.1 | 31.5 | 29.7 | 30.2 |
| 1986 | 7.7 | 15.4 | 14.5 | 15.5 | 21.0 | 20.0 | 21.7 | 22.2 |
| 1987 | 5.7 | 5.3 | 6.5 | 4.7 | 2.2 | 0.5 | 3.7 | 4.7 |
| 1988 | 9.3 | 11.3 | 11.9 | 15.4 | 20.7 | 23.2 | 21.7 | 22.8 |
| 1989 | 29.6 | 35.9 | 36.4 | 35.2 | 27.7 | 25.2 | 26.1 | 25.1 |
| 1990 | -0.9 | -0.3 | 0.2 | 0.3 | -5.5 | -8.1 | -6.8 | -7.6 |
| 1991 | 44.8 | 41.2 | 38.4 | 46.6 | 25.9 | 24.6 | 22.6 | 25.6 |
| 1992 | 4.3 | 5.0 | 5.2 | 5.9 | 8.7 | 13.8 | 10.6 | 14.4 |
| 1993 | 3.4 | 2.9 | 1.5 | -0.5 | 14.4 | 18.1 | 18.5 | 13.5 |
| Ten-Year Average | | | | | | | | |
| Annualized | 10.0 | 12.6 | 12.9 | 14.0 | 14.6 | 15.8 | 15.8 | 16.9 |
| Arithmetic | 13.1 | 14.9 | 15.0 | 15.9 | 15.1 | 15.9 | 15.8 | 17.0 |
| Standard Deviation | 14.8 | 15.1 | 14.4 | 15.9 | 11.3 | 11.5 | 10.7 | 10.8 |
| Beta | 1.17 | 1.09 | 1.08 | 1.14 | 0.89 | 0.90 | 0.91 | 0.84 |

The fundamentals of the value indexes point up the differences that a definition can create. The heavy utility weighting in the Wilshire index influences many of the valuation parameters, causing the lowest P/E and price-to-book values, along with the highest yield. The price-to-book sort has some impact on the fundamentals as well. The S&P/BARRA and Russell indexes have lower historical earnings growth, ROEs, and ROAs compared to the screen-based indexes.

## Growth Differs from Value in Many Ways

The value indexes tend to be much more heavily weighted in financials and utilities (although the weightings vary dramatically based on how the indexes are constructed and from which universe), where dividend yields tend to be higher and P/Es and price-to-book ratios are lower. Consumer cyclicals also figure more heavily in value than in growth, as does energy. Value tends to have a much lower weighting than growth in consumer staples, consumer services, and health care, where P/Es tend to be higher.

## Value has Outperformed Growth over Time

Since 1979 value has done much better, on average, than growth, with a lower standard deviation of annual returns. S&P/BARRA's ten-year annualized average return for value is 15.8% as compared to 12.9% for growth. Although return levels differ, all the index pairs show a similar spread between growth and value returns. Most years seem to be dominated by one style or the other. Most recently, 1991 has been dubbed a growth year, while 1992 and 1993 were value years. Returns for growth and value have been similar in only two or three years out of the past 10: 1979, 1982, and 1985. (Exhibits 1, 2, and 3 present the historical returns on a cumulative and relative basis for the eight indexes.)

One of the most noticeable differences between growth and value indexes is their sector exposures. The growth indexes have over 30% of their weighting in consumer services and consumer staples, while the value indexes tend to fall below 10% in those groups. Among other sector differences are heavier technology and health care weightings for growth and the overabundance of financial, utility, and energy issues for value.

The growth indexes tend to include more large names (because value indexes generally contain "cheaper" stocks), which is borne out in the larger weighted-average capitalization figures and the greater percentage of the index in names over $10.0 billion in market cap.

Value tends to have lower P/E, price-to-book, and price-to-sales ratios, and lower growth rates as well. Dividend yields for value are higher, as is the percentage of companies that are dividend-paying. Stocks in the growth portfolios tend to be traded more actively; the weighted-average daily trading volume is almost double that of value.

## THE MID-CAP STYLE BENCHMARKS

The notion of mid-cap investing existed only in the minds of a few prior to S&P's launch of its index in May 1991. Wilshire was first out of the box with its screen-based portfolios in late 1991, and the PSI style indexes were developed in mid-1993. S&P/BARRA launched its price-to-book sort-based indexes on the S&P MidCap 400 in April 1994. Rounding out the field, Frank Russell Company offered its style indexes in June 1994. Exhibits 9-16 cover the details regarding the three mid-cap indexes for which data are available.

### Mid-Cap Growth Shows Sizable Variations

The size profile is one of the more striking differences of the three mid-cap growth indexes. This is one of the major starting points in the choice of style benchmark — choose one that is invested in companies similar in size to the managed portfolio. As a result of the very different selection universes, the weighted-average market value ranges from $2.0 billion for S&P to $950 million for PSI. In addition, over 50.0% of the weight of the S&P/BARRA Growth index is in companies over $1.5 billion in capitalization; Wilshire totals 23.7%, and PSI 14.4%, with no companies over $3.0 billion.

## Exhibit 9: Mid-Cap Growth Indexes

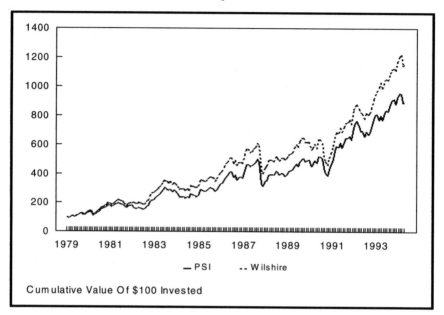

Cumulative Value Of $100 Invested

## Exhibit 10: Mid-Cap Value Indexes

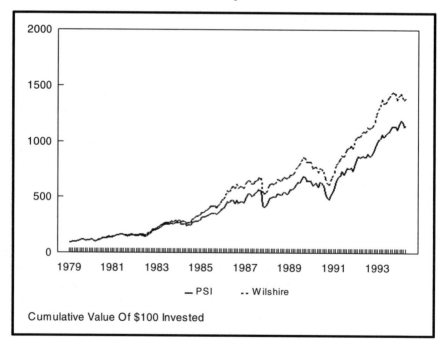

Cumulative Value Of $100 Invested

## Exhibit 11: Mid-Cap Growth Relative to Value

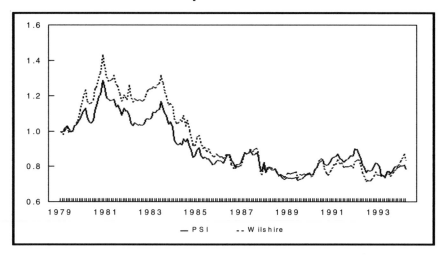

The stock exchange distribution shows a bias toward NYSE issues, with over 60.0% weightings for the S&P/BARRA and Wilshire indexes, but only a 48.2% weighting for PSI. This weighting is quite a bit different from the large-cap growth indexes. Nasdaq picks up a bit of weight when moving into the mid-cap universe. PSI's growth index is 48.3% Nasdaq issues, while the other indexes top 30.0%.

The initial universe and creation methods generate interesting differences in macroeconomic sector weightings. Health care and basic industry illustrate this. The price-to-book sort-based S&P/BARRA index has 17.2% of its weight in basic industry and only 9.3% in health care. The two indexes that are screen-derived show much heavier weightings in health care — 19.3% and 14.1% for PSI and Wilshire, respectively, compared to 6.2% and 13.2%, respectively, in basic industry. The fact that many cyclicals are trading at the high end of the price-to-book range puts them into growth at this point in the business cycle, but they don't usually have the growth rates to pass the screening criteria for the PSI and Wilshire indexes.

Although the valuation criteria (P/E, price-to-book, and price-to-sales) for the growth indexes are comparable, there are some differences worth mentioning. The more industrial orientation of the S&P/BARRA index creates a higher debt-to-capital ratio as these companies tend to have more leverage than health care and technology names. Additionally, this index has a much higher percentage of companies that are dividend paying and has a higher yield as well. The net result of the growth-oriented screens are higher historical growth rates for the PSI and Wilshire indexes.

## Exhibit 12: Descriptive Characteristics of Mid-Cap Style Benchmarks

|  | Mid-Cap Growth | | | Mid-Cap Value | | |
|---|---|---|---|---|---|---|
|  | PSI | S&P/BARRA | Wilshire | PSI | S&P/BARRA | Wilshire |
| Number of Companies | 391 | 167 | 167 | 395 | 233 | 123 |
| First Full Year of Return | 1976 | 1992 | 1978 | 1976 | 1992 | 1978 |
| Index Rebalancing | Semiannually | Semiannually/As Needed | Quarterly | Semiannually | Semiannually/As Needed | Quarterly |
| Return Calculation | Principal and with Income | With Income | With Income | Principal and with Income | With Income | With Income |
| Exchange Distribution |  |  |  |  |  |  |
| Nasdaq | 48.3% | 34.5% | 33.1% | 19.0% | 16.4% | 24.7% |
| NYSE | 48.2 | 63.3 | 62.2 | 79.7 | 81.8 | 75.3 |
| AMEX | 3.5 | 2.2 | 4.7 | 1.3 | 1.8 | — |
| Total Capitalization | $292.6 Bil | $230 Bil | $164.0 Bil | $344.1 Bil | $232 Bil | $115.3 Bil |
| Average Size |  |  |  |  |  |  |
| Weighted Mean | $950.2 Mil | $2.0 Bil | $1.2 Bil | $1.1Bil | $1.8 Bil | $1.1 Bil |
| Mean | 748.4 Mil | 1.4 Bil | 982.3 Mil | 871.2 Mil | 1.0 Bil | 937.4 Mil |
| Median | 624.8 Mil | 1.1 Bil | 855.8 Mil | 782.6 Mil | 722 Mil | 935.6 Mil |
| Size Range |  |  |  |  |  |  |
| Largest | $1.9 Bil | $6.4 Bil | $5.0 Bil | $1.9 Bil | $8.0 Bil | $1.9 Bil |
| Smallest | 316.3 Mil | 154.0 Mil | 236.9 Mil | 316.2 Mil | $54.0 Mil | 372.9 Mil |

Note: Data are as of December 31, 1993 for all indexes except S&P which are as of April 29, 1994.

Source: Prudential Securities Inc.

## Exhibit 13: Size Distribution of Mid-Cap Style Benchmarks (Market-Cap-Weighted)

|  | Mid-Cap Growth (%) | | | Mid-Cap Value (%) | | |
|---|---|---|---|---|---|---|
|  | PSI | S&P/BARRA | Wilshire | PSI | S&P/BARRA | Wilshire |
| Large $3.0B - $10.0B | — | 23.7 | 3.0 | — | 14.8 | — |
| Medium-Large $1.5B - $3.0B | 14.4 | 31.5 | 20.7 | 22.0 | 28.8 | 10.1 |
| Medium $750M - $1.5B | 46.4 | 34.9 | 55.3 | 50.7 | 34.3 | 66.9 |
| Medium-Small $250M - $750M | 39.2 | 9.7 | 20.8 | 27.3 | 20.2 | 23.1 |
| Small $100M - $250M | — | 0.2 | 0.1 | — | 1.7 | — |
| Very Small Less than $100M | — | — | — | — | 0.1 | — |

Note: Data are as of December 31, 1993.

Source: Prudential Securities Inc.

# Exhibit 14: Macroeconomic Sector Breakdown of Mid-Cap Style (Market-Cap-Weighted)

| | Mid-Cap Growth (%) | | | Mid-Cap Value (%) | | |
|---|---|---|---|---|---|---|
| | PSI | S&P/BARRA | Wilshire | PSI | S&P/BARRA | Wilshire |
| Basic Industry | 6.2 | 17.2 | 13.2 | 16.8 | 11.4 | 7.1 |
| Business Services | 4.5 | 7.7 | 4.8 | 3.1 | 3.9 | 2.9 |
| Capital Spending | 3.0 | 4.7 | 3.1 | 2.1 | 4.7 | 1.9 |
| Conglomerates | 0.6 | 0.4 | 0.6 | 0.1 | 0.6 | 1.3 |
| Consumer Cyclical | 2.7 | 3.7 | 7.6 | 4.0 | 0.9 | 4.0 |
| Consumer Services | 22.2 | 17.0 | 19.7 | 12.1 | 2.9 | 5.2 |
| Consumer Staples | 0.8 | 4.5 | 1.8 | 3.3 | 4.2 | 0.3 |
| Energy | 4.4 | 5.3 | 3.4 | 7.1 | 5.5 | 8.6 |
| Financial Services | 9.1 | 6.5 | 10.8 | 30.0 | 25.6 | 33.3 |
| Health Care | 19.3 | 9.3 | 14.1 | 4.3 | 4.4 | — |
| Technology | 25.0 | 20.7 | 19.2 | 5.5 | 10.5 | 4.5 |
| Utilities | 1.7 | 3.0 | 1.7 | 10.7 | 25.4 | 31.0 |

Note: Data are as of December 31, 1993 for all indexes except S&P/BARRA which are as of April 29, 1994.

Source: Prudential Securities Inc.

# Exhibit 15: Fundamental Characteristics of Mid-Cap Style Benchmarks

| | Mid-Cap Growth | | | Mid-Cap Value | | |
|---|---|---|---|---|---|---|
| | PSI | S&P/BARRA | Wilshire | PSI | S&P/BARRA | Wilshire |
| LTM* P/E | 24.1 | 22.9 | 21.4 | 14.3 | 17.2 | 13.0 |
| LTM* P/E - W/O Negative Earnings | 26.3 | 23.5 | 24.1 | 15.0 | 16.7 | 14.0 |
| P/E - I/B/E/S Forecast EPS | 19.1 | 19.7 | 18.5 | 13.0 | 14.0 | 12.4 |
| Price To Book | 4.0 | 4.0 | 3.9 | 2.0 | 1.8 | 1.6 |
| Price To Sales | 2.0 | 2.0 | 1.8 | 1.1 | 1.2 | 1.1 |
| Debt To Capital | 25.6 | 31.9 | 28.0 | 51.0 | 46.8 | 50.9 |
| Dividend Yield | | | | | | |
| % Of Companies | 36.2 | 65.6 | 54.0 | 77.7 | 77.9 | 100.0 |
| Mean | 0.3 | 1.0 | 0.6 | 2.5 | 3.2 | 4.2 |
| P/E To Growth | 1.8 | 1.4 | 1.1 | 1.6 | 2.3 | 2.1 |
| I/B/E/S Forecast Growth | 21.0 | 18.8 | 17.8 | 10.6 | 10.1 | 8.0 |
| Historical 5-Year EPS Growth | 19.6 | 15.3 | 20.0 | 5.5 | 4.8 | 3.8 |
| Historical 5-Year Sales Growth | 19.3 | 17.8 | 18.7 | 6.6 | 7.4 | 5.9 |
| Return On Equity | 17.7 | 18.8 | 18.2 | 12.5 | 10.3 | 12.1 |
| Return On Assets | 9.2 | 9.8 | 9.2 | 4.3 | 3.2 | 3.5 |
| Average Daily Trading Volume (Thu.) | 257 | 401 | 196 | 148 | 179 | 75 |

Note: Data are as of December 31, 1993 except S&P/BARRA which are as of April 29, 1994. Averages are weighted by capitalization.
* Latest 12 Months.

Source: Prudential Securities Inc., IBES Inc., and Compustat.

## Exhibit 16: Annual Returns of Mid-Cap Style Benchmarks (Percent Returns)

| Year | Mid-Cap Growth (%) | | | Mid-Cap Value (%) | | |
|---|---|---|---|---|---|---|
| | PSI | S&P | Wilshire | PSI | S&P | Wilshire |
| 1984 | -9.3 | — | -4.6 | 8.0 | — | 18.3 |
| 1985 | 30.6 | — | 30.2 | 34.7 | — | 38.7 |
| 1986 | 12.1 | — | 14.8 | 14.6 | — | 23.2 |
| 1987 | -4.9 | — | -5.4 | -5.6 | — | -5.9 |
| 1988 | 13.5 | — | 15.1 | 26.7 | — | 23.0 |
| 1989 | 24.7 | — | 22.0 | 20.5 | — | 21.5 |
| 1990 | -7.3 | — | -12.9 | -16.6 | — | -16.4 |
| 1991 | 56.4 | — | 55.4 | 47.2 | — | 48.5 |
| 1992 | 11.7 | 6.9 | 12.3 | 23.0 | 16.0 | 22.6 |
| 1993 | 14.8 | 13.7 | 15.8 | 16.6 | 13.4 | 12.8 |
| **Ten-Year** | | | | | | |
| Annualized Average | 12.8 | — | 12.8 | 15.5 | — | 17.2 |
| Arithmetic Average | 14.2 | — | 14.3 | 16.9 | — | 18.6 |
| Standard Deviation | 18.8 | — | 18.7 | 17.6 | — | 17.9 |
| Beta | 1.25 | — | 1.24 | 1.00 | — | 0.82 |

Source: Prudential Securities Inc.

## Mid-Cap Value Shows More Consistency

The mid-cap value indexes show a bit more consistency between them in terms of exchange distribution and size. The lion's share of the companies trade on the NYSE, but the percentages range from 75.3% for Wilshire to 81.8% for S&P/BARRA. Nasdaq has the remainder of the companies, with the AMEX accounting for less than 2.0% (actually 0% in the case of the Wilshire Value index). The weighted-average market cap for the S&P/BARRA index is heavily influenced by only a few names, as the mean and median values are very close to the other indexes.

The greatest discrepancies in sector weightings are in the utilities and basic industry areas. Wilshire's yield requirement generates a 31.0% weighting for the utility sector, and the S&P 400 MidCap index's heavy exposure to utilities relative to other mid-cap indexes causes these issues to fall into its value index. PSI has the smallest utility weighting at 10.7%. PSI also has the heaviest weighting in basic industry (16.8%) because the normalized P/E screen is specifically designed to allow cyclical companies to remain in value regardless of the stage of the business cycle. Wilshire shows the lightest weighting in this sector at 7.1%. Consumer services and technology also show variation across the indexes.

From a valuation perspective, the S&P/BARRA index has the highest P/E ratios of the three value indexes on both a trailing and a forecast basis. Wilshire, with its yield requirement, has 100% dividend-payers and the highest yield of the three indexes at 4.2%. In terms of fundamentals, there is little difference in either the historical growth rates or the return on equity/asset values.

## What Distinguishes Mid-Cap Growth From Mid-Cap Value?

Mid-cap value is dominated by NYSE companies, with 75%-80% trading on this exchange. In mid-cap growth, Nasdaq takes on a bigger role, accounting for 48.3% of the PSI portfolio, 33.1% of the Wilshire index, and 34.5% of the S&P/BARRA index.

In two of the three indexes, growth includes more large issues than value. This shows up in the capitalization characteristics and in the size distribution as well. The mean market value for the S&P mid-cap growth index is $1.4 billion, compared to $1.0 billion for the value index. Additionally, 55.2% of its growth index is made up of companies over $1.5 billion in size, compared to 43.6% for value.

Over the past ten years, and as well as the longer term, mid-cap value has beaten mid-cap growth by any measure. On a ten-year annualized basis, value is up 17.2%, according to Wilshire, compared to 12.8% for growth. This can at least in part be explained by the economic environment of generally falling interest rates between 1984 and 1993. The heavy utility and financial weighting in value makes it more interest sensitive and likely to benefit more than growth from declining interest rates. The long-term relative performance could reverse during a period when interest rates climb steadily. Additionally, growth tends to be more volatile, as indicated by greater standard deviation and higher beta. Of course there are times when growth shines, most recently in 1991 when the two growth indexes available were both up over 55.0%.

Technology ranks as the heaviest sector in PSI and S&P/BARRA, and is second in the Wilshire. PSI has the heaviest weighting at 25.0%, while Wilshire's is 19.2%. Consumer services is also a sizable component of the growth portfolios with a 22.2% weight in the PSI index, 19.7% in Wilshire, and 17.0% in S&P/BARRA. Health care also tends to be a heavy component of the growth universe, with a 19.3% weighting in the PSI index.

The mid-cap value portfolios have very heavy weightings in financial services and utilities compared to the growth indexes. The Wilshire portfolio tips the scales at 64.3% in these two groups; S&P/BARRA follows at 51.0%, while PSI shows a combined weighting of

40.7%. Beyond these two groups there are many differences. Basic industry also has a fair representation in the value indexes at 16.8% for PSI, 11.4% for S&P/BARRA, and 7.1% for Wilshire.

Fundamentally, the value portfolios have lower valuation figures on P/E (trailing or forward), price-to-book, and price-to-sales. Naturally, the growth portfolios have substantially higher historical sales and earnings growth rates and higher ROE and ROA as well. Typically, growth stocks have little debt and finance their expansion through equity offerings and internally-generated growth. This is evident in the much lower debt-to-capital ratios for the growth portfolios. The mid-cap value indexes, like their large-cap counterparts, have many more dividend-paying companies and higher yields than their small-cap counterparts. Growth stocks have substantially higher average daily trading volumes.

## THE SMALL-CAP STYLE BENCHMARKS

For a number of years, Wilshire Asset Management was the sole purveyor of growth and value style indexes for the small-cap sector of the market. In mid-1993, both Frank Russell (with style portfolios based on the Russell 2000) and Prudential Securities developed benchmarks. S&P launched their own small-cap index in October 1994 and may create style indexes at some point in the future. Exhibits 17-24 describe the characteristics of the small-cap style indexes.

### How Do The Growth Portfolios Compare With One Another?

Across the three growth portfolios many characteristics are comparable, perhaps more so than in the other two size sectors. All three small-cap growth indexes find the heaviest distribution of companies in the medium-small ($250-$750 million) grouping, and over 50.0% of the names trade on Nasdaq. PSI has the highest weighting in Nasdaq stocks at over 67.0%. Average sizes do vary, however. Wilshire has the highest weighted average-market cap at $621.6 million; PSI's is smallest at $262.8 million.

The screening methodology, with its emphasis on growth rates, tends to weight the indexes more heavily in sectors with high growth (such as technology). PSI is 24.0% technology and Wilshire has a 25.2% representation in the group, while Russell has only a 17.0% weighting. Consumer services also shows a distinct difference. This sector constitutes 16.2% of the Russell Growth index, but is 19.5% of PSI's and 21.7% of Wilshire's. On the other side of the coin, Russell includes more financial services issues, with an 11.8% weighting, compared to 8.4% and 9.7% for Wilshire and PSI, respectively.

## Exhibit 17: Small-Cap Growth Indexes

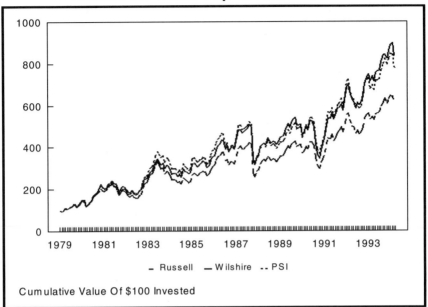

Cumulative Value Of $100 Invested

## Exhibit 18: Small-Cap Value Indexes

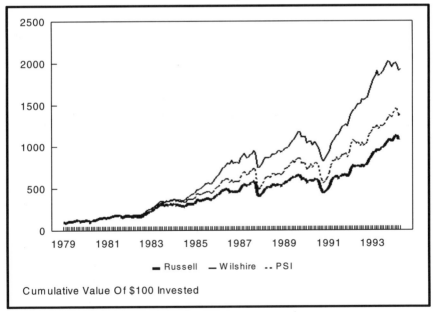

Cumulative Value Of $100 Invested

## Exhibit 19: Small-Cap Growth Relative to Value

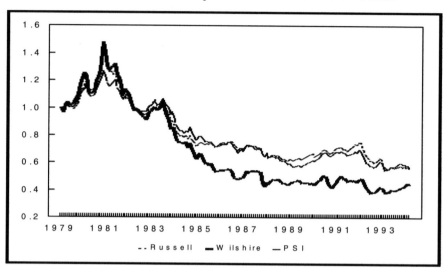

Fundamentally, a few differences stand out among the small-cap growth indexes. The valuations are all comparable, whether one looks at P/E, price-to-book or price-to-sales. All have debt-to-capital ratios of over 20.0%. Russell's index shows the lowest trailing five-year earnings and sales growth rates at 14.6% apiece, while Wilshire has the highest of over 20.0% for both. PSI has the lowest ROE and ROA at 13.9% and 7.4%, respectively. Wilshire fills out the other end of the spectrum, with values of 17.2% for ROE and 9.3% for ROA.

## The Value Indexes Aren't Look-a-likes

More than 50% of the stocks in the Wilshire and PSI small-cap value indexes are listed on the NYSE, while Russell shows 45.6%. All three portfolios have their highest concentration in stocks of the medium-small category. The Wilshire index has the highest market-cap profile with a weighted average of $531.4 million, and PSI has the smallest at $268.8 million.

Sector distribution points up the major deviation in the style portfolios. The low P/E, high-yield screen of Wilshire generates very heavy weightings in the financial services and utilities sectors. As of year-end 1993, the Wilshire value portfolio had 38.8% in financial services and 22.2% in utilities, or 61.0% of the portfolio. Russell and PSI also show a heavy financial concentration at 32.9% and 29.5%, respectively, but their utilities weighting is only 7.9% (Russell) and 3.1% (PSI). As a result of its concentration in two sectors, Wilshire has almost no weight in technology at 1.7%, compared with 9.8% for PSI and 9.5% for Russell.

# Exhibit 20: Descriptive Characteristics of Small-Cap Style Benchmarks

| | Small-Cap Growth | | | Small-Cap Value | | |
|---|---|---|---|---|---|---|
| | PSI | Russell | Wilshire | PSI | Russell | Wilshire |
| Number of Companies | 511 | 1,415 | 298 | 422 | 1,494 | 198 |
| First Full Year of Return | 1976 | 1984 | 1978 | 1976 | 1984 | 1978 |
| Index Rebalancing | Semiannually | Annually | Quarterly | Semiannually | Annually | Quarterly |
| Return Calculation | Principal and with income | Principal and with income | With income | Principal and with income | Principal and with income | With income |
| Exchange Distribution | | | | | | |
| Nasdaq | 67.0% | 59.3% | 55.0% | 42.7% | 48.2% | 38.9% |
| NYSE | 26.2% | 33.9% | 41.3% | 52.1% | 45.6% | 59.7% |
| AMEX | 6.8% | 6.8% | 3.7% | 5.2% | 6.2% | 1.4% |
| Total Capitalization | $111.3 Bil | $285.2 Bil | $132.2 Bil | $94.6 Bil | $282.1 Bil | $76.3 Bil |
| Average Size | | | | | | |
| Weighted Mean | $262.8 Mil | $345.4 Mil | $621.6 Mil | $268.8 Mil | $325.0 Mil | $531.4 Mil |
| Mean | 217.8 Mil | 201.5 Mil | 443.5 Mil | 224.2 Mil | 188.8 Mil | 385.4 Mil |
| Median | 193.5 Mil | 145.7 Mil | 349.7 Mil | 202.4 Mil | 134.9 Mil | 324.3 Mil |
| Size Range | | | | | | |
| Largest | $465.2 Mil | $1.4 Bil | $1.3 Bil | $465.8 Mil | $1.4 Bil | $1.1 Bil |
| Smallest | 94.0 Mil | 2.3 Mil | 68.4 Mil | 95.5 Mil | 2.3 Mil | 76.7 Mil |

Note: Data are as of December 31, 1993.

Source: Prudential Securities Inc.

# Exhibit 21: Size Distribution of Small-Cap Style Benchmarks (Market-Cap-Weighted)

| | Small-Cap Growth (%) | | | Small-Cap Value (%) | | |
|---|---|---|---|---|---|---|
| | PSI | Russell | Wilshire | PSI | Russell | Wilshire |
| Large $3.0B and over | — | — | — | — | — | — |
| Medium-Large $1.5B - $3.0B | — | — | — | — | — | — |
| Medium $750M - $1.5B | — | 6.0 | 36.5 | — | 4.3 | 23.6 |
| Medium-Small $250M - $750M | 53.1 | 53.2 | 51.4 | 54.0 | 52.0 | 60.3 |
| Small $100M - $250M | 44.1 | 30.0 | 11.7 | 44.8 | 31.6 | 15.8 |
| Very Small Less than $100M | 2.7 | 10.9 | 0.4 | 1.2 | 12.2 | 0.4 |

Note: Data are as of December 31, 1993.

Source: Prudential Securities Inc.

## Exhibit 22: Macroeconomic Sector Breakdown of Small-Cap Style Benchmarks (Market-Cap-Weighted)

| | Small-Cap Growth (%) | | | Small-Cap Value (%) | | |
|---|---|---|---|---|---|---|
| | PSI | Russell | Wilshire | PSI | Russell | Wilshire |
| Basic Industry | 6.2 | 8.8 | 8.5 | 10.1 | 11.9 | 6.3 |
| Business Services | 4.3 | 6.2 | 4.3 | 2.8 | 4.6 | 4.1 |
| Capital Spending | 3.6 | 6.2 | 4.2 | 4.6 | 6.3 | 3.8 |
| Conglomerates | 0.3 | — | 0.2 | 0.5 | — | — |
| Consumer Cyclical | 2.7 | 4.4 | 6.1 | 5.2 | 4.1 | 5.8 |
| Consumer Services | 19.5 | 16.2 | 21.7 | 16.8 | 12.0 | 9.9 |
| Consumer Staples | 1.8 | 2.1 | 1.1 | 3.7 | 1.9 | 1.2 |
| Energy | 5.1 | 4.7 | 2.9 | 3.2 | 3.1 | 6.2 |
| Financial Services | 9.7 | 11.8 | 8.4 | 29.5 | 32.9 | 38.8 |
| Health Care | 20.3 | 18.0 | 17.1 | 5.8 | 6.0 | — |
| Technology | 24.0 | 17.0 | 25.2 | 9.8 | 9.5 | 1.7 |
| Utilities | 1.6 | 4.5 | 0.1 | 3.1 | 7.9 | 22.2 |
| Note: Data are as of December 31, 1993. | | | | | | |

Source: Prudential Securities Inc.

## Exhibit 23: Fundamental Characteristics Of Small-Cap Style Benchmarks

| | Small-Cap Growth | | | Small-Cap Value | | |
|---|---|---|---|---|---|---|
| | PSI | Russell | Wilshire | PSI | Russell | Wilshire |
| LTM* P/E | 27.1 | 29.6 | 23.2 | 14.6 | 20.1 | 13.2 |
| LTM* P/E - W/O Negative Earnings | 25.2 | 24.8 | 25.2 | 14.9 | 15.9 | 13.8 |
| P/E - I/B/E/S Forecast EPS | 18.1 | 18.5 | 18.6 | 12.3 | 14.3 | 12.1 |
| Price-to-Book | 3.5 | 3.6 | 3.8 | 1.8 | 1.7 | 1.6 |
| Price-to-Sales | 1.7 | 1.9 | 1.8 | 0.9 | 1.1 | 1.0 |
| Debt-to-Capital | 21.4 | 28.5 | 23.6 | 38.7 | 39.4 | 49.4 |
| Dividend Yield | | | | | | |
|    % Of Companies | 21.0 | 40.0 | 31.9 | 54.2 | 50.8 | 99.5 |
|    Mean | 0.2 | 0.7 | 0.3 | 1.4 | 1.9 | 4.0 |
| P/E To Growth | 1.0 | 1.2 | 1.0 | 1.2 | 1.4 | 1.7 |
| I/B/E/S Forecast Growth | 24.1 | 20.4 | 20.5 | 12.9 | 13.0 | 9.0 |
| Historical 5-Year EPS Growth | 18.3 | 14.6 | 21.2 | 2.2 | 1.5 | 2.1 |
| Historical 5-Year Sales Growth | 19.8 | 14.6 | 20.8 | 7.0 | 8.3 | 6.1 |
| Return On Equity | 13.9 | 15.1 | 17.2 | 11.6 | 7.8 | 12.5 |
| Return On Assets | 7.4 | 8.3 | 9.3 | 4.0 | 2.5 | 3.4 |
| Average Daily Trading Volume (Thu.) | 111 | 135 | 172 | 73 | 77 | 42 |
| Note: Data are as of December 31, 1993. Averages are weighted by capitalization. * Latest 12 Months. | | | | | | |

Source: Prudential Securities Inc., IBES Inc., and Compustat.

# Exhibit 24: Annual Returns of Small-Cap Style Benchmarks (Percent Returns)

| Year | Small-Cap Growth (%) | | | Small-Cap Value (%) | | |
|------|-----|---------|----------|-----|---------|----------|
| | PSI | Russell | Wilshire | PSI | Russell | Wilshire |
| 1984 | -13.0 | -15.8 | -9.0 | 6.3 | 2.3 | 22.1 |
| 1985 | 28.9 | 31.0 | 26.5 | 34.1 | 31.1 | 43.9 |
| 1986 | 3.3 | 3.6 | 10.1 | 11.6 | 7.4 | 23.5 |
| 1987 | -11.7 | -10.5 | -8.9 | -9.9 | -7.1 | -3.1 |
| 1988 | 17.4 | 20.4 | 19.3 | 32.2 | 29.5 | 22.4 |
| 1989 | 21.1 | 20.2 | 18.9 | 16.3 | 12.4 | 18.1 |
| 1990 | -14.3 | -17.4 | -19.0 | -22.3 | -21.8 | -19.4 |
| 1991 | 54.1 | 51.2 | 56.8 | 51.0 | 41.7 | 49.0 |
| 1992 | 9.7 | 7.8 | 13.2 | 25.6 | 29.1 | 29.2 |
| 1993 | 14.4 | 13.4 | 18.0 | 18.2 | 23.8 | 14.1 |
| Ten-Year | | | | | | |
| Annualized Average | 9.2 | 8.5 | 10.8 | 14.4 | 13.2 | 18.3 |
| Arithmetic Average | 11.0 | 10.4 | 12.6 | 16.3 | 14.8 | 20.0 |
| Standard Deviation | 20.3 | 20.6 | 20.5 | 20.4 | 18.8 | 19.1 |
| Beta | 1.26 | 1.17 | 1.30 | 1.04 | 0.90 | 0.71 |

Source: Prudential Securities Inc.

Wilshire's yield requirement shows up in the 99.5% dividend-paying companies compared with 50.8% for Russell and 54.2% for PSI. In addition, the yield is more than twice as high as the other portfolios at 4.0%, compared to 1.9% for Russell, and 1.4% for PSI. Russell has the highest valuation characteristics according to P/E and price-to-sales but also has the highest forecast growth rates. All three small-cap value indexes show similar single-digit five-year historical earnings and sales growth rates.

## Small-Cap Growth And Value Are Far From Similar
In the small-caps, the growth portfolios have a higher percentage of companies that trade on Nasdaq, while value portfolios are more heavily weighted with NYSE issues. In the case of sectors, the small-cap growth portfolios have heavy weightings in consumer services, health care, and technology, with negligible weights in utilities. The value portfolios are dominated by financial services, utilities, and consumer services issues, with very low health care weightings.

The past ten years have been kinder to value than to growth in the small-cap universe. The value indexes' annualized average returns range from 13.2% to 18.3%, while the growth indexes have returned between 8.5% and 10.8%. Taking an even longer look back in time we can see a similar performance spread between the two styles. While the betas of the value indexes are quite a bit lower than those of growth, it is interesting to note that standard deviations of return have been more comparable. Whereas some years are particularly good for value (1992, for example), there have been few years in which a provider's small-growth index has beaten its small-value index.

With combined weightings of at least 35.0%, technology and health-care dominate the small-cap growth indexes. By comparison, the PSI and Russell value indexes have a 15.5% weighting. Small-cap growth also has a heavy representation in consumer services.

There is no escaping the fact that small-cap value is overloaded with financial services issues — whichever construction methodology is used. In Russell's value index the weighting is 32.9% compared to 11.8% for their growth index. Basic industry is another sector where the value index has a heavier weighting, generally. For Russell and PSI it is 11.9% and 10.1%, respectively, and the corresponding growth indexes have less than 9.0% representation.

From a valuation point of view, the small-cap growth indexes trade at higher multiples than the value indexes. In fact, the price-to-book ratios for growth are almost twice those of value. Where value stands out is in higher debt-to-capital ratios, dividend yields, and number of dividend-payers. Of little surprise is the fact that the historical and projected growth rates for the small-cap growth indexes are much higher than those of value. Historical growth rates show dramatic differences. For instance, the Russell value index's historical earnings growth rate is 1.5%, compared to 14.6% for its growth index. Small-cap value also has lower ROEs and ROAs.

# APPENDIX

## METHODOLOGY USED TO CALCULATE FUNDAMENTAL CHARACTERISTICS

The calculation of fundamental characteristics for a benchmark can be an onerous task. Many methodologies can be employed and many different measures calculated. Suppliers constantly try to provide the most accurate and representative calculations.

One of the main problems in calculating benchmark fundamentals has to do with exclusion of outliers. Outliers are numbers that are so different from the rest of the numbers that they have a distorting effect on measures of central tendency. The meaningfulness of such excessively high or low numbers is questionable. In addition, outliers are often extreme because calculation of that particular ratio is considered inappropriate because of a particular circumstance, occurrence, or accounting peculiarity. For example, many people exclude all negative earnings in the calculation of P/E or exclude heavily leveraged financial companies when calculating debt-to-capital.

We chose to use the same interquartile range methodology adopted by the Frank Russell Company in excluding outliers. The advantages of this methodology are that:

1. It does not automatically assume data at the top and bottom of the distribution are outliers.

2. It can be applied consistently as a quantitative method for all fundamental characteristics.

### Calculating the Critical Points
The upper and lower critical points — that is, the highest and lowest value to be included in the calculation are calculated for a global universe of stocks that includes both small — and large-cap stocks. The Frank Russell Company uses the Russell 3000 as its universe, while we use the combined PSI small-cap and large-cap universes.

### The Interquartile Range
The interquartile range, or IQR, is calculated by subtracting the value of the fundamental characteristic of the company at the 75th percen-

tile from the value of the fundamental characteristic of the company at the 25th percentile.

***The Critical Values.*** We multiply the IQR by three, then add it to the value of the 75th percentile and subtract it from the value of the 25th percentile to form the critical values. All values higher than the upper critical value and lower than the bottom critical value are excluded as outliers.

***Notes On Fundamental Data.*** Fundamental data are taken from Compustat, I/B/E/S, or Value Line via Factset as of December 31, 1993. We use latest 12-month earnings for LTM P/E and I/B/E/S fiscal-year 1 estimates for forecast EPS. For P/E to growth, we use P/E with forecast EPS and I/B/E/S long-term growth estimates. Return-on-equity and return-on-assets are for the last 12 months. Debt to capital uses long-term debt, and the average daily volume is for the 40 days prior to December 31, 1993.

***Averages.*** We recommend the harmonic average for ratios of "something" per "something else." A harmonic average is also best for ratios for which a low number is considered good but a negative number is considered bad or not meaningful (for example, P/E, P/E to growth, and price-to-book). Our harmonic average is a weighted harmonic average.

# CHAPTER 3

# RETURN-BASED STYLE ANALYSIS

*STEVE HARDY*
*PRESIDENT*
*ZEPHYR ASSOCIATES, INC.*

## THE THEORY

William F. Sharpe, a 1990 Nobel Prize winner in economic science, developed the theory of return-based style analysis.[1] This theory asserts that a manager's investment style, both past and present, can be determined by comparing the manager's returns to the returns of a number of selected indexes. The beauty of the theory is its simplicity, speed, and accuracy. There is no need to look at the individual holdings in a manager's portfolio to determine investment style; information can be obtained simply by analyzing the manager's monthly or quarterly returns.

An example of the theory in its simplest form will probably be helpful. Assume you are given a manager's quarterly returns from January 1, 1983 to March 31, 1994. Your job is to determine what kind of investment manager generated these returns. At this point, you don't know whether this is a stock, bond, or real estate manager, or whether the manager is dealing with international or domestic securities. In fact, you know absolutely nothing about the "mystery manager."

The only other information you have at your disposal is returns for a number of generic indexes that measure various asset classes. These indexes include the Morgan Stanley EAFE Index, the Lehman Brothers Government and Corporate Bond Index, the S&P 500 Index, and the four Russell Style Indexes (the Russell 1000 Large Growth, the Russell 1000 Large Value, the Russell 2000 Small Growth, and the Russell 2000 Small Value).

---

[1] William F. Sharpe, "Determining a Fund's Effective Asset Mix," *Investment Management Review* (November/December 1988), pp. 59-69.

First, you compare the pattern of the manager's returns to the pattern of the Lehman Corporate Bond Index. To compare these returns statistically, you calculate the $R^2$, which is the squared correlation between the manager and the index. You notice first that the $R^2$ of the manager's returns to the bond index is a very low 3.9%. You repeat the calculation with the other asset class indexes, and find $R^2$s with EAFE, 19.9%, and S&P 500, 82.6%. With an $R^2$ of 82.6% for the S&P 500, it should be obvious that the manager is a domestic equity manager.

You next want to know what particular investment style the manager follows. Although there are many different ideas of what constitutes style, you limit consideration of domestic equity styles to two general categories — value versus growth, and small versus large. You define four investment styles: large-capitalization value, large-capitalization growth, small-capitalization value, and small-capitalization growth. To represent these styles, you can use Russell's Style Indexes.

You can now compare the manager's returns to the returns of the four Russell Style Indexes in the same way you compared them to asset class returns. The resulting $R^2$s are as follows:

| Style Index | $R^2$ to Manager (%) |
|---|---|
| Large Growth | 82.4 |
| Large Value | 78.2 |
| Small Growth | 91.7 |
| Small Value | 84.4 |

You can now see that the manager tracks the Russell Small Cap Growth Index most closely, with a 91.7% $R^2$. It is safe to say that that the manager is a small-cap growth domestic equity manager.

When we talk about looking at a manager's pattern of returns, we don't necessarily mean performance in terms of the manager's total returns compared to the total returns of the index. Managers may wonder, "If I'm a growth manager, and growth underperformed value during a given period, but I did well during that period, then would I be mistaken for a value manager?" The answer to that question is *no*.

It makes no difference how well a manager performs over a particular period, since it is the month-to-month, or quarter-to-quarter pattern of those returns that identifies the manager's style. It is this pattern that Bill Sharpe refers to as a "manager's tracks in the sand".

To demonstrate that performance in terms of annualized returns has nothing to do with the $R^2$, Exhibit 1 plots returns for the mystery manager and the four Russell Style Indexes. Exhibit 2 compares annualized returns for each index along with the respective $R^2$s to the mystery manager. It is important to note that the index with the highest $R^2$, Small Growth, is the index that is the farthest from the mystery manager in terms of the annualized returns for this period.

# Exhibit 1: Performance of Mystery Manager versus Russell Style Indexes
## In-Sample Simulation

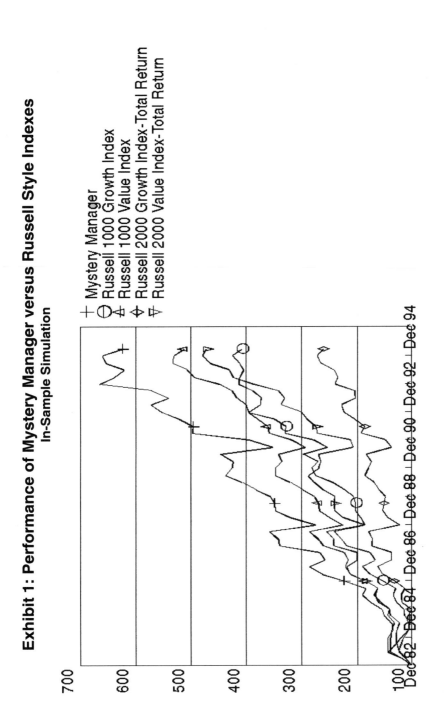

## Exhibit 2: Return Comparison

| Index/Manager | $R^2$ (%) | Annualized Returns |
|---|---|---|
| Mystery Manager | 100.00 | 17.67 |
| Large Growth | 82.40 | 13.31 |
| Large Value | 78.20 | 15.65 |
| Small Growth | 91.70 | 8.86 |
| Small Value | 84.04 | 14.78 |

Very few managers can be classified as pure small-cap growth, large-cap value, and so on. Rather, managers tend to be shades of styles. To determine what shades of the four styles a manager may be, we apply a more sophisticated procedure. Using a quadratic optimizer, we find what *combination* of style indexes gives us the highest tracking or $R^2$ to the manager's returns.

When we do this with the mystery manager, we find the optimum combination of style indexes to be 19.5% Large Growth, 26.8% Small Value, 53.6% Small Growth, and nothing in Large Value. This combination of Russell Style Indexes has an $R^2$ of 94.8% to the manager's returns. The higher we can get the $R^2$, the more information we can get about the manager's style. The information we can't get (the difference between 100% and 94.8%) can best be attributed to the manager's stock selection.

Exhibit 3 is a style chart we have developed that allows us to represent a manager's style graphically. The style chart measures value-to-growth on the horizontal axis and size on the vertical axis. The four corners are represented by the four Russell Style Indexes. The upper left-hand corner is the Large Value Index; the upper right-hand corner is the Large Growth Index; the lower right-hand corner is the Small Growth Index; and the lower left-hand corner is the Small Value Index. These reference points allow us to determine a manager's style by seeing where the manager's style point falls on the chart. The mystery manager's style point falls in the small-cap growth quadrant.

So far, we have taken 11 years of quarterly returns to calculate one style point for the entire period. Next, we would like to know how consistent this manager's style has been, and how much it has changed over this period of time. To do this, we will look at a series of style points generated over a number of rolling 12-quarter periods (if we were using monthly data, we would use a series of rolling 36-month periods).

## Exhibit 3: Manager Style

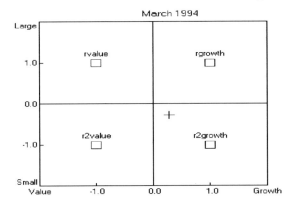

We calculate our first style point by calculating the $R^2$ on the first 12 quarters of data. We then move that 12-quarter window each quarter, thereby calculating one style point for each of these periods until we have calculated the most recent style point, which would be based on the most recent 12 quarters of data. This generates 34 style points on the manager style chart (see Exhibit 4). Each style point is represented by a cross. The crosses get larger in size as time passes. So, the smaller crosses represent the manager's earlier style, and the larger crosses represent the more recent style.

In this example, we can see that the mystery manager's earliest style was large growth. The style then began to move to small-/medium-cap value and, more recently (over the past four to five years), the style has consistently remained small-cap growth. This analysis took only a few seconds on a 486 laptop computer. Imagine how much time it would take if we were to analyze the holdings in each of these portfolios for each of these 34 quarters!

## USING STYLE INDEXES TO BUILD CUSTOMIZED BENCHMARKS

I have explained how we can identify a manager's style in terms of percentages of style indexes. We can also use those same indexes and percentages to construct a customized benchmark. If we want to construct one benchmark for the manager over the entire time frame, that benchmark would be 19% Large Growth, 27% Small Value, and 54% Small Growth. We can build such a composite style benchmark using the Russell indexes. Exhibit 5 shows the performance of such a benchmark compared to the manager's actual returns. For comparison's sake, we also include the returns for the S&P 500 Total Return Index.

## Exhibit 4: Manager Style

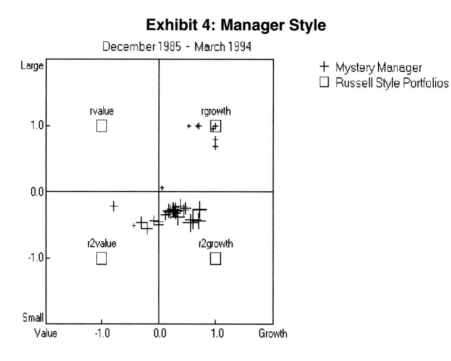

## Exhibit 5: Performance / Cumulative Excess Return

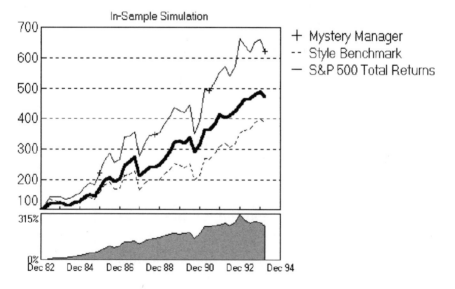

There are several problems with this benchmark. First of all, it does not in any way reflect how the manager's style has changed over time. If the manager today is much larger or has changed investment philosophies, or if there has been a turnover in portfolio managers, that manager's style may be much different today from ten years ago. In this case, building a benchmark for today that includes ten-year-old data doesn't make sense. On the other hand, if we simply look at what the manager has done over the last six months or the year, we may be looking at too short a period of time to determine style accurately. We believe that the most reasonable window to use when building a manager's benchmark is about three years, so with this in mind I use a 12-quarter window to build a benchmark for the mystery manager.

There is one other problem with a static ten-year benchmark: It is created after the fact. A benchmark, by definition, should be specified in advance of the period in which it is to be used to judge the manager's performance. To accomplish this, we build our benchmark "out-of-sample" by taking the first 12 quarters of returns to determine what the benchmark will be for the next, or the 13th quarter. This is done at the beginning of the 13th quarter and not at the end. In this way, we are determining the benchmark in advance and predicting what the manager's style will be on the basis of the past three years. Our out-of-sample benchmark has the following characteristics:

1. The benchmark is dynamic in that it will always represent the manager's style over the past 12 quarters.
2. The benchmark is specified in advance by being "out-of-sample."
3. The benchmark is investible, since one could invest in passive portfolios designed to replicate the Russell style indexes.

Exhibit 6 compares the performance of the out-of-sample benchmark (dashed line) to the actual performance of the mystery manager (line with crosses). The shaded area at the bottom of the graph is the cumulative excess return that the manager has achieved over and above the style benchmark. I believe this represents the manager's skill primarily in stock selection within his or her particular style.

## Exhibit 6: Performance / Cumulative Excess Return

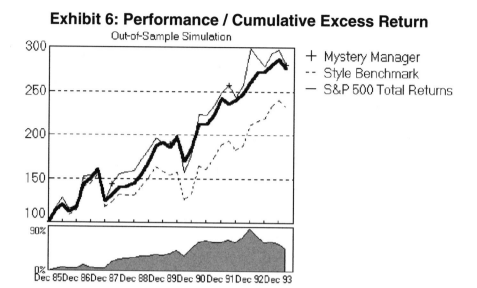

One doesn't hire an active manager and pay active management fees for "market-like" returns, because the same results can be achieved for much less money through an index fund. Similarly, one does not hire an active manager to deliver "style index-like" returns, as those too can be realized through investing in passive portfolios designed to replicate style indexes. We do, however, hire active managers and pay active management fees for a manager's skill in stock selection. This skill is seen in a manager's ability to select stocks that provide above-average performance within a particular style. It is this excess return over the style benchmark that warrants active management fees. This excess return can be measured only by developing proper style benchmarks. This important fact is revolutionizing the investment management profession.

One word of caution. Our discussion so far assumes that most managers have a fairly consistent style. If changes in style happen, they are usually fairly subtle and occur gradually. To the extent that this is true, the type of style analysis we have described can work very well. A small minority of managers, however, attempt to get their value added from rotating among sectors and styles, and predicting what particular sector or style will do well in the future. In this case, a manager's skill may lie more in the prediction of style or sector returns than in stock selection. Our style analysis and benchmark creation may not be suitable for analyzing such a manager. For true sector or style rotators, a more appropriate benchmark would be a broad-based benchmark such as the S&P 500 or the Russell 3000.

Our style analysis will spot a true sector rotator very quickly. First, the history of style points will fall all over the style graph, instead of clustering in one area as the mystery manager did. Second, the $R^2$ calculated to determine the validity of the benchmark will be low, particularly when calculated out-of-sample. In other words, it should be almost impossible to predict the future on the basis of the past because the manager's style is not consistent, and there will also be a very high turnover in the benchmark. The calculation of the benchmark is dynamic, since it is always based on the past 12 quarters of data. The typical annualized turnover in the style benchmark averages about 20% to 30% for a manager whose style is reasonably consistent, while the turnover for a true sector rotator will be much higher (typically over 100%).

I've noticed that a number of managers who call themselves sector rotators still tend to cluster in one particular style. To the degree that the manager's style can be predicted accurately out of sample, this approach is still relevant. It boils down to ignoring what managers call themselves and simply looking to see what they have been and are doing. Since most institutional pension plan sponsors hire specialty style managers, this concern over sector rotators should not be great.

## TESTING STYLE BENCHMARKS

So far our discussion of this methodology has been anecdotal. I have taken one real manager's returns to demonstrate that we can identify a manager's asset class and investment style. But is this approach valid enough to work on a large number of managers? More specifically,

1. Can we predict a manager's future style by looking at the manager's past style?
2. Can we build customized style benchmarks out-of-sample that capture more information and are better than a broad-based generic benchmark such as the S&P 500?

To answer these questions, I conducted a study using the Mobius Database, which is a commercial database that includes quarterly returns for over 1,200 domestic equity managers. I include only those managers who had quarterly returns for the last eight years, thereby creating a universe of 869 managers. Using a 12-quarter window, I do an out-of-sample style analysis and build a benchmark each quarter for five years. I do this for each manager.

I do not include the performance for the in-sample portion of data, which constitutes the first 12 quarters. Therefore, all of the returns for the benchmarks and style points are created out-of-sample. The first 12 quarters are used to predict what the style and the benchmark will be for the 13th quarter. Then the 12th-quarter window must move one quarter, so that quarters 2 through 13 are used to predict the 14th quarter. This process is continued for each of the 869 managers for a total of 20 predictions per manager. The accuracy of the predictions and the quality of the benchmarks can be determined by looking at the out-of-sample $R^2$s of the benchmarks to each of the manager's actual returns.

Exhibit 7 shows a scatter diagram for each of the 869 managers. The $R^2$ of the style benchmark is measured on the horizontal axis and the $R^2$ of the S&P 500 on the vertical axis. If there were little difference between the style $R^2$s and the market $R^2$s, the points on the graph would generally fall along the diagonal line. Note that the great majority of managers fall below the diagonal line, which indicates that the style $R^2$s are higher than the market $R^2$s. The average $R^2$ to the style benchmark for all of the managers is 83.7%; the average $R^2$ to the S&P 500 is only 76.43%. Since there are a number of extreme outliners that could skew the data, we also looked at the median $R^2$s, which are 87.25% and 80.61%, respectively, for the style benchmarks and the S&P 500.

In short, this study demonstrates that manager styles can be predicted on the basis of historical returns and that, for manager performance, custom-blended style benchmarks are superior to the S&P 500.

## STYLE ANALYSIS FOR THE TOTAL EQUITY FUND

Plan sponsors typically hire a number of managers for each asset class. For large funds, it is not uncommon to find a number of managers for each domestic equity style. When a plan has a dozen or more domestic equity managers, how does one determine the style of the total equity portfolio? This is done by simply aggregating the equity managers' styles in their respective weights and performing a style analysis for the total fund. The style of the total equity fund can then be compared to the style of the plan sponsor's overall benchmark, which is generally a market benchmark such as the S&P 500 or Russell 3000.

## Exhibit 7: Style Benchmarks Versus S&P 500 Out-of-Sample $R^2$s for 869 Managers

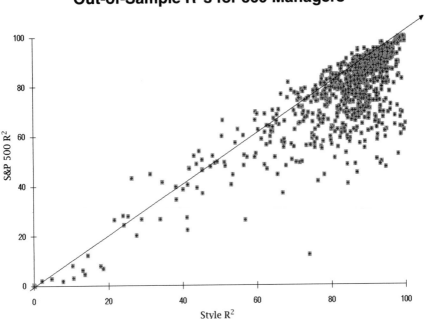

Any deviation in style away from the market benchmark represents a "bet" by the plan sponsor. That plan sponsor "bet," whether intentional or not, is determined by the kind or style of managers hired and the amount of money allocated among them.

Exhibit 8 shows the style point for a total domestic equity portfolio (the circle). In this case, the plan sponsor hired only large growth equity managers. The benchmark for the total equity fund is the Russell 3000 (the cross). In this example, the plan sponsor has made a big bet toward large growth. The Style Advisor software program determines the optimum portfolio, in terms of style, that the plan sponsor should invest in to remove this bet. In other words, investing in this portfolio would bring the style point of the plan sponsor's equity portfolio as close to the style point of the benchmark (the Russell 3000) as possible.

This new portfolio, which we call a *custom core portfolio* (also referred to as a completeness fund in Chapter 8) is represented by the diamond and is primarily all large value. This is a simple and extreme example, but it does demonstrate how the style of a fund can be analyzed and how a style bias can be removed if desired.

## Exhibit 8: Total Domestic Equity Portfolio Manager Style

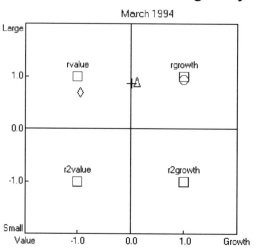

March 1994

+ Russell 3000 Index-Total Return
○ Total Domestic Equity Portfolio (LG)
△ 50% in Custom Core
◊ Custom Core Portfolio ( 50%)
□ Russell Style Portfolios

At first blush, it may seem as if the plan sponsor is just converting its total fund into one big index fund. But this is not the case. Remember, each particular active manager is expected to add value by beating a specific benchmark. If the managers in the aggregate are successful in accomplishing this goal, and the plan sponsor makes no significant bet away from the market benchmark, then, by definition, the total equity fund will outperform the market benchmark.

Any style bias represents a risk, and risk represents an opportunity for extra return. Sponsors who feel they have skill in predicting what investment styles will do well in the future can make such bets just as easily as they can move away from them. Whether a plan sponsor wants to make a style bet or remove a style bet, return-based style analysis as described here can be an extremely useful tool.

The style bets of plan sponsors can have dramatic return implications for the total fund. Many plan sponsors who choose not to make such bets do so because they believe that, over time, investment style return differences will even out, and that any good or bad total performance should be attributed to the managers. Although it is true that investment styles tend to smooth out over time, the length of time is beyond the threshold that most plan sponsors use when evaluating managers. This rationale has led to the somewhat common practice of changing managers every four to five years.

## Exhibit 9: Annualized Rates of Return
## for Rolling Five-Year Periods Using Russell Style Indexes

| Five-year Period | Large-cap Value | Large-cap Growth | Small-cap Value | Small-cap Growth | S&P 500 |
|---|---|---|---|---|---|
| 3/89-3/94 | 11.60 | 13.07 | 12.73 | 10.36 | 12.17 |
| 3/88-3/93 | 14.84 | 16.55 | 13.62 | 10.24 | 15.58 |
| 3/87-3/92 | 9.04 | 11.43 | 6.74 | 5.49 | 10.41 |
| 3/86-3/91 | 11.15 | 13.33 | 5.22 | 4.72 | 13.28 |
| 3/85-3/90 | 16.77 | 16.39 | 10.66 | 8.22 | 17.55 |
| 3/84-3/89 | 18.33 | 15.65 | 13.76 | 8.30 | 17.45 |
| 3/83-3/88 | 17.43 | 11.80 | 13.76 | 4.18 | 15.52 |
| 3/82-3/87 | 27.04 | 24.14 | 26.68 | 19.69 | 26.48 |
| 3/81-3/86 | 19.62 | 14.13 | 22.48 | 9.97 | 17.40 |
| 3/80-3/85 | 19.98 | 14.75 | 27.62 | 17.46 | 17.80 |
| 3/79-3/84 | 16.32 | 13.10 | 23.87 | 18.09 | 15.18 |

Exhibit 9 shows the annualized returns for the four investment styles measured over rolling five-year periods. Suppose a plan sponsor hired a small-cap growth manager in the first quarter of 1987, gave that manager five years to perform, and evaluated the performance after the first quarter of 1992. Let's assume that the small-cap growth manager's annualized performance was 8%. If the plan sponsor compares that to the S&P 500 (which was 10.41%) it might conclude that the manager is a poor performer. Yet Exhibit 9 shows us that annualized returns for small-cap growth during that period were only 5.49%. Hence the small-cap growth manager who provided 8% annualized returns was probably in the top quartile of the universe of small-cap growth managers for the period. Does it make sense to fire a manager simply because that manager's style is out of favor, even though the manager has demonstrated skill within a style?

Let's take another example. Suppose the plan sponsor hires a small value manager during the first quarter of 1979, and then five years later realizes that the manager has provided an average annual return of 20% during this period. Compared to the S&P 500, with only 15.18% annualized return, this manager looks like a genius. Compared to the Russell Small Value Index (which returned 23.87%), however, the performance looks quite different; the manager beat the market, but did not demonstrate skill within the style. This manager would be a much better candidate for replacement than the small-cap growth manager in the first example.

One of the primary purposes of using appropriate benchmarks to measure managers is to keep plan sponsors from making the mistakes that so many have made in the past of firing good managers and hiring or holding onto mediocre or poor-performing managers.

## RETURN-BASED ANALYSIS
## FOR INTERNATIONAL MANAGERS

Just as we use style indexes to analyze domestic equity managers, we can use regional or country indexes and currencies to analyze international managers. This topic is more fully discussed in Chapter 9 and 10. To demonstrate this, I've taken the monthly returns from a well-known international mutual fund and compared them to the Financial Times European Index, the Financial Times Pacific Basin Index, and the Baring Emerging Market Index. I ran this analysis from August 1988 through March 1994.

The allocation among the regional indexes that gives the highest $R^2$ to the manager is shown in Exhibit 10. Exhibit 11 plots an index constructed of this particular blend of indexes that tracks the international manager's returns quite closely. The $R^2$ of the index to the manager's returns is 88.5%, while the $R^2$ of the EAFE Index to the manager's returns is only 81.1%.

If we want to create an index with a much higher $R^2$, we can do so by using a number of country indexes. Along with the countries, we can also include currencies allowing the optimizer to go either long or short. Exhibit 12 shows an asset allocation based on such an analysis, where we have used ten countries, three currencies, and one emerging market index.[2] This exhibit shows the optimum percentages in each of the countries and currencies, which gives an $R^2$ of 92.2%. Exhibit 13 shows the benchmark plotted (dashed line) alongside the manager's actual returns.

So far, I've avoided calling this index a benchmark. Most international managers make country bets, and it is from these bets that they get a good portion of their value added. To include those bets in the benchmark is not fair to the manager, particularly when this is done in-sample. When we attempt to predict manager country bets out-of-sample using their past bets, the $R^2$ drops significantly because such predictions are inaccurate.

---

[2] Salomon Brothers Indexes: Countries: sihkb — Hong Kong, sijab — Japan, sinzb — New Zealand, sinlb — Netherlands, simab — Malaysia, siukb — United Kingdom, sispb — Spain, siwgb — Germany, sifrb — France, sicab — Canada. Currencies: exjapa — Japan, exgerm — Germany, exbrit — Britain. Emerging market index: bemi — Baring Emerging Market Index.

## Exhibit 10: Region Attribution Analysis
## Asset Allocation Analysis

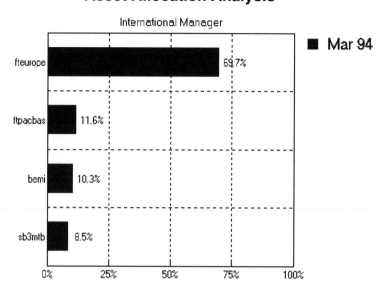

International Manager

■ Mar 94

- fteurope — 69.7%
- ftpacbas — 11.6%
- bemi — 10.3%
- sb3mtb — 8.5%

## Exhibit 11: Region Attribution Analysis
## Performance / Cumulative Excess Return

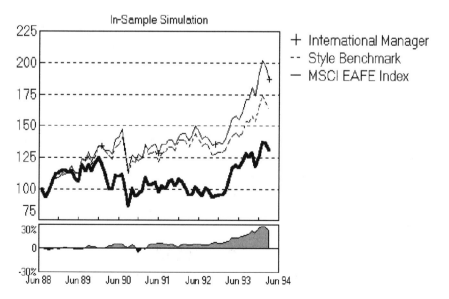

In-Sample Simulation

+ International Manager
-- Style Benchmark
— MSCI EAFE Index

## Exhibit 12: Country Attribution Analysis
## Asset Allocation Analysis

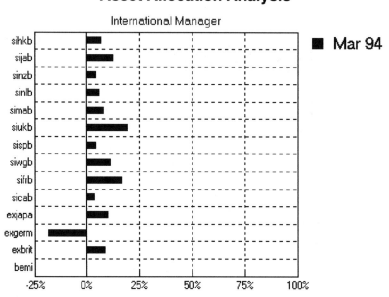

## Exhibit 13: Country Attribution Analysis
## Performance / Cumulative Excess Return

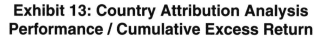

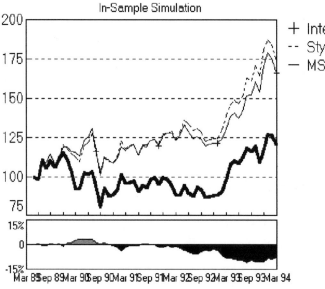

This analysis is intended more as an attribution analysis, in order to determine where an international manager has added value. In this example, stock selection appears to be neutral to negative. This can be seen as the difference between the country and currency index we have constructed versus the manager's actual returns, which are slightly lower. This manager has significantly outperformed the EAFE Index because of superior country weightings.

## CONCLUSION

I believe return-based style analysis has revolutionized and will continue to revolutionize the way plan sponsors analyze their existing and potential money managers. For years, it has been a laborious and expensive process to analyze a manager's style, reconstruct the manager's style history, and build a customized style benchmark. The task was typically done by an outside consultant, who had to analyze portfolio holdings for a number of periods. In fact, because of the labor intensity and sophistication of this process, few consultants attempted to build customized benchmarks for managers. Instead, they chose simply to use a market benchmark such as the S&P 500. I submit that this unsophisticated approach resulted in many unnecessary manager changes and cost plan sponsors millions of dollars in terms of additional and unnecessary expenses.

With the sophisticated software and manager databases currently available, a plan sponsor can apply return-based style analysis to any number of managers and build customized style benchmarks in a matter of minutes. A plan sponsor can also scan a database of 1,000 managers and quickly isolate those with the necessary style who have demonstrated skill within that style. Plan sponsors can also analyze the style of their total fund to be sure they have not taken any unwanted style bets because of the kinds of managers selected.

The idea started with Sharpe. The technology that allows plan sponsors to take advantage of Sharpe's work has been developed by others. These innovations are recent, and the possibilities have only begun to be realized.

# CHAPTER 4

# EQUITY STYLE CLASSIFICATION SYSTEM

*JON A. CHRISTOPHERSON, PH.D.*
*SENIOR RESEARCH ANALYST*
*FRANK RUSSELL COMPANY*

*DENNIS J. TRITTIN, CFA*
*DIRECTOR — ALPHA STRATEGY GROUP*
*FRANK RUSSELL COMPANY*

## INTRODUCTION

Managers with similar investment philosophies or "styles" will, on average, perform more like each other than like the overall market or like managers pursuing other styles (or we would have a distinction without a meaning). Performance similarities are to be expected, because these managers share similar portfolio characteristics and factor exposures that are priced or rewarded in the market.

Equity style classifications play several roles for investment practitioners. First, equity style is an important input in design and maintenance of an aggregate portfolio strategy. Second, style classifications serve as a useful guide for selection of managers to fill particular roles in a multiple-manager context. Third, they provide a framework for appraising the extent to which managers are adhering to their investment disciplines and, therefore, the roles for which they were hired. Finally, style classifications enable far more effective performance evaluations, whether versus indexes or peer group universes.

This chapter focuses on a model-driven method for determining manager style classification — the U.S. Equity Style Classification System (SCS). We describe the evolution of this rule-based system, which produces manager classifications, through examination of the various ways that a manager could be deemed value, growth, market-oriented, or small capitalization, given certain key aspects of the manager's equity portfolio.

First we review the traditional approaches to the task of classification, with their attendant difficulties. This is followed by an examination of the most popular current method of determining style — correlational analysis. Next is a description of the new approach used in SCS. We evaluate its performance by comparing its machine-based classifications to the manual classification of analysts. We also examine the utility of SCS in evaluating managers and managing aggregate funds.

## REASONS FOR CREATION
## OF THE STYLE CLASSIFICATION SYSTEM

The SCS or any quantitative method for style classification is useful for analysis of large numbers of managers for several reasons. Quantitative methods allow us to:

1. Provide a more systematic approach to style classification and reduce the judgment element.
2. Appraise persistence and purity of style quantitatively.
3. Check if an existing style classification has been carried out by analysts.
4. Provide an early warning of potential changes in style that can expose plan sponsors to unwanted fund risk.
5. Improve plan diversification by quantifying a sponsor's exposure to various styles, which, in turn, will reduce the likelihood of unintended factor bets in the aggregate portfolio.

Traditionally, Russell analysts have used a variety of methods to identify styles of investment management. An analysis of portfolio characteristics relative to both the market and to other managers over time has been the prime tool for assigning managers to styles. Descriptions of the investment process (including key security selection criteria and portfolio construction principles) are also important contributors. Descriptions of the process and the portfolio characteristics should match. As a final check, performance correlations are also computed to identify the Russell style index and universe that best explains manager returns.

Despite the care taken, the manager classification process is an imprecise science. There is no infallible, unambiguous method for classifying managers. Because classification fundamentally involves the naming and categorization of things, there is an element of arbitrariness in any classification system. This is because manager styles, in reality, represent a continuum, not discrete "boxes."

## APPROACHES TO THE CLASSIFICATION PROBLEM

There are a number of traditional quantitative methodologies for classifying observations into groups. Our purpose here is not to review individual methods as they could be applied to the problem of manager classification. We focus only on the methods attempted and the difficulties encountered using them.

### Multivariate Methods
A wide variety of multivariate methods have been used for the classification of subjects into groups. The approaches reviewed briefly in the Appendix include discriminant function analysis, cluster analysis, factor analysis, logistics regression (logit), and neural networks. All of the multivariate techniques explored have certain features in common. First, they are quantitatively empirical. This means that the classification process and coefficients are based upon specific observations rather than on general principles or theoretical assumptions. All but neural networks have inherently linear mathematical models. They all suffer from the "simultaneity" and training set problems.

### The Simultaneity Problem
Suppose a man is trying to figure the probability of locating a purple Corvette in California. A mathematical model that tells him that 10% of all Corvettes are in California and that 10% of all Corvettes are purple is of little use. What he wants to know is the conditional probability of the car being purple once he knows that it is a California Corvette. Unfortunately, multivariate techniques simultaneously evaluate all criteria as if there is no relationship between whether a Corvette is purple and whether it is found in California. The forced inclusion of classification variables whether relevant or not is a central problem of all multivariate techniques when applied to the classification task.

Because equity characteristics are often conditionally dependent, simultaneity is a problem. For example, a dividend yield of zero is common for growth stocks, but it also occurs for many low-priced value companies in distress. Consider a manager who has a low price-to-book ratio, low dividend yield, high sector concentration, and very high price/earnings ratio. A simultaneous consideration of factors could lead to a conclusion that this is a growth manager because of the very high P/E ratio, perhaps so high that it dominates all other factors. This menu of characteristics, however, is common among "contrarian value" investors, who typically invest in companies with depressed earnings (thus, high P/E ratios and no dividends). In these two instances the high P/E is misleading, and the simultaneous consideration of portfolio characteristics will lead to a classification error.

As another example, consider a manager with a market-like price-to-book ratio, low dividend yield, high P/E, and very low sector deviation. Under a simultaneous consideration methodology, this manager, because of the high P/E ratio and the low dividend yield, may be viewed as a growth manager. Yet, "market-oriented" is probably the most appropriate classification, because the low sector deviation is likely to overwhelm the valuation factors and produce performance more highly correlated with the broad market. Again, the simultaneous consideration of portfolio characteristics can lead to a classification error.

Mathematically, most multivariate methodologies are linear and simultaneously consider all variables. For example, a discriminant function value for an observation (a manager) is calculated according to Equation (1):

$$d_i = b_1 x_{i1} + b_2 x_{i2} + \ldots + b_j x_{ij} \tag{1}$$

where:   $d_i$ = value of a discriminant function;

$b_j$ = weight associated with the key criterion variable j;

$x_{ij}$ = value of key criterion variable for the subject i on variable j (e.g., P/E, P/B, etc.).

In Equation (1), $b_1$, $b_2$ . . ., $b_n$ are all included in the calculation of $d_i$. One cannot conditionally compute $d_i$. That is, one cannot use $b_2$ only if $b_1$ is high and ignore it otherwise.

Given Equation (1), one can clearly see why multivariate techniques would yield different classifications from an analyst's classification. Analysts focus on a few key variables in a manager's portfolio and then use other variables as supporting data to either confirm or reject their tentative classification, i.e., to refine their classification. They do not simultaneously consider all information because experience has shown that portfolio characteristics must be judged in context.

## Training Set Difficulties

Most multivariate classification techniques begin with training sets or groups of observations that are similar within the group and different across groups. These sets require very specific, formal, quantitatively measured variables, so that the methodologies can empirically derive the coefficients for their mathematical equations. Unfortunately, training sets are difficult to create and maintain, and they can contaminate the classification process in unintended ways. Let's explore some of these difficulties.

Members of a style in the training set are not all equally pure examples of the style. You can imagine it is not an easy empirical task to assign weights to managers to reflect their purity of style even when you think you know the managers. It is worse when you are unsure about the "purity" of the manager's style, or if the purity changes with time and you fail to notice it. One chooses training sets to maximize their purity, but this is, in fact, difficult to achieve.

To make matters worse, a manager's degree of style purity often wanders over time. We observe that a manager's portfolio characteristics tend to change over time (i.e., they may become more and then less purely representative of a style). Therefore, the integrity of the multivariate method's coefficients may be jeopardized as the training set fluctuates.

Among the most common reasons for unstable portfolio characteristics are:

1. Changes in portfolio strategy in response to market conditions, sector/stock/factor valuations, and the like. These bets may be short- or long-term in nature.
2. Changes in the investment philosophy, process, or personnel. New members of an investment team may have different definitions of what constitutes value, which may fundamentally alter portfolio traits.
3. Major changes in assets under management. Manager size affects portfolio characteristics in areas such as market capitalization, diversification, and the number of holdings.
4. Substantial periods of underperformance, which jeopardize the firm's business. Managers sometimes lose their nerve and begin changing investment strategy in an effort to improve short-term performance.

Finally, from an end user's point of view, multivariate techniques are problematical. There is no easy way to describe why a manager is classified in a particular manner. Discussions of factor loadings and discriminant function scores are obscure for even the experienced practitioner, and present obstacles to the analyst and sponsor.

These drawbacks to multivariate techniques do not mean they are not useful for classification, but only that their use in the equity manager style application is ineffective.

## Correlational Methods of Style Classification

The *effective mix* method introduced by Sharpe assesses style on the basis of asset class return pattern analysis.[1] This is a complete system of plan management and performance measurement based upon the analysis of covariance structures in manager return patterns over historical time periods. Sharpe believes that style analysis is the determination of a manager's effective asset mix. Fundamentally, these methodologies are all based on the analysis of covariance structures and/or correlation coefficients among manager returns and index returns.[2] The number of indexes varies, as does the form of presentation, but, the analysis of correlations is key to all of them.

The effective mix methodology uses quadratic optimization of asset class returns to match a manager's return pattern as closely as possible. The *style point* methodology of Tierney and Winston optimizes the correlations of a manager's return with its proprietary index returns in two-dimensional space.[3]

Implicit in return pattern analysis is the assumption that future returns at time t + 1 will behave like returns up to time t. The relationship between factor exposures and returns is circular — factor exposures lead to returns, hence returns indicate factor exposures. Sharpe uses the phrase, "The manager behaves as if...," which seems to imply a relationship between returns and factor exposures.[4] The assumption that return patterns imply a certain set of factor exposures is a very important one, which we will see is not always the case.

Several caveats surface with correlational analysis, but for reasons of space we will focus on only two problems that affect the determination of style. The first is the susceptibility of returns to noisy data. The second caveat has to do with style dynamics.

---

[1] William F. Sharpe "Determining a Fund's Effective Asset Mix," *Investment Management Review* (December 1988), pp.59-69.

[2] William F. Sharpe "Asset Allocation: Management Style and Performance Measurement," *Journal of Portfolio Management* (Winter 1992), pp 7-19. David Tierney and Kenneth Winston "Using Generic Benchmarks to Present Manager Styles," *Journal of Portfolio Management* (Summer 1991), pp 33-36.

[3] Tierney and Winston, "Using Generic Benchmarks to Present Manager Styles," *op. cit.*

[4] Sharpe, "Determining a Fund's Effective Mix," *op. cit.*

# The Confounding of Specific Risk and Style in Manager Returns

Firm-specific risk causes managers with identical investment strategies, but different portfolios, to obtain approximately, but not exactly, the same returns. Any distribution of monthly quarterly stock returns by style index membership for all stocks in the Russell 3000® Index will reveal a high degree of variability and overlap of stock returns among the style indexes. There is variation in the average return to each style index, and there is variation around those means. Assuming all the stocks in a style are taking similar risk exposures, the variability in return around the average comes from variations around average risk exposures and firm-specific risk.

Managers pursuing a given style can be viewed as selecting samples of stocks from the style index distributions. Given the variability of returns within one style, managers pursuing the same style are likely to have returns that vary from the index and from those of other managers employing the same style. Furthermore, the longer the window of measurement, the more a manager's portfolio average return will approach the underlying style index return.[5] This means that, on average, managers' long-run returns will be closer to their style index return than to some other style index return — but not in every case and perhaps not in the short run.

We are likely often to see large-capitalization behavior of some small stocks because in any single time period some small-capitalization stocks will *just happen by chance* to correlate more highly with a large-cap stock index than they do with a small-cap stock index. If we rely only on the correlations, we could be led by the methodology to believe the stocks have factor exposures they do not have.

To demonstrate this potential misspecification, we took five years of quarterly returns ending in the first quarter of 1988 for 180 managers (20 of whom are small-cap managers) and correlated these returns with the Russell 1000® Index returns over the same period. We then note whether the manager correlates most highly with a large-cap index or the small-cap index. We then apply the same procedure to the manager's returns over the subsequent five years of quarterly returns ending in the first quarter of 1993. Exhibit 1 presents these results.

---

[5] Since a manager's portfolio over time can be viewed as a series of samples drawn from lognormal stock return distributions, we know, from the central limit theorem, that the mean of the manager's returns will approach the mean of the underlying style index return distribution.

## Exhibit 1: Comparison of Manager Correlations Over Two Consecutive Five-Year Periods
### Columns: 5 Years Ending First Quarter 1993
### Rows: 5 Years Ending First Quarter 1988

|  | Correlates Highest with R2000 in 1993 | Correlates Highest with R1000 in 1993 | Totals |
|---|---|---|---|
| Correlates Highest with R2000 in 1988 | 11 | 12 | 23 |
| Row% | 47.8 | 52.2 |  |
| Correlates Highest with R1000 in 1993 | 14 | 143 | 157 |
| Row% | 8.9 | 91.1 |  |
| Totals | 25 | 155 | 180 |
| Column% | 13.9% | 86.1% | 100.0% |

The upper set of numbers to the left in Exhibit 1 represents the numbers and percentages of times that all managers who correlated more highly with the Russell 2000® than with the Russell 1000® in the initial five year period also correlated highest with the Russell 2000 in the subsequent five-year period. Eleven managers fall into this category, which is 47.8% of the total of 23 managers who correlated with the Russell 2000 in the first time period. The second cell in the first row shows that 12 (52.2%) of those 23 managers who correlated with the Russell 2000 in the first time period did not in the second time period.

The lower set of numbers shows the same kind of analysis for managers who correlated most highly with the large-cap indexes. In this case, of 157 managers, only 14 (8.9%) correlated with the small cap index in the second time period, while 143 (91.1%) correlated with the large-cap indexes in both time periods.

These data illustrate that specific risk, or noise, is in not only the stocks' underlying manager portfolios but also in the returns of manager portfolios. Even in large portfolios, the noise does not cancel out, leaving only true style exposure. The specific risk cumulates up to the portfolio level and causes some managers to correlate with a style index other than their universe style index.

*Correlation analysis can induce factor identification error and, by extension, plan risk. This error occurs because the correlational analysis cannot tell the difference between noise and true factor exposures.*[6]

Since the sources of return variation are confounded, one cannot know how serious this specific risk problem is, or if it even exists at all, using correlational analysis.

## Blindness to Style Dynamics

Style changes are important to managing plan risk. Forecasts can be accurate when styles are stable, i.e., when there is no change in style, but they can be wrong when styles shift or drift or when cycles occur. Correlation analysis tends to be blind to style dynamics. The reasons for this follow inexorably from the nature of the method.

In correlational analysis, correlations are computed over a window — in the case of effective mix, 60 months. In such windows, the most recent time point is as important as the most remote time point. If a style shift occurs, this shows up in the most recent time point. As the effects of the change in style cumulate over time, a larger proportion of the observations reflect this new style. Gradually the proportion of points reflecting the old style become smaller, and the effective mix solution changes.

Inevitably, there is a delay in the recognition of a style change with effective mix methods. The length of the delay will be a function of the severity of the style shift and the extent to which the styles are differentially rewarded.

Exhibit 2 presents an example of an effective mix error over a long period of time. In this time-series graph, the vertical axis shows the probability that the portfolio is of some given style. The solid black line shows that the probability of the manager being small-cap drops over time. The $\hat{R}_{EM}$ and $\hat{R}_{SCS}$ are the conditional forecast of the manager's return in the second quarter of 1992 using the weights at the last time style was assessed. This should be compared with the actual R for the manager. The old market-oriented data points are just about out of the 60-month window, but effective mix continues to include these old data in assigning current style, and evaluates the manager incorrectly. The conditional forecast error of SCS is less than the conditional forecast error of the effective mix solution. Effective mix is better, in most cases, than simply using broad indexes but it can provide misleading conclusions and is prone to late identification of style shifts.

---

[6] As an aside, correlational analysis can also attribute stock-picking ability, i.e., alpha, to index behavior. Style index returns that differ from those expected from factor exposures may not be random. Appearing and disappearing factors (i.e., oil shock exposure — a nonpriced factor) may be priced for a certain period of time and then disappear. These factors may produce systematic positive or negative shocks to a style index return for a reasonable period of time. See Barr Rosenberg, "Choosing a Multiple Factor Model," *Investment Management Review* (September 1987), pp. 33-35. and Nai-fu Chen, Richard Roll, and Stephen A. Ross, "Economic Forces and the Stock Market," *Journal of Business* (59) pp. 383-403.

## Exhibit 2: Growth Style Classification

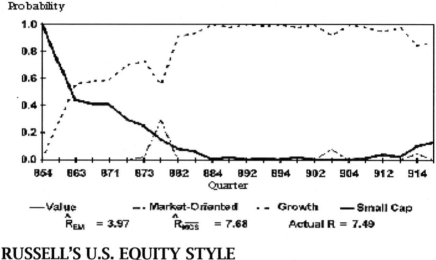

Probability

—Value      — · Market-Oriented      · · Growth      — Small Cap

$\hat{R}_{EM}$ = 3.97          $\hat{R}_{MOS}$ = 7.68          Actual R = 7.49

## RUSSELL'S U.S. EQUITY STYLE CLASSIFICATION SYSTEM (SCS)

When we were not able to find a satisfactory style assessment using covariance structures alone, we turned toward a new way based on portfolio characteristics. The SCS is an "expert system" that determines the probability of membership in four equity styles. It is based on an analysis of market-relative and style-relative portfolio characteristics. Given our discussion of the need for a conditional decision-making model, the system is based on emulating the thought processes of equity analysts. The system has a number of advantages.

1. It uses a decision tree approach that applies a series of confirming judgments to preliminary classifications. The sequential decision-making methodology takes a conditional probability approach.

2. It evaluates equity characteristics and derives probabilities of membership in each of Russell's four equity styles (Growth, Market-Oriented, Value, and Small-Capitalization) on the basis of the deviation of key fundamental factors from those of selected Russell indexes. Hence, it takes a market-relative approach that is responsive to changes in the characteristics of the broad market. The probability approach also reflects the idea that manager styles are best viewed as a continuum.

3. It is based on factors deemed most powerful in explaining manager performance. It is a broadly based empirical system that also incorporates diversification characteristics.

4. It classifies managers into the style with the highest probability, while apportioning the probability into the four styles based on their relative "purity."

5. It presents a clear rationale for classification. Users can identify the path (and variables) that are most influential in the classification. Hence, the system produces intuitively comprehensible results.

6. It classifies managers chronologically in a series of snapshots to reveal the variations in classification over time. Therefore, it serves as an early warning system of change in manager style.

More than 20 logic paths used by analysts have been identified that lead to style classifications. Given the manager's portfolio characteristics relative to selected Russell indexes and an appraisal of economic sector diversification, the probability that the manager follows any one of the paths is computed. Many of the paths lead to the same style classification. All the paths are cumulated into the four basic style groups. Managers are assigned to the style group to which they have the highest total probability of belonging.

The following sections review the variables and decision rules, classification paths, and examples of the classification system in action.

## Key Variables in the Classification Process

Six variables are used to classify managers into the four equity styles. Most of these variables are judged in market-relative terms to control for changing market conditions.

The first — and most critical — variable in the classification process is the *percentage of the manager's portfolio in the Russell 2500™ Index*. The second variable is *price-to-book* value. This is the most important variable in determining manager style (after size criteria) in that it is a more stable measure of value than P/E. The third variable is *dividend yield*. While dividend yield is largely a function of corporate dividend policy, it is a more stable measure than P/E. The fourth variable is the *price-to-earnings ratio*, which tends to confirm or refine the valuation assessment in P/B and dividend yield. The fifth variable is *return on equity (ROE)*. This variable is incorporated into the SCS to permit "growth-at-a-price" managers to be classified as market-oriented.

The final variable is the *sector deviation measure*. This measures the size of the aggregate portfolio's economic sector exposures relative to the sector weightings of the Russell 3000. The role of the sector deviation measure variable is to override or moderate preliminary growth or value classifications if the portfolio is very diversified. Sector diversification can overwhelm the growth or value characteristics as an explanation for performance.

## CLASSIFICATION LOGIC PATHS AND THE COMPOSITE DECISION TREE

The central logic of Russell's classification process is the argument that classification is best accomplished through a sequential or conditional decision-making process using the six key variables. There are many possible sequences in which to evaluate the six key variables. Obviously, we do not consider all possible combinations. For convenience, we call such sequences of evaluation of data "paths" through the data. This raises the question of which of these paths are chosen and why.

The style classification decision tree is shown in Exhibit 3. It is basically a directed graph in which the boxes indicate decision points (i.e., variable tests), and the arrows indicate the sequence of decisions. The medium-gray lines beginning at the top of the graph and running down the center to the bottom of the graph show the decision path for a classic market-oriented manager. The heavy black arrows running down the left-hand side of the graph outline the classic path to a value style classification, and the light gray arrows running down the right-hand side of the graph outline the classic path to a growth style classification. The smaller black arrows indicate variations off the classic paths, with small-cap being a path all its own.

An easy way to view this graph is to consider each line between variable evaluation points as a water pipe and each decision point as a valve or set of valves. Depending on the values of the manager's portfolio characteristics, the valves are set at completely closed or fully open or somewhere in between.

Exhibit 3: Style Classification Decision Tree

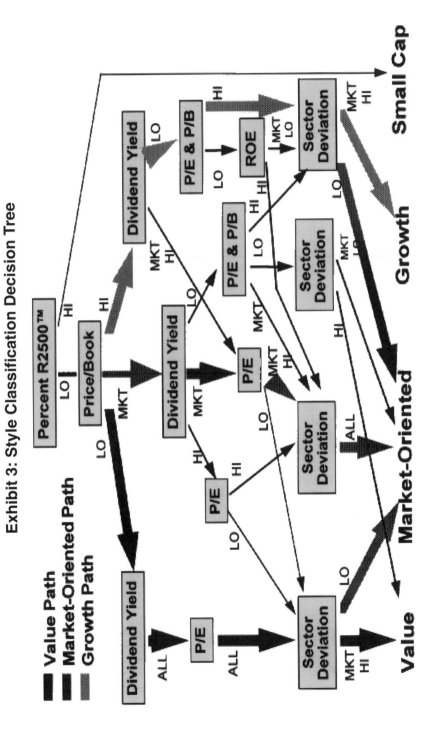

Now picture the manager classification process as a procedure where you pour in at the top a glass of water representing 100% of the probability of style membership. Depending on the settings of the valves, the water pours through the pipes in various ways. If the value of a key characteristic for a manager is high relative to the market, the "high" valve is open and the "low" valve is closed, so all the water flows down the pipe leading from the high valve. For example, the first decision point at the top has two valves — a low and high valve — that will be set depending on the percentage of the manager's portfolio in the Russell 2500 index.

All the pipes end up leading to one of four buckets at the bottom. The amount of water in each bucket represents the probability of membership in each style at a particular time.

## Redirecting Initial Classifications

In Exhibit 4, we demonstrate how the primary probabilities of style membership based on price-to-book can be overridden by subsequent portfolio characteristics. This capability to evaluate information conditionally makes the SCS unique among style classification methodologies. For example, if the price to book is market level, a clear value or growth orientation is not indicated; rather, the market-oriented style is indicated. To be certain, the influences of dividend yield and P/E ratio in the next two decision levels are examined to confirm or reject this preliminary decision. These pieces of information could steer the initial classification probabilities in new directions.

If the dividend yield is low, let us follow through on this path. A low dividend yield is typical of growth managers. At the P/E decision point on this path, we reconsider P/B since low P/Es can exist when cyclical companies are at peak earnings. We bias the P/E evaluation back toward market-oriented on this path. If the P/E is sufficiently low, we may have a value manager with a low dividend yield. If the P/E-P/B is market-like, and the sector deviation is low, then market-oriented is indicated. In this case, the combination of the probabilities associated with various levels of dividend yield, P/E ratio, and sector deviation can override or redirect the flow of probabilities indicated by the initial price-to-book.

## Determining Probabilities Of Group Membership

Central to the approach taken in the SCS is deciding the probabilities at each decision point in the chains of classification reasoning, or, using our water flow analogy, setting the degree of openness for each of the valves that control the flow of probabilities. The basic building blocks of the classification process are each manager's portfolio characteristics relative to the large-cap market. Given a manager's key portfolio characteristics, such as price-to-book, we establish a link between a specific level of price-to-book and a specific probability of style of management.

Exhibit 4: Style Classification Decision Tree

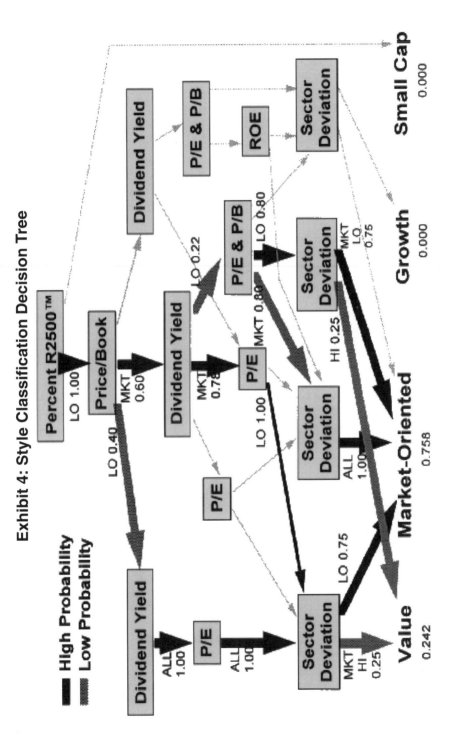

*Portfolio Characteristics and Style Membership:* About 70% of the value managers in Russell's large-capitalization value universe have a P/B lower than about 1.7 standard deviations below the market, and only 4% have a P/B lower than 3.0 standard deviations below the market. Consequently, it is reasonable to say that the probability that a manager who has a P/B equal to -0.3 sigma is a value manager is about 10%. Furthermore, the probability that a manager who has a P/B equal to -3.0 sigma is a value manager is 100%. In other words, the lower the P/B, the higher the probability the manager is a value manager.

Examination of the growth universes shows a similar cumulative frequency distribution of P/B. The same logic applies to the relationship between values of P/B and the probability a manager will be classified as growth.

We would expect market-oriented managers to have market-level P/Bs and be approximately normally distributed around the mean. As the managers' P/B moves away from the market in either direction, the probability of classification as a market-oriented manager decreases.

Given the distributions of P/B in the style universes, we have determined that the relationship between portfolio characteristics and the probabilities of a style membership is inherently nonlinear. The probability that a manager is a value manager increases as the price-to-book drops below the market level price-to-book, but it does not decline linearly; i.e., the probability of value classification does not increase 5% as the price-to-book drops 5% below market. Rather, the probability of market-oriented classification remains fairly constant as long as the price-to-book is reasonably close to market. But, as the price-to-book moves away from the flat spot around the market mean, the probability of value classification climbs very rapidly (and, conversely, the market-oriented probability drops off rapidly).

These empirical observations are represented in the function shown in Exhibit 5.

# Nonlinear Probability Functions
## Versus Traditional Screening

The curved line in Exhibit 5 represents a more realistic probability of membership function. As the P/B ratio moves from below the market to above the market, the probability rises or drops toward one or zero. In a sense, then, the nonlinear probability functions that are used in the manager classification methodology can be seen as a loose interpretation of classic screen, or hurdle, methodology.

## Exhibit 5: Breakpoint Method versus Non-linear Probability Function for Determining Style Membership

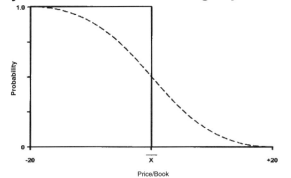

The relationship between probability of group membership based on portfolio characteristics is in sharp contrast to traditional screening methods. The screening of stocks on levels of characteristics, such as the market-relative P/B ratio, is implicitly a step-probability function, where the probabilities of group membership change abruptly as the characteristic approaches and passes a screening breakpoint, such as a market value.

In Exhibit 5, we represent a screening probability function with the square lines. The probability of being value is 1.0 when the P/B ratio is below the market and drops to zero when the P/B is above the market. The probability of membership when P/B is exactly equal to the market is not defined — or, rather, is left vague.

The yes/no (or screen or hurdle) approach is widely used in the investment industry, but it is arbitrary.[7] It can also be misleading because it assumes that any value above the cutoff is equal in weight to all other values above the cutoff, when, in fact, that is not the way most people think. In reality, the higher the value of the manager, the more convinced most analysts would be about the manager's style classification.

## Multiple Branches and Probabilities

Consider again the decision tree in Exhibit 3 and the empirical cumulative frequency charts in Exhibits 2, 3, and 4. Note that the branch for the price-to-book variable in Exhibit 3 has three arrows leading from it. How do we decide the probabilities associated with each of the arrows leading from this branch in Exhibit 3?

---

[7] This cliff of breakpoint methodology was used in the creation of the original Russell Style Indexes (Kelly Haughton and Jon A. Christopherson "Equity Style Indexes: Tools for Better Performance Evaluation and Plan Management," *Russell White Paper*,1989).

## Exhibit 6: Value of Characteristics

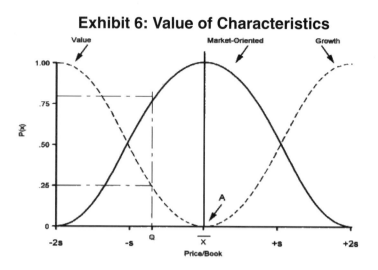

Exhibit 6 helps show how a given manager portfolio characteristic is evaluated in terms of the probability that it is value oriented, market-oriented, or growth-oriented. This logic is at the heart of the SCS probability assignment.

The probabilities associated with the market-oriented path, (the center branch of Exhibit 3), follow the market-oriented curve in Exhibit 6. If the manager's price-to-book is at the market, the function will have a probability equal to 1.0. Using the valve and pipe analogy, the valve will be set fully open. As a manager's price-to-book moves away from the market, the probability of market-oriented falls. When the price-to-book is at or below the pole for value, the probability of market-oriented falls to zero (the valve is fully closed), and the value probability goes to 1.0 (the value valve is fully open).

The growth curve in Exhibit 6 shows the probabilities for the growth (or high branch) of the P/B decision point in Exhibit 3. Again, at the value style index median, the probability of growth style is zero; it remains zero until the price-to-book reaches the market. As the price-to-book moves above the market, the probability of the growth path begins to increase, and by the time it reaches the growth style index median, the probability of growth is 1.0.

The value curve in Exhibit 6 shows the probabilities associated with the left-hand branch, or the value path. It mirrors the growth form and complements the lower half of the market-oriented form.

## Exhibit 7: Style Shift Example

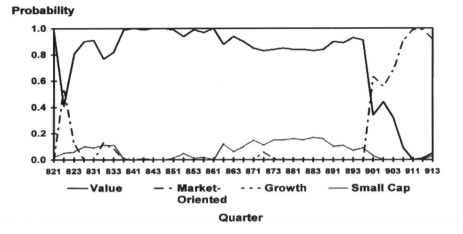

Probability

821 823 831 833 841 843 851 853 861 863 871 873 881 883 891 893 901 903 911 913

——Value        — - Market-      - - - Growth        —— Small Cap
                   Oriented

Quarter

We emphasize that in this exhibit, and in SCS generally, *the characteristics are judged in market-relative terms*. The market-relative approach allows the system to adapt to changing market characteristics and to assign the most accurate probabilities of style membership through time. Clearly, a manager's absolute portfolio characteristics are heavily influenced by changes in the overall market's valuation.

## TIME SERIES ANALYSIS OF STYLE CLASSIFICATION

One of the most important and useful features of the SCS is its ability to analyze style classifications over time. The system allows the user to monitor portfolios on a period-by-period basis to ensure the manager is delivering the product he or she expects. This is a key difference between SCS and correlational methods. The SCS looks only at the current portfolio to make its style assessment and is not influenced by a portfolio's history. SCS therefore provides an early warning system for managers who are altering major aspects of their portfolios. The SCS helps an investor hiring new managers to appraise persistence and purity of style through time.

Exhibit 7 is a graph of the time series, from December 1982 to September 1991, of classifications of a value manager. It is a visual depiction of the longitudinal stability of the manager's classification. Firm analysts had classified the manager as value for some time, yet the system determined the style was market-oriented as of April 1, 1990. Why the discrepancy?

## Exhibit 8: Manager Excess Performance Correlations* with Russell Indexes Before and After Style Shifts

|  | Before Style Shift | After Style Shift |
|---|---|---|
| Russell 1000® Index | -0.386 | +0.19 |
| Russell 1000® Value Index | +0.421 | -0.17 |
| *Excess returns of the Russell 3000® Index | | |

Subsequent in-depth research by analysts revealed some interesting things about this manager. Poor performance caused the investment committee to become conscious of the manager's heavy sector bets and value orientation relative to the market. The manager subsequently adjusted its process to ensure that portfolios had more market-like exposures. Thus, the system was successful in identifying changes in the portfolio characteristics that were at odds with the manager's value history, and the manager was then classified as market-oriented.

Not coincidentally, the manager's performance subsequent to early 1991 shows higher tracking versus the Russell 1000 and weaker tracking with the Russell 1000 Value Index. Exhibit 8 shows the monthly excess return correlations of the manager before and after the style shift. Before the style shift, the manager correlated negatively with the Russell 1000 but flipped signs after the style shift. The reverse pattern holds for the manager's performance versus the Russell 1000 Value Index.

Exhibit 9 shows the performance patterns in terms of excess returns around the Russell 3000. The horizontal line is the Russell 3000 return so that the manager returns and the Russell 1000 Value Index are excess returns around the line. Before the style shift point, the manager's excess returns tracked the excess returns of the Russell 1000 Value Index, and after the style shift point, excess returns track the Russell 3000 with less variation. (Note: This result is consistent with the relationship between equity characteristics and subsequent performance mentioned at the beginning of the chapter.)

As an aside, this manager also reinforces one point about the instability of training sets. Managers may make changes to their process or take short-term bets away from a normal position. Hence, a manager who historically is a pure example of a given style may become less so in other periods. If this manager were to be used in a training set, it is plain to see how its inclusion would distort the classification equations and introduce noise into the process.

## Exhibit 9: One-Quarter Rolling Excess Returns
### Manager With Style Shift and Corresponding Russell Indexes
### Versus Russell 3000

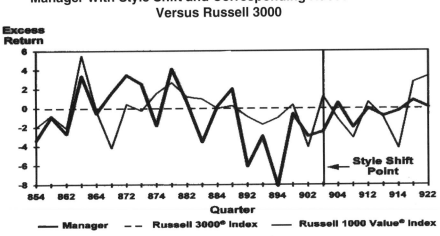

The method used in Exhibit 10 to plot the manager in growth/value space and large-cap/small-cap space is based on a scaling of the SCS probabilities so that the value and growth probabilities scale from -1 to +1 with market-oriented at zero. The probability of small-capitalization is similarly scaled, with zero meaning mid-cap.

Exhibit 10 describes the movement of another confounding value manager. Originally the manager was classified as a small-cap manager. As you can see in the graph, the manager has slowly drifted up in capitalization and has also wandered between value and growth several times. The value/growth wandering is consistent with the manager's particular definition of value and is not deemed a problem, but the drift in capitalization is not what was expected or desired. After instructions to the manager to maintain the small-cap orientation, the SCS confirmed in the following quarter that the manager had complied with the mandate.

## PERFORMANCE OF THE CLASSIFICATION SYSTEM VERSUS ANALYSTS

If the SCS works adequately, we would expect the machine-generated classifications to correlate highly with Russell equity analysts' classifications. Where there are disagreements, these should be understandable, given the propensity of some managers to wander around their overall style.

## Exhibit 10: Position of Manager in Growth/Value and Large-/Small-Cap Space

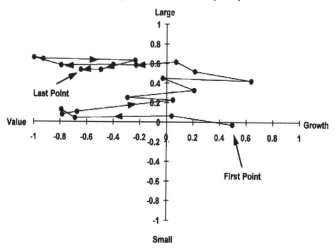

Exhibit 11 is a contingency table of the Russell analyst style classifications compared with the SCS classifications at a particular time, December 31, 1990 (see the Appendix for discussion of the data). At the left are the analysts' classifications, and across the top are the system's classifications. The diagonal cells of the table in Exhibit 11 contain the number of agreed-upon classifications. Numbers off the diagonal are disagreements.

For now, let's focus on what the diagonal of the exhibit tells us. The first observation is that the ability to classify managers varies by style. For example, in the growth universe, SCS correctly matches 45 out of 53 managers, or 84.9% of the managers. For the market-oriented universe of 79 managers, SCS does less well; the system correctly classifies only 50, or 63.3%. For the value universe of 67 managers, SCS correctly classifies 58, or 86.6%. In the small-capitalization universe of 65 managers, 59 are correctly classified, for a very high 90.8% correct classification rate.

Overall, the system correctly matches 212 out of 264 managers, or 80.3%. Whether 80% for this time period is an adequately high percentage of classifications is not abundantly clear (again recognizing that the SCS classifications are for one particular time, while analysts evaluate multiple periods). Ideally, we would like to see 100% correct classifications, although 80% is acceptable. We must examine the 53 disagreements to be able to make an adequate judgment.

## Exhibit 11: Russell Analyst Style Classification
## Versus SCS Style Classification

| Analyst Classification | Growth | Market-Oriented | Value | Small-Capitalization | Total |
|---|---|---|---|---|---|
| | 45 | 8 | 0 | 0 | 53 |
| Growth | 84.91% | 15.09% | 0.00% | 0.00% | 20.00% |
| | 7 | 50 | 22 | 0 | 79 |
| Market-Oriented | 8.86% | 63.29% | 27.85% | 0.00% | 29.81% |
| | 0 | 7 | 58 | 2 | 67 |
| Value | 0.00% | 10.45% | 86.57% | 2.99% | 25.38% |
| | 6 | 0 | 0 | 59 | 65 |
| Small-Capitalization | 9.23% | 0.00% | 0.00% | 90.77% | 24.53% |
| | 58 | 65 | 80 | 61 | 264 |
| Total | 22.97% | 24.62% | 30.30% | 23.11% | 100.0% |

| Statistics: | |
|---|---|
| | 0.0001 |
| Chi square = p(x) | 465.9 |
| Percentage of agreement | 212/264 = 80% |
| Disagreement or misclassification | 53/264 = 20% |

It is encouraging to note that of the eight misclassified growth managers, all are assigned to market-oriented, a close neighbor in terms of style. Of the 29 market-oriented misclassifications, seven are misclassified as growth, and 22 are misclassified as value. Again, these are neighboring classifications and not unexpected at a particular time periods as market-oriented managers periodically "wander" about the adjacent styles. Of the nine misclassified value managers, seven are misclassified as market-oriented, and two as small capitalization. It is important to note that no value manager was classified as growth and no growth managers are classified as value managers.

The errors, when they occurred, are to neighboring classifications, as in the case of the manager shown in Exhibit 10. The chi square for this exhibit is 462, which indicates that this pattern is unlikely to be generated by a random process. The lambda asymmetric R/C correlation coefficient for categorical tables is 0.71, indicating a strong relationship between the Russell analyst classifications and the SCS classification system.

## Time Series Analysis of Disagreements

Clearly, the manager we saw in Exhibit 9 cannot be considered to represent a classification error by the SCS. Rather, that manager performance exhibits a pattern that the system is designed to detect. SCS calls the analyst's or sponsor's attention to managers who take significant bets away from their normal pattern. In this particular case, the manager's normal pattern is to oscillate between market-oriented and growth styles, thereby presenting considerable classification difficulties and demonstrating the utility of systematic analysis. Some managers do wander around their normal style, and others seem to change the basic nature of their portfolios permanently. The market-relative approach of the system allows us to identify and track these types of managers.

A review of classification discrepancies shown in Exhibit 12 underscores the points we made earlier about the difficulties of using training sets and the issue of inconsistency in manager style. Exhibit 12 shows the average long-term probabilities of each of the mismatched managers. A time series analysis of the SCS was run for each manager and the average probabilities for each style are reported. The highest average probability is italicized and shaded. In the last column is a code assigning a reason for the disagreement.

We have given one or two codes to the discrepancy based on a visual inspection of the time series graph. Of the 54 disagreements, 30 appear to be the result of managers wandering away on a short-term basis from their long-run average style; 24 managers appear to have changed their styles or to be in the process of doing so. Given the analysis of disagreements, the SCS classifies over 90% of the managers correctly.

## ADVANTAGES OF THE SCS METHOD

The new SCS outlined here is a systematic and unbiased means of appraising equity style. Its distinctive features give it advantages over other systems for a variety of reasons.

### Features of SCS

1. SCS provides a series of checks and balances in the classification process in a conditional decision-making framework, which tends to reduce the dominance of odd data combinations.

2. SCS appraises the evolution in a manager's style through time in a market-relative fashion.

3. SCS avoids the "simultaneity problem" inherent in other linear multivariate methodologies.

4. SCS reflects the style biases inherent in many managers' styles.

## Exhibit 12: Time Series Analysis of Misclassifications

| Analyst Classification | SCS Classification | Average Probabilities* | | | | Reason for Error ** |
|---|---|---|---|---|---|---|
| | | VL | MO | GR | SC | |
| VL | MO | 0.57 | 0.25 | 0.00 | 0.08 | V |
| MO | VL | 0.87 | 0.13 | 0.00 | 0.00 | V |
| MO | VL | 0.36 | 0.64 | 0.00 | 0.00 | V |
| MO | VL | 0.59 | 0.38 | 0.03 | 0.00 | S |
| GR | MO | 0.06 | 0.34 | 0.60 | 0.00 | V |
| MO | VL | 0.76 | 0.24 | 0.00 | 0.00 | S, A |
| VL | MO | 0.75 | 0.25 | 0.00 | 0.00 | S |
| MO | VL | 0.19 | 0.81 | 0.00 | 0.00 | V |
| MO | VL | 0.88 | 0.09 | 0.00 | 0.03 | A |
| SC | GR | 0.00 | 0.02 | 0.32 | 0.66 | V, S |
| MO | VL | 0.72 | 0.08 | 0.07 | 0.13 | S |
| MO | VL | 0.81 | 0.19 | 0.00 | 0.00 | A |
| SC | GR | 0.00 | 0.10 | 0.35 | 0.55 | V |
| MO | VL | 0.63 | 0.21 | 0.00 | 0.16 | S |
| GR | MO | 0.02 | 0.22 | 0.76 | 0.00 | S |
| VL | SC | 0.42 | 0.00 | 0.00 | 0.58 | V, A |
| VL | MO | 0.83 | 0.17 | 0.00 | 0.00 | V |
| MO | VL | 0.57 | 0.25 | 0.02 | 0.16 | V, S |
| SC | GR | 0.00 | 0.01 | 0.26 | 0.73 | V, S |
| MO | VL | 0.86 | 0.14 | 0.00 | 0.00 | S |
| GR | MO | 0.02 | 0.49 | 0.49 | 0.00 | V |
| MO | GR | 0.10 | 0.26 | 0.44 | 0.20 | V, S |
| MO | VL | 0.47 | 0.53 | 0.00 | 0.00 | V |
| MO | VL | 0.34 | 0.48 | 0.13 | 0.05 | V |
| VL | MO | 0.96 | 0.04 | 0.00 | 0.00 | S |
| MO | VL | 0.37 | 0.59 | 0.04 | 0.00 | S |
| SC | GR | 0.00 | 0.00 | 0.30 | 0.70 | S |
| GR | MO | 0.02 | 0.17 | 0.66 | 0.15 | V |
| MO | VL | 0.37 | 0.17 | 0.38 | 0.09 | V |
| MO | GR | 0.02 | 0.23 | 0.75 | 0.00 | S |
| VL | MO | 0.52 | 0.45 | 0.00 | 0.03 | V |
| MO | VL | 0.30 | 0.70 | 0.00 | 0.00 | S |
| GR | MO | 0.05 | 0.67 | 0.23 | 0.05 | S |
| MO | VL | 0.75 | 0.25 | 0.00 | 0.00 | V |
| SC | GR | 0.00 | 0.00 | 0.52 | 0.48 | V |
| MO | GR | 0.00 | 0.37 | 0.56 | 0.07 | S |
| SC | GR | 0.00 | 0.00 | 0.17 | 0.83 | S |
| VL | GR | 0.80 | 0.08 | 0.06 | 0.06 | V |
| MO | GR | 0.03 | 0.26 | 0.67 | 0.04 | S |
| VL | MO | 0.60 | 0.40 | 0.00 | 0.00 | V |
| MO | VL | 0.41 | 0.43 | 0.16 | 0.00 | V |
| MO | VL | 0.16 | 0.36 | 0.14 | 0.34 | V |
| GR | MO | 0.00 | 0.10 | 0.90 | 0.00 | S |

## Exhibit 12 (Continued)

| Analyst Classification | SCS Classification | Average Probabilities* | | | | Reason for Error ** |
|---|---|---|---|---|---|---|
| | | VL | MO | GR | SC | |
| GR | MO | 0.04 | 0.16 | *0.66* | 0.14 | V |
| MO | VL | *0.49* | 0.45 | 0.01 | 0.05 | V, S |
| MO | GR | 0.00 | *0.59* | 0.41 | 0.00 | S |
| MO | GR | 0.02 | 0.39 | *0.57* | 0.00 | V |
| MO | GR | 0.02 | 0.08 | *0.80* | 0.10 | V |
| VL | SC | 0.46 | 0.00 | 0.00 | *0.54* | V |
| MO | VL | *0.58* | 0.38 | 0.04 | 0.00 | V |
| MO | VL | 0.31 | *0.35* | 0.19 | 0.15 | V |
| VL | MO | *0.87* | 0.13 | 0.00 | 0.00 | S |
| GR | MO | 0.02 | *0.48* | 0.39 | 0.11 | V |

\* Average overall style probability indicates that average membership over time coincides with analyst's classification.

\*\* Codes for errors:
   V = Variable-style membership or short-term tactical move.
   A = Analyst misclassification.
   S = Probable style change not yet noted by analyst.

5. SCS provides improved understanding of the rationale behind manager classifications. The reasons for classification are traceable, clear, and understandable.

6. SCS does not require a time series of training sets to estimate the parameters of its mathematical model.

7. SCS responds immediately to fundamental shifts in managers' portfolios.

## Benefits of SCS

SCS provides a variety of potential benefits to users:

1. It provides an ongoing validation of a manager's style and strengthens confidence in establishment of the proper benchmark for a manager.

2. It provides an early warning system of manager style change.

3. It provides systematic input to the classification process for managers and consequently reduces the element of judgment.

4. It improves the understanding of a manager's biases, style volatility, and style evolution, thereby enhancing the correct assignment of a manager to an investment role.

5. It provides a method to aggregate the style exposures of all managers in a fund and help spot style gaps and imbalances. This should allow sponsors to reduce a fund's unintended factor exposure risk.

## CONCLUSIONS

In our review of approaches to the difficult problem of classifying managers into equity styles of investment, we have explored the limitations and difficulties of using standard multivariate classification methods and the analysis of past return patterns. A new approach to classify managers uses nonlinear probability functions to assign probabilities to paths in a decision tree, which produces style classifications. The SCS classifications largely coincide with Russell analysts' classifications. An analysis of disagreements confirms that styles are more volatile for certain managers than for others.

The system takes an innovative approach to classification in general and to manager classification in particular. This is an important issue because the proper matching of managers with investment assignments is fundamental to the achievement of plan objectives. The system allows for the monitoring of manager investment style for consistency over time and allows the identification of major shifts in strategy or portfolio characteristics.

# APPENDIX

## The Data Analyzed

The style classification for each manager is assigned by analysts in the Russell Equity Research group. Four universes are maintained: value, market-oriented, growth, and small-capitalization. The classifications are based on long-term analysis of a manager's portfolio characteristics and in-depth manager research.

The SCS classifications are based on data analysis of the manager's equity portfolio characteristics as drawn from the Russell M204 equity profile database as of December 31, 1990.

Data for 265 managers were collected for each of the Russell style universes. Managers in each style are:

| | |
|---|---|
| Value | 68 |
| Market-Oriented | 79 |
| Growth | 53 |
| Small-Capitalization | 65 |
| Total | 265 |

## Alternative Classification Methods

The best known classification method is discriminant function analysis. Discriminant function analysis is a methodology that seeks to examine the covariance structures among a set of variables (e.g., price-to-book, dividend yield, etc.) for one or more groups of subjects.[8] The covariance structures are mathematically transformed to produce discriminant functions.

These functions can be seen as artificial variables that maximize the distance between group centroids.[9] Essentially, the methodology produces a set of linear equations with coefficients/weights for each variable that produce scores on a discriminant function for each subject. The discriminant function scores, in turn, can be interpreted in terms of the probability of group membership based on the location of the observation relative to the group centroids. The observation is

---

[8] Covariance structure refers to the pattern of correlations or covariations among a set of variables as found in a correlation or covariance matrix.

[9] A centroid is a group center or a point in m-dimensional space corresponding to the multidimensional mean of the members of the group over m variables. The centroid can thus be seen as the center of gravity of a group in a space defined in terms of the variables of interest.

classified into the group with which it has the highest probability of membership (or in the group to whose center it is the closest). The discriminant function coefficients developed using a training set can be used, along with the relevant data, to classify new observations whose group membership is not known.

An alternative approach is cluster analysis. The cluster analysis procedure computes distance scores across all the observations based on the similarity of observations over the values of relevant variables. The observations are grouped according to their distances to groups. In other words, clusters are formed by grouping together observations that have the smallest within-group mean distance. Rather than developing a set of mathematical rules for classifying subjects, as in discriminant analysis, cluster analysis directly groups subjects sequentially. A variety of grouping constraints can be specified. The various clustering methods are differentiated on the basis of grouping constraints and distance measures.

Another multivariate approach is factor analysis. The original objective of factor analysis was to reduce the dimensionality of a covariance matrix of variables, i.e., to reduce the number of variables by creating abstracts or artificial variables from two or more variables.[10] Factor analysis can be used for classification only if the covariance structure reduces to a few factors, and the observations load on the factors in a way that is consistent with the classification of the observations.[11] In this sense, factor analysis can be seen as a cousin of discriminant function analysis.

Another approach is to use logistics regression (logit).[12] In this approach, equations are developed depending on whether the observations are in a class or not. By estimating a series of logit equations for each class, one can produce the probability of membership in each class. An observation is then classified on the basis of the highest probability. In this sense, logit is also akin to discriminant function analysis. The major difference is that in discriminant function analysis, the probabilities of group membership sum to 1.0, while in logit analysis the sum of probabilities is normally greater than 1.0. Research indicates logit is superior to discriminant function analysis, particularly when the criterion variables are not distributed normally.

---

[10] Dimensionality refers to the number of variables (dimensions) on which subjects are measured.

[11] Loadings are like correlations between the original variables and the new artificial variables or factors. They indicate how much of the variable is captured by the factor.

[12] Logit refers to loglinear models in which the dependent variable is an odds ratio of categorical data (e.g., the conditional ratio of favorable to unfavorable observations). It is a method for creating regression style models when the variables are categorical.

Finally, neural networks — a new artificial intelligence approach — assist in rapid pattern recognition. Neural network methodology develops a series of decision rules and coefficients that produce scores on whether or not an observation belongs in a group. In this sense, it is akin to logit analysis. Some have argued that neural networks are superior to discriminant function analysis or any other kind of multivariate technique because neural networks are inherently nonlinear, while all the other multivariate empirical classification methods reviewed are linear.

All these multivariate techniques have certain features in common. The first is that they are empirical. This means that the classification process and coefficients are based upon observations rather than on *a priori,* or theoretical, assumptions. All the multivariate techniques also consider all factors in the classification process simultaneously.

Discriminant function analysis, logit analysis, and neural networks all use training or test sets to develop the classification rules or equations.[13] Factor analysis and cluster analysis also use training sets, in that as one judges the factor loadings in factor analysis or the groups in cluster analysis (in terms of whether the observations group together as one would expect them to load or cluster). This direct or indirect reliance on a training set is one inescapable factor in empirical multivariate methods — you cannot use the methods without a training set.

Efforts to develop a model for style classification based on multivariate discriminant function analysis were frustrating. While we were able to classify the training sets with 100% accuracy, the system was not sufficiently robust when applied out of sample to nontraining set managers. After extensive analysis to understand why this was the case, two key problem areas were identified — simultaneity and training sets.

---

[13] Training sets or test sets are collections of observations that have been correctly classified in some way. The variables associated with the correct classifications (or criterion variables) are thought to contain information that the multivariate statistical techniques can extract and formulate into a set of rules (in the form of equations) that can be used to classify unclassified observations.

# CHAPTER 5

## STYLE RETURN DIFFERENTIALS: ILLUSIONS, RISK PREMIUMS, OR INVESTMENT OPPORTUNITIES

RICHARD ROLL, PH.D.
ALLSTATE PROFESSOR OF FINANCE
ANDERSON GRADUATE SCHOOL OF MANAGEMENT
UNIVERSITY OF CALIFORNIA, LOS ANGELES
AND CO-CHAIRMAN
ROLL AND ROSS ASSET MANAGEMENT CORPORATION

The author thanks Laura Field, Stephen A. Ross, and Ivo Welch for constructive comments and suggestions and Ken Mayne for expert assistance.

## POSSIBLE EXPLANATIONS OF INVESTMENT STYLE RETURNS

For both the investor and the finance researcher, the single most important unanswered question about equity style investing is the origin of historically observed differential returns. There seem to be at least three possibilities:

1. Return differentials across investment styles are statistical aberrations. They do not reflect differences in *expected* returns and are thus not likely to be repeated.

2. Return differentials are risk premiums. They *do* reflect differences in expected returns, but this is compensation for risk.

3. Return differentials represent market opportunities. Not only are they statistically significant, but they occur above and beyond any measurable risk. Investing according to style can thus be expected to earn extra return without bringing any additional exposure to loss.

99

These explanations are not mutually exclusive; each one could have some degree of empirical relevance.

Many empirical studies of style investing, including other chapters in this volume, have uncovered seemingly significant statistical differences in the returns of portfolios classified by price/earnings ratio, market capitalization, book/market ratio, and other indicia of style. Yet the first explanation above is not completely moribund. Taken individually, each empirical study employs sound econometric methods and draws scrupulously correct inferences from the data. But taken as an aggregate, the studies are far from independent investigations.

The historical record of observed returns is limited, and there are more professional data miners than data points. Just by chance, all this mining over the years could have uncovered fool's gold. This view is championed persuasively by Fischer Black.[1] Unfortunately, it is difficult to know whether data mining can completely explain style-specific results and what, if anything, we can do to correct the problem.

Beyond the data-mining issue, various studies have argued that the empirical results may be tainted by selection bias or by aberrations in the data. For instance, Kothari, Shanken, and Sloan find evidence that survivorship bias in COMPUSTAT data, the usual source of accounting information, may affect subsequent returns, particularly among small firms.[2] Brown, et. al. argue that survivorship histories of individual firms can bias performance studies; they apply this to mutual fund performance, but the effect is more generally applicable.[3]

If we are willing to assume that style investment results are not simply statistical aberrations, then the second and third possible explanations listed above can be subjected to empirical enquiry. By assuming some rational model of risk and return, and deriving empirical measures of risk, it is conceptually straightforward to ascertain whether risk premiums account totally for return differences across investment styles, conditional on the validity of the assumed risk/return model.

---

[1] Fischer Black, "Return and Beta," *Journal of Portfolio Management* (Fall 1993), pp. 8-18.
[2] S. P. Kothari, Jay Shanken, and Richard G. Sloan, "Another Look at the Cross-section of Expected Stock Returns," Working Paper, William E. Simon Graduate School of Business Administration, University of Rochester (December 1992).
[3] Stephen J. Brown, William Goetzmann, Roger G. Ibbotson, and Stephen A. Ross, "Survivorship Bias in Performance Studies," *The Review of Financial Studies* (1992, Number 4), pp. 553-580.

The purpose of this chapter is to present such an investigation in the context of Ross's Arbitrage Pricing Theory (APT) of risk and return.[4] The APT has become one of the standard paradigms of risk/return finance in the sense that it now appears in most investments textbooks, is frequently cited in journal articles, and is employed in practice for portfolio selection and capital budgeting.

More important for our purpose here, the APT has the potential to explain investment style returns because it is a multi-factor theory. Many studies have found several distinct dimensions of style. For example, Fama and French document that both market capitalization (Size) and the ratio of book-to-market equity (B/M) are associated with cross-sectional differences in return.[5] They also find that the single-factor Capital Asset Pricing Model (CAPM) fails to explain any of the cross-sectional average return differences.[6]

Since portfolios classified along two style dimensions appear to have different expected returns (assuming this has not been produced by data-mining), a risk/return model with at least two risk premiums would seem *a priori* to have the greatest chance of empirical success.[7] Investment style literature mentions a number of possible dimensions; in addition to Size and B/M, earnings/price, leverage, sales growth, price momentum, and seasonals are among the suggested proxies for cross-sectional differences in returns.[8] Also, it seems reasonable to anticipate that still unknown styles may eventually be discovered, thereby adding to dimensionality burden of any rationally-based risk/return model.

Beyond Size and B/M, there is little agreement about the materiality of other indicia of style. Fama and French, for example, present evidence that earnings/price and leverage are unimportant when Size and B/M are taken into account.[9] Sharpe's method of return attribution based on investment styles has only two dimensions for *domestic*

---

[4] Stephen A. Ross, "The Arbitrage Theory of Capital Asset Pricing," *Journal of Economic Theory* (December 1976), pp.341-360.

[5] Eugene F. Fama and Kenneth R. French, "The Cross-Section of Expected Stock Returns," *Journal of Finance* (June 1992), pp.427-465.

[6] The Capital Asset Pricing Model was originated by William F. Sharpe, "Capital Asset Prices: A Theory of Market Equilibrium Under Conditions of Risk," *Journal of Finance* (September 1964), pp.425-442, and John Lintner, "The Valuation of Risk Assets and the Selection of Risky Investments in Stock Portfolios and Capital Budgets," *Review of Economics and Statistics* (February 1965), pp.13-37.

[7] Technically, a single risk premium model could explain the results, but only with a different parameterization than has previously been employed.

[8] The APT has already been used with some degree of success to explain the size anomaly. See K.C. Chan, Nai-Fu Chen, and David A. Hsieh, "An Exploratory Investigation of the Firm Size Effect," *Journal of Financial Economics* (September 1985), pp.451-471.

[9] *Op. cit.*

equities, Size and growth/value, the latter measured by B/M.[10] Sharpe gives other style dimensions for fixed-income assets and lists foreign equities as a separate style dimension for domestic U.S. investors. This is perfectly adequate for most U.S. investors, but one might wonder whether equities in non-U.S. markets display return differences across such attributes as Size and B/M, or whether other variables are more important.

Although it is a controversial conclusion, the empirical APT literature generally agrees that several distinct factors are associated with risk premiums. Many studies provide evidence of between two and five factors, while others suggest fewer or more.[11] Given the preponderance of evidence in favor of five or fewer factors, this chapter simply *assumes* that five factors are relevant for domestic U.S. equities. The power of statistical tests will be reduced by an incorrect assumption about the true number of factors. Additionally, if there are actually *more* than five relevant factors, the tests will be biased in favor of concluding that the risk/return model (the APT) is inadequate; i.e., the tests will be biased in favor of the market inefficiency hypothesis. If there are five or fewer factors, however, no particular bias will occur.

## THE EXPERIMENTAL DESIGN

Eight U.S. domestic equity portfolios were formed by classifying individual stocks along three style dimensions: large or small Size, high or low earnings per share/price (E/P), and high or low book equity/market equity (B/M). The first and third dimensions are known to produce material *ex post* return differences in past sample periods, and the second dimension is a popular focus of practical growth/value style

---

[10] William F. Sharpe, "Asset Allocation: Management Style and Performance Measurement," *Journal of Portfolio Management* (Winter 1992), pp.7-19.

[11] Supporting the presence of a single dominant factor is Charles Trzcinka, "On the Number of Factors in the Arbitrage Pricing Model," *Journal of Finance* (June 1986), pp.347-368. Trzcinka concludes that other factors may be present, but that the first factor is by far the most important. Supporting the presence of a limited number of factors, but more than one, are Stephen Brown and Mark Weinstein, "A New Approach to Testing Asset Pricing Models: The Bilinear Paradigm," *Journal of Finance* (June 1983), pp.711-743. Supporting a large number of factors are Phoebus J. Dhrymes, Irwin Friend, and N. Bulent Gultekin, "A Critical Re-examination of the Empirical Evidence on the Arbitrage Pricing Theory," *Journal of Finance* (June 1984), pp.323-346. Supporting the presence of just a single factor in some countries and several factors in other countries are John E. Hunter and T. Daniel Coggin, "The Correlation Structure of the Japanese Stock Market: A Cross-National Comparison," Working Paper, Investment Department, Virginia Retirement System (August 1994).

investing.[12] In an effort to avoid using information not available to market participants, classification into style groups was accomplished using accounting data (B and E) pertaining to a period at least four months prior to the classification date.[13] All listed NYSE and AMEX and OTC stocks available from the CRSP database on the classification date were included in one of the eight portfolios.[14]

Every stock with available information was sorted by each of the three style dimensions, and then assigned to one of eight portfolios, depending on whether it was in the lowest or highest half of all stocks for that dimension. If Size, E/P, and B/M had been cross-sectionally uncorrelated, this would have resulted in an equal number of stocks in each portfolio. There was, however, some cross-sectional dependence among these indicia, so the eight style portfolios contain unequal numbers. Exhibit 1 shows the number of stocks per portfolio over the sample period, chosen rather arbitrarily to cover the latest available decade, April 1984 through March 1994.[15]

The plotting convention used in Exhibit 1 is followed throughout the chapter. Low (high) Size portfolios are represented by narrow (wide) lines, low (high) E/P portfolios by dashed (solid) lines, and low (high) B/M portfolios by grey (black) lines. Each portfolio is labeled with a three-character designator, where the first character is for Size, the second character is for E/P, and the third character is for B/M; in each case the character is "L" for low or "H" for high. For example, the HLH portfolio includes stocks in the half of all stocks with larger market capitalization, the half with lower earnings per share/price, and the half with higher book equity/market equity. As Exhibit 1 shows, even the portfolio with the smallest number of stocks included more than 100 individual issues in every period, and most portfolios had at least 200 most of the time.[16]

---

[12] In the practitioner literature, both B/M and E/P are considered indicators of "growth" versus "value" equities.

[13] The analysis was repeated using an eight-month lag, to make absolutely certain that no hindsight crept in; the results are qualitatively similar.

[14] Center for Research in Securities Prices, Graduate School of Business, University of Chicago. Subsequent to the latest available CRSP date (December 1992), the data were supplemented with the proprietary database of Roll and Ross Asset Management Corporation. Accounting data (for earnings and book equity) were also obtained from the latter source.

[15] Actually, there is some rationale for the choice of sample period. It was limited to ten years so that earlier data might constitute a hold-out sample should someone want to check the intertemporal robustness of results reported here. Also, the later part of the sample period here has not yet been used in other studies. For instance, the data period in Fama and French, op. cit., ends in December 1990. Thus, more than three years of our sample is not subject to the charge that it has already been data-mined.

[16] Because of missing accounting information, not every stock with returns could be included in a portfolio. Also, stocks with negative earnings or negative book values in a given period were discarded from the sample in that period.

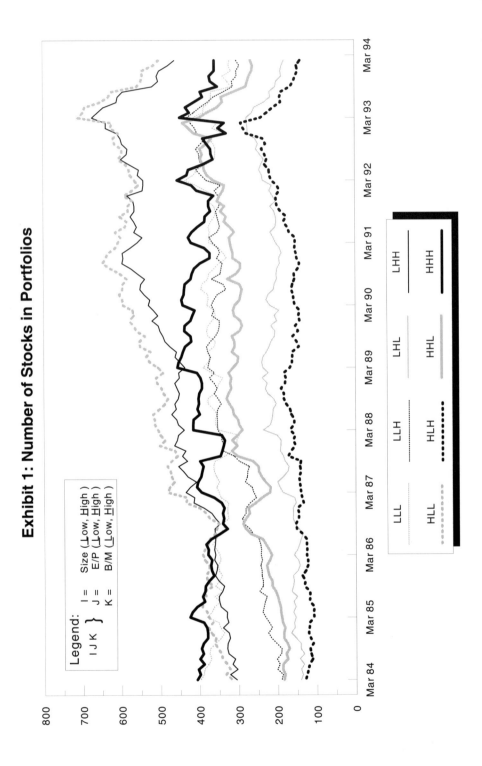

Exhibit 1: Number of Stocks in Portfolios

After all stocks were assigned to style portfolios, value-weighted averages of the three indicia of style were calculated for each portfolio at the beginning of each sample month.[17] These averages are plotted over the sample period in Exhibits 2, 3, and 4, for Size, E/P, and B/M, respectively.

The efficacy of the classification scheme can be observed in these exhibits. Ideally, all four portfolios in a given class for a particular dimension should have similar mean values for their common attribute and should differ markedly from the four portfolios in the other class. For instance, the four portfolios with low Size, but with high and low E/P and B/M, should have similar average market capitalization and materially different market capitalization than the four portfolios with high Size. Exhibit 2 shows this to be the case: The four portfolios LLL, LLH, LHL, and LHH all have average market capitalization in the $30 to $100 million range. Their average market cap is far from that of the four portfolios in the high group, whose average market cap hovers around $10 billion.

Similar clustering is apparent for E/P and B/M in Exhibits 3 and 4. The low E/P portfolios have average E/P values around 0.05 while the high E/P portfolios, although somewhat more diverse within their category, have average E/Ps around 0.10 to 0.15. Low B/M values are around 0.4, while high B/M values are between 0.8 and 1.20. One noticeable regularity in all cases is the greater dispersion in mean attribute values in the high groups, whether it be Size, E/P, or B/M. In the case of Size, this is probably attributable to one or two extremely large stocks moving from low to high E/P or from low to high B/M, or vice versa, as stocks are reassigned to portfolios month by month. In the cases of E/P and B/M, the cause is less apparent, but it might be due simply to greater price volatility in low-priced stocks.

## STYLE PORTFOLIO INVESTMENT PERFORMANCE OVER THE PAST DECADE

### Differences in Raw Returns

Value-weighted total returns for all eight portfolios were calculated over each month subsequent to a classification date. At the end of that month, stocks were reclassified and the portfolios were reformed. Total return investment levels, assuming reinvestment of cash dividends and other distributions, are plotted in Exhibit 5, along with the corresponding cumulative total return level for the S&P 500 Index, also including dividends.

---

[17] That is, weighted averages were calculated for Size, E/P, and B/M, with the weights proportional to each stock's market capitalization at the beginning of the month.

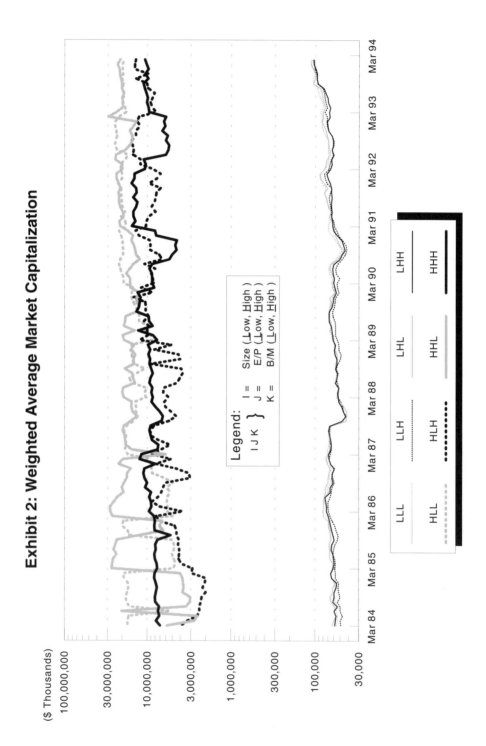

Exhibit 2: Weighted Average Market Capitalization

Legend:
I J K } I = Size (Low, High)
J = E/P (Low, High)
K = B/M (Low, High)

LLL    LLH    LHL    LHH
HLL    HLH    HHL    HHH

($ Thousands)

# Exhibit 3: Mean Earnings/Price

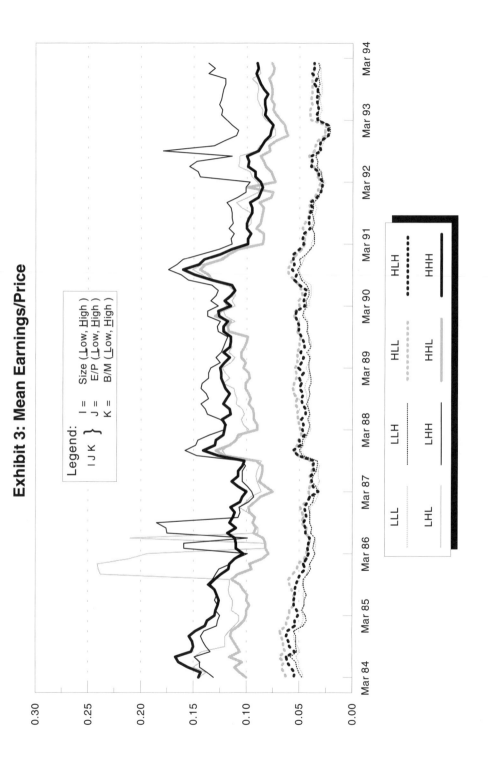

Legend:

$$I\,J\,K \left.\right\}$$   I =   Size (Low, High)
J =   E/P (Low, High)
K =   B/M (Low, High)

LLL       LLH       HLL       HLH
LHL       LHH       HHL       HHH

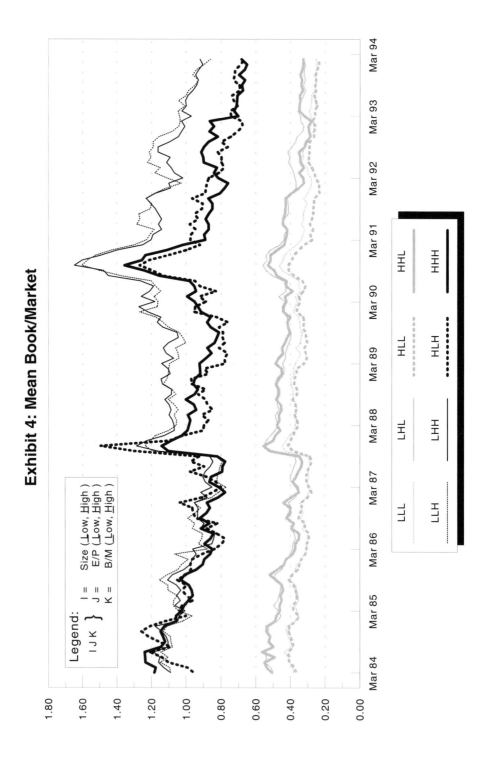

Exhibit 4: Mean Book/Market

# Exhibit 5: Style Portfolio Investment Value

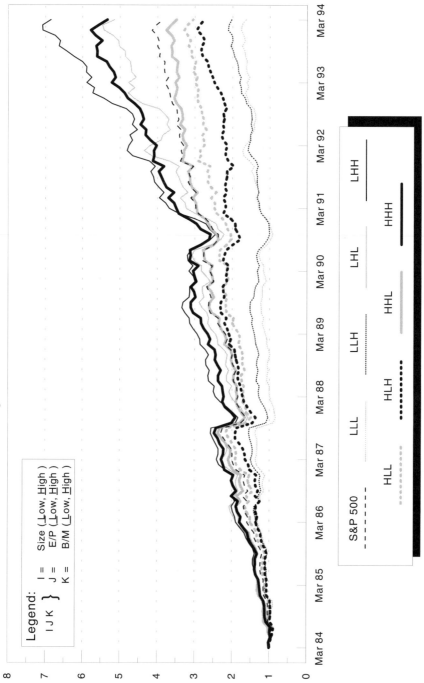

Legend:
I J K } I = Size (Low, High)
J = E/P (Low, High)
K = B/M (Low, High)

During this decade, the best-performing portfolio was LHH: small market cap, high E/P, and high B/M. In conformance with other empirical reports, this is essentially a "value" portfolio, but one composed of small stocks. Small stocks per se, however, were not necessarily ideal investments during this decade; the worst-performing portfolio was LLL, small market cap, low E/P, and low B/M. Here are the relative rankings of the eight style portfolios and of the S&P 500:

| Rank | Accumulated Value of One Dollar* | Style | | |
|---|---|---|---|---|
| | | Size | E/P | B/M |
| 1 | $6.85 | Low | High | High |
| 2 | $5.34 | High | High | High |
| 3 | $5.15 | Low | High | Low |
| S&P 500 | $3.96 | — | — | — |
| 4 | $3.49 | High | High | Low |
| 5 | $3.05 | High | Low | Low |
| 6 | $2.76 | High | Low | High |
| 7 | $2.02 | Low | Low | High |
| 8 | $1.64 | Low | Low | Low |

*That is, a dollar invested on March 31, 1985, would have accumulated to this amount on March 31, 1994, assuming reinvestment of dividends.

The numbers show a dramatic range of investment results, from a compound annual return of 5.07% for the worst portfolio to 21.2% for the best. The S&P's compound annual return was 14.8%. The three style portfolios that outperformed the S&P 500 were all in high earnings per share/price groups. Two of the three had small market cap, but so did the two lowest-ranked portfolios. The book equity/market equity style dimension displayed a middle ground of performance. Although the two best-performing portfolios had high B/M, so did portfolios that ranked sixth and seventh. For this particular sample period, these raw returns suggest a conclusion that the E/P style dimension was the most important.

## Is Style Performance Significant?

Are differences in style portfolio investment returns statistically significant? If so, can they be ascribed to differences in risk? To answer both these questions, we shall implement a particularly tractable version of the statistical technique known as the *analysis of variance*. The technique employs a pooled time series/cross-section regression with appropriately chosen explanatory risk variables plus "dummy" variables used to classify the returns along style dimensions.[18] A "dummy" variable takes on the values zero or one depending on the class to which the dependent variable belongs. Thus, since we have three style dimensions, we shall employ three dummy variables; each dummy variable has the value zero or one, depending on whether the observed return is in the low or high group. For example, if an observed return were in a low Size, high E/P, and low B/M portfolio, the dummy variable triplet would be 0,1,0. The exact form of the regression equation is

$$R_{j,t}\text{-}R_{f,t} = \alpha_{LLL} + \alpha_{Size}D_{Size} + \alpha_{E/P}D_{E/P} + \alpha_{B/M}D_{B/M} + \varepsilon_{j,t} \qquad (1)$$

where $R_{j,t}$ is the return on style portfolio j in month t, $R_{f,t}$ is the riskless rate, $D_i$ is the dummy variable for style dimension i, and $\varepsilon_{j,t}$ is a regression disturbance. Note that the regression intercept has subscript "LLL" (for low Size, low E/P, and low B/M). For this combination of styles, all three dummy variables are zero.

Our first regression pools the monthly excess returns[19] (for 120 months) on all eight style portfolios. These returns comprise the 960 observations of the dependent variable in the pooled regression. The explanatory variables are 960 dummy variable triplets, each one describing the particular style for the corresponding monthly portfolio return. Exhibit 6 presents the results.

The regression coefficients indicate the marginal contribution produced by having a high value of the style attribute, holding constant other style dimensions, in percent per month. The t-statistic measures whether the coefficient is reliably nonzero, a test of statistical significance. To be specific, the Size dummy's coefficient of 0.0177 indicates that an extra 1.77 basis points *per month* would have been earned in the sample decade simply by investing in large-rather than small-cap stocks, *ceteris paribus*. The t-statistic is only 0.0551, however; this indicates that the extra investment return of 1.77 basis points is not statistically significant.

---

[18] For a general treatment of pooling time series and cross-sectional data using dummy variables, see George G. Judge, R. Carter Hill, William E. Griffiths, Helmut Lütkepohl, and Tsoung-Chao Lee, *Introduction to the Theory and Practice of Econometrics* (New York: John Wiley & Sons, 1988), Section 11.4, pp. 468-479.
[19] The excess return is the total monthly return on the portfolio less the return on a U.S. Treasury bill that had one month to maturity at the beginning of the month.

**Exhibit 6: Eight Style Portfolios on Style Dummy Variables**
Pooled Time Series/Cross-Section Regressions
April 1984 - March 1994, Monthly

| | Size | E/P | B/M |
|---|---|---|---|
| Intercept | Dummy Variables | | |
| $\alpha_{LLL}$ | $\alpha_{Size}$ | $\alpha_{E/P}$ | $\alpha_{B/M}$ |
| 0.25038 | 0.01771 | 0.65012 | 0.13867 |
| (0.77930) | (0.05512) | (2.0235) | (0.43160) |

| | |
|---|---|
| Sample Size | 960 |
| Adjusted $R^2$ | 0.001337 |
| F-statistic for Regression (3/956) | 1.4280 |
| Durbin-Watson | 1.7046 |

t-statistics in parentheses.

Along the E/P dimension, the extra investment return was 65 basis points per month (!), and its t-statistic was 2.02. This indicates that the earnings/price style did produce reliably different returns, and they were sizable; 65 basis points per month implies an annual incremental return of approximately 7.80% simply from investing in stocks in the higher half of E/P ratios each month, holding constant other styles.

The results for B/M are less dramatic. The incremental return from buying high B/M stocks was 13.9 basis points per month. This is certainly nothing to ignore, but the t-statistic of 0.432 provides little assurance that differential return along this style dimension was statistically reliable.

## Adjusting for Risk

The results in Exhibit 6 are based on raw returns; they are not risk-adjusted. Also, they are subject to a technical difficulty. The analysis of variance assumes that the observations are independent.[20] We know, however, that this is unlikely in our case because we have pooled monthly returns from eight portfolios observed over the same sample period. A glance at Exhibit 5 shows that the market values of these portfolios fluctuate together with considerable regularity. Most

---

[20] If the observations are dependent, the regression is misspecified because the disturbances are not "spherical." This induces bias in the estimated standard errors and t-statistics, although not in the coefficients.

large diversified portfolio values correlate positively because they are subject to *common* factors, either a single market factor as in the CAPM or several macroeconomic factors, as predicted by the APT. To remove the dependencies among the style portfolios and thereby make our inferences more reliable, we ought to remove the sources of the dependence. It turns out that we can do this simultaneously with correcting for differences in risk across the portfolios.

Our method is to include either a market factor or a set of APT factors as additional explanatory variables in the pooled time series/cross-sectional regressions, along with the dummy variables for style already reported. In addition, we shall include a set of cross-product terms between the dummy variables and the factors. These cross-product terms will effectively control for differences in risk.

To see how this works, let's first start in the context of the simplest model, a single-factor risk/return market model inspired by the CAPM. As an example, consider a portfolio with a particular style, say, LHL for low market cap, high E/P, and low B/M. We can write its single-factor market model as

$$R_{LHL,t} - R_{f,t} = \alpha_{LHL} + \text{ß}_{LHL}(R_{M,t} - R_{f,t}) + \varepsilon_{LHL,t} \qquad (2)$$

where the subscript f denotes the riskless return, M denotes the single-factor market return, and $\varepsilon$ is a regression disturbance.

Notice that both $\alpha$, the intercept, and ß, the slope coefficient, have subscripts denoting the portfolio's style. The style subscript on ß signifies that a portfolio's style can conceivably influence its market risk. Since returns are measured in excess of the riskless rate, the style subscript on $\alpha$ signifies that style might provide an expected return *not* accounted for by risk, an "extra-risk" return. Differing values of ß would support risk as the explanation of style investment returns, while differing values of $\alpha$ would support an investment opportunity such as pricing inefficiency as their source.

There is a potentially different equation such as (2) for each style portfolio; this is captured by interportfolio variation in the values of $\alpha$ and ß. These values can be estimated directly from a pooled time series/cross-sectional regression by using the dummy variable method. We need both intercept and slope dummy variables. The complete regression equation with a single market factor is

$$
\begin{aligned}
R_{j,t} - R_{f,t} = \ &\alpha_{LLL} + \alpha_{Size}D_{Size} + \alpha_{E/P}D_{E/P} + \alpha_{B/M}D_{B/M} + \qquad (3) \\
&\text{ß}_{LLL}(R_{M,t} - R_{f,t}) + \text{ß}_{Size}D_{Size}(R_{M,t} - R_{f,t}) + \\
&\text{ß}_{E/P}D_{E/P}(R_{M,t} - R_{f,t}) + \text{ß}_{B/M}D_{B/M}(R_{M,t} - R_{f,t}) + \varepsilon_{j,t}
\end{aligned}
$$

## Exhibit 7: Eight Style Portfolios on Single-Factor Market (S&P 500) Risk
### Pooled Time Series/Cross-Section Regressions
### April 1984 - March 1994, Monthly

| | Base | Size | E/P | B/M |
|---|---|---|---|---|
| | (LLL) | Dummy Variables | | |
| Intercept | | | | |
| $\alpha$ | 0.55014 | 0.02278 | 0.68232 | 0.24481 |
| | (-3.5107) | (0.14537) | (4.3543) | (1.5623) |
| Market Risk | | | | |
| $\beta$ | 1.0609 | -0.006721 | -0.04267 | -0.14067 |
| | (30.880) | (-0.19564) | (-1.2419) | (-4.0944) |

| | |
|---|---|
| Sample Size | 960 |
| Adjusted $R^2$ | 0.76894 |
| F-statistic for Regression (7/952) | 456.91 |
| Durbin-Watson | 1.7373 |

t-Statistics are in parentheses.

Note that $D_i$ is zero for each i with style dimension LLL (low Size, low E/P, and low B/M). For this combination of styles, only the intercept $\alpha_{LLL}$ and market factor excess return $[\beta_{LLL}(R_{M,t}-R_{f,t})]$ will appear with nonzero values. The incremental effect on risk (relative to LLL) of any other combination of styles will be empirically measured by the sum of $\beta$'s whose subscripts bear the style description. Similarly, the extra-risk incremental return from a style combination different from LLL will be empirically measured by the corresponding $\alpha$'s with style-descriptive subscripts. The statistical significance, if any, of different styles can be measured directly by the t-statistics of these slope and intercept dummy variable coefficients. Finally, the validity of the inferences can be checked by examining the correlations of residuals across style portfolios.

Exhibit 7 presents the empirical results from fitting Equation (3) using the eight style portfolios and a decade of monthly observations. The market factor is the total return on the S&P 500 index. The return units are percent per month. The market factor is highly significant, as would be expected in a time series model where the dependent variable is a well diversified portfolio. All three of the slope dummy coefficients are negative, although only $\beta_{B/M}$ is highly significant. This implies that higher book equity/market equity style portfolios have less market risk.

The intercept dummy variable coefficients have larger t-statistics than when Equation (1) was fit to the same data without a market factor. This is somewhat surprising, because a possible reason for the significance of style return differences in Equation (1) is differing market risks; thus, one might have predicted *a priori* that adjusting for risk would eliminate the significance. Yet the contrary is true. The intercept dummy coefficient, $\alpha_{E/P}$, has a similar magnitude in the two regressions, 65.0 versus 68.2 basis points in regressions (1) and (3), respectively; but it now has a considerably larger t-statistic, 4.35. This result indicates that style investing along the E/P dimension has been reliably profitable over the past decade, above and beyond single-factor market risk.

Regression model (3) explains more than three-quarters of the monthly variability in style portfolio returns across time and across the eight combinations of style. Most of the explained variability is attributable to the market factor. However, a single market risk factor may not be adequate to fully capture the multidimensional risks that may be underlying style investment returns. Can a multi-factor APT risk model do better?

Using the method of Connor and Korajczyk (hereafter CK), five factors were extracted from the entire data sample of individual equity excess returns.[21] The CK method has the great advantage of handling virtually any number of individual assets; the computations involve inversion of a covariance matrix with only as many rows and columns as the number of time series observations, in our case 120 X 120. The extracted factors have monthly observations that can be scaled in units equivalent to monthly rates of return. Connor and Korajczyk show that the first factor is similar to a large market index, although it is equal-weighted rather than value-weighted like the S&P 500. The second and higher CK factors are approximately unrelated to the first factor and to each other. They are constructed as combinations of systematic risks other than general market risk.

Once the time series of APT factor returns is available, we can employ the same procedure as before, but now we can be more precise about the possibility of multiple risks as sources of style portfolio returns. The pooled time series/cross-sectional regression will now have a total of 23 explanatory variables: 3 intercept dummy variables, the 5 APT factors, and 15 slope dummy variables (three for each of the five factors). The regression equation is

[21] Gregory Connor and Robert A. Korajczyk, "Performance Measurement with the Arbitrage Pricing Theory: A New Framework for Analysis," *Journal of Financial Economics* (March 1986), pp.373-394. See also Gregory Connor and Robert A. Korajczyk, "Risk and Return in an Equilibrium APT: Application of a New Test Methodology," *Journal of Financial Economics* (September 1988), pp. 255-289.

## Exhibit 8: Eight Style Portfolios on Five APT Risk Factors
### Pooled Time Series/Cross-Section Regressions
### April 1984 - March 1994, Monthly

|  | Base | Size | E/P | B/M |
|---|---|---|---|---|
|  | (LLL) | Dummy Variables | | |
| Intercept | | | | |
| $\alpha$ | 0.5348 | -0.1323 | 0.6130 | 0.2945 |
|  | (-5.4807) | (-1.3556) | (6.2825) | (3.0182) |
| APT Risks | | | | |
| $\beta_1$ | 1.0136 | -0.1025 | -0.0274 | -0.1160 |
|  | (54.7160) | (-5.5314) | (-1.4815) | (-6.2605) |
| $\beta_2$ | 0.2863 | -0.3027 | -0.0658 | -0.0072 |
|  | (15.4570) | (-16.3400) | (-3.5526) | (-0.3908) |
| $\beta_3$ | 0.1158 | -0.2452 | 0.0696 | -0.0465 |
|  | (6.2549) | (-13.2430) | (3.7619) | (-2.5104) |
| $\beta_4$ | 0.0576 | -0.1788 | -0.0037 | 0.1468 |
|  | (3.1093) | (-9.6569) | (-0.2016) | (7.9268) |
| $\beta_5$ | -0.0958 | 0.0563 | 0.0391 | 0.0365 |
|  | (-5.1762) | (3.0397) | (2.1103) | (1.9705) |

| | |
|---|---|
| Sample Size | 960 |
| Adjusted $R^2$ | 0.91427 |
| F-statistic for Regression (23/936) | 445.64 |
| Durbin-Watson | 1.7053 |

t-statistics are in parentheses.

$$R_{j,t} - R_{f,t} = \alpha_{LLL} + \alpha_{Size}D_{Size} + \alpha_{E/P}D_{E/P} + \alpha_{B/M}D_{B/M} + \quad (4)$$
$$\sum_k [\beta_{LLL,k}F_{k,t} + \beta_{Size,k}D_{Size}F_{k,t} +$$
$$\beta_{E/P,k}D_{E/P}F_{k,t} + \beta_{B/M,k}D_{B/M}F_{k,t}] + \varepsilon_{j,t}$$

where $F_{k,t}$ is the observed excess return on factor k in month t. The summation extends for k=1,...,5, over the five factors. All the slope coefficients, including those associated with slope dummy variables, must now have k subscripts to denote the factor with which they are associated. Exhibit 8 presents the results.

The explanatory power has increased substantially over the single-factor market model regression; the adjusted R-square is 0.914. Also, each of the five slope coefficients for style portfolio LLL (low size, low E/P, and low B/M), is statistically significant. Among the 15 dummy variable slope coefficients, 11 have t-statistics whose absolute values are greater than 2, the usual rule-of-thumb value for reliability. This implies that there are substantial and statistically significant differences in APT risks among style portfolios. The differences are not confined just to the first factor (which is like a single broad market factor); nine of the large t-statistics are associated with factors two through five. Thus, it seems reasonable to conclude that adding more factors gives us more ability to distinguish risk differences among investment styles.

Despite better ability to measure risk empirically, or, better said, *because* of this ability, the intercept dummy variable coefficients are now even more statistically significant. The intercept dummy variable for E/P has a coefficient of 0.613 (basis points of extra risk-adjusted return per month) with a t-statistic of 6.28. The intercept dummy for B/M has a coefficient of 0.295 with a t-statistic of 3.02. The coefficient for size, however, remains insignificant.

The inescapable conclusion: Controlling for multiple dimensions of risk by using a five-factor APT model does not eliminate return differences across investment styles. Indeed, it strengthens the effect. According to the empirical methods here, risk does vary substantially across investment styles, but risk alone does not explain differences in return. Higher values of both E/P and B/M are usually associated with "value" stocks as opposed to "growth" stocks. Value portfolios outperformed growth portfolios over the past decade, and the performance is not attributable to CAPM (single-factor) or APT (five-factor) risk.

## Risk and Return Profiles for Style Portfolios

To get a feeling for risk and return differences across style portfolios, a simple expedient is to calculate their overall profiles from the dummy variable coefficients. Remember that we have eight style portfolios, denoted IJK, where I represents Size, J represents E/P, and K represents B/M. I, J, and K can be either low (L), or high (H) on the style attribute. For example, portfolio HLH has large (high) market capitalization stocks, low earnings per share/price stocks, and high book equity/market equity stocks. The dummy variables are 0 for L and 1 for H; thus, the dummy variable triplet corresponding to HLH is 1,0,1.

To obtain the estimated risk coefficient of portfolio HLH for, say, the first factor, multiply each coefficient by its dummy variable value and add it to the base coefficient, $\beta_{LLL,1}$; e.g., $\beta_{HLH,1} = 1.0136 + 1(-0.1025) + 0(-0.0274) + 1(-0.1160) = 0.795$.

Thus, the first factor risk coefficient for a portfolio with large-cap stocks, low E/P stocks, and high B/M stocks is considerably less than 1.0. This might have been partly anticipated because a coefficient of 1.0, given the Connor/Korajczyk factor method, would be the first factor coefficient for an equal-weighted portfolio and $ß_{HLH,1}$ is for large-cap stocks. But notice in the adjustment above that a slightly greater contribution to the reduction in the coefficient comes from B/M than comes from Size. High B/M stocks also have lower first-factor risk.

The dummy variable slope coefficients in Exhibit 8 have an interesting pattern across the factors. For the Size slope dummies, the first four factors have negative and highly significant coefficients. Thus, large-market cap stocks have less APT risk on these four factors. For the fifth factor, the Size dummy coefficient is positive and significant, but this is swamped by the first four factors. As might have been anticipated, the overall volatility induced by systematic factors is greater for small than for large stocks.

Among the E/P slope dummies that are significant, factor 2 is negative, while factors 3 and 5 are positive. This mixed pattern makes it all the more surprising that the *intercept* dummy for E/P becomes so much more significant when going from a single-factor model to a multiple-factor model. Evidently, high E/P stocks are more susceptible to some risk sources and less susceptible to others compared to low E/P stocks. Although the overall difference in volatility is not particularly dramatic between low and high E/P portfolios[22], holding constant the other style dimensions, the ability to control for multiple risk sources substantially improves the ability to detect extra-risk performance.

The slope dummy coefficients corresponding to B/M are significantly negative for the first and third factors and positive for the fourth and fifth. The coefficient is insignificant for the second factor. Overall, high B/M stocks are somewhat less volatile; the volatility difference is more obvious than in the case of the E/P dimension. Again, as in the case of E/P, controlling for multiple risk sources renders

---

[22] The sample standard deviations of returns, in percent per month, are as follows for the eight style portfolios (for ease of comparison, organized by matching pairs holding constant the other style dimensions):

| Low Size | | High Size | | Low E/P | | High E/P | | Low B/M | | High B/M | |
|---|---|---|---|---|---|---|---|---|---|---|---|
| LLL | 5.84 | HLL | 4.82 | LLL | 5.84 | LHL | 5.67 | LLL | 5.84 | LLH | 4.92 |
| LLH | 4.92 | HLH | 4.63 | LLH | 4.92 | LHH | 4.73 | LHL | 5.67 | LHH | 4.73 |
| LHL | 5.67 | HHL | 4.61 | HLL | 4.82 | HHL | 4.61 | HLL | 4.82 | HLH | 4.63 |
| LHH | 4.73 | HHH | 4.21 | HLH | 4.63 | HHH | 4.21 | HHL | 4.61 | HHH | 4.21 |

the return difference along the B/M dimension more statistically reliable. Unlike E/P, risk control also increases the average return differential attributable to B/M.

Exhibit 9 presents a pictorial view of the risk coefficients and extra-risk returns across the eight style portfolios. The numbers depicted in Exhibit 9 consist of the base coefficient ($\alpha_{LLL}$ for the intercept and $\beta_{LLL,k}$ for the slope on factor k) plus the appropriate dummy variable coefficients. As can also be seen from the pattern of dummy variable coefficients in Exhibit 8, smaller Size is associated with algebraically larger risk coefficients on factors 1 through 4 and a smaller coefficient on factor 5. Larger E/P is associated with slightly smaller risk coefficients on the first and second factors and slightly larger coefficients on the third and fifth factors. Larger B/M is associated with smaller risk coefficients on the first and third factors and larger coefficients on the fourth and fifth factors. There is clearly a variety of APT risk profiles among the style portfolios, and the variation is statistically significant.

But perhaps the most striking chart is the bottom panel of Exhibit 9, which presents the extra-risk return of the eight style portfolios. Increasing either E/P or B/M had a monotonic impact on extra-risk return, holding Size constant. The largest extra-risk returns for either small- or large-cap stocks are in portfolios in the highest class of *both* E/P and B/M, while the worst-performing portfolios are in the lowest class of both these measures. The performance rankings by style are close to, but slightly different from, the rankings presented earlier based on raw returns. One notable departure concerns the lowest ranking portfolio in Exhibit 9, style HLL. On the basis of raw returns, it is ranked fifth out of eight. This is a bit puzzling because larger-cap stocks have *lower* risks on the first four factors.

## Correcting for Cross-Sectional Dependence
In pooled time series/cross-section regressions, the standard errors of the estimated coefficients are affected by cross-sectional dependence in the regression disturbances. The regression residuals, sample estimates of the true but unobservable disturbances, display considerable dependence in Equation (1), the regression that makes no correction for risk. All the correlations in residuals across style portfolios are positive.[23] Their average value is 0.861, and eight of them exceed 0.9.

---

[23] Among the 8 style portfolios there are 28 pairwise correlations.

## Exhibit 9: Estimates from Pooled
## Time Series/Cross-Section Regression

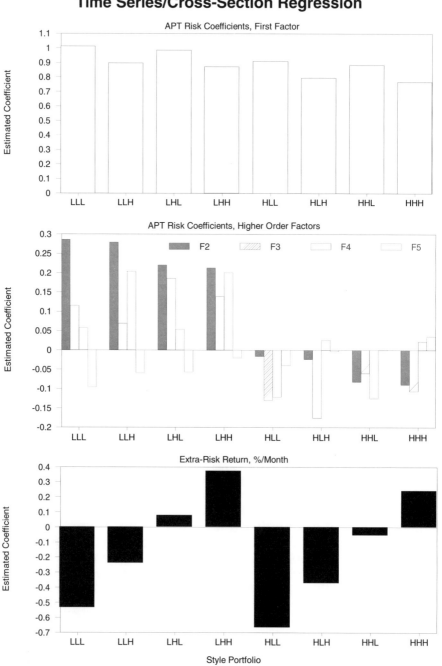

After correcting for single-factor market risk in regression (3), all these correlations are closer to zero, although six of them are still larger than 0.5, and the average is 0.287. After correcting for the five APT risk factors in regression (4), only three (of 28) exceed 0.4 and the average value is 0.115. This is the expected result; most of the cross-portfolio dependence is attributable to common factors.

Even though the degree of cross-portfolio dependence is considerably reduced by removing systematic comovement, there could still remain enough dependence to bias inferences. A formal test of whether the 8 X 8 correlation matrix of the residuals from regression (4) is diagonal is rejected at the 0.001 significance level.[24] Although the correlations are small in magnitude, this test result implies that at least some of them are statistically significantly nonzero.

To be sure that the remaining cross-sectional dependence does not bias our inferences, we apply the "Seemingly-Unrelated Regressions" (SUR) method of Zellner to the eight style portfolio returns and the associated APT factors.[25] In SUR, a separate regression model, with possibly distinct coefficients, is estimated for each style portfolio; simultaneously, cross-regression dependence in the residuals is taken into account when computing standard errors and t-statistics.

The first step in SUR is simply to fit ordinary least squares (OLS) separately for a regression of the type:

$$R_{j,t}\text{-}R_{f,t} = \alpha_j + \sum_k [\beta_{j,k} F_{k,t}] + \varepsilon_{j,t} \tag{5}$$

where j denotes the style portfolio, (j = LLL, LLH,..., HHH). There are eight separate regressions in this case, one for each style. Then an 8 X 8 cross-sectional covariance matrix is formed from the $\varepsilon$'s, the OLS residuals. The estimated covariance matrix is then employed in a generalized least squares *multivariate* regression, which provides revised estimates of the coefficients. A new set of residuals is then computed, and the process is repeated. Most of the time, there is little variation in the coefficient estimates after a few iterations.[26]

---

[24] The test was derived by T. S. Breusch and A. R. Pagan, "The Lagrange Multiplier Test and its Applications to Model Specification in Econometrics," *Review of Economic Studies* (1980), pp.239-254. It is based on the asymptotic Chi-square distribution of the sum of the correlation coefficients.

[25] Arnold Zellner, "An Efficient Method of Estimating Seemingly Unrelated Regressions and Tests of Aggregation Bias," *Journal of the American Statistical Association* (1962), pp.348-368. A convenient discussion is in Judge, *et al., op. cit.,* Chapter 11.

[26] Three iterations and the SHAZAM econometrics software were used here. See *SHAZAM User's Reference Manual Version 7.0* (New York: McGraw-Hill), Chapter 25.

## Exhibit 10: Eight Style Portfolios on Five APT Risk Factors
### Seemingly-Unrelated Regressions, April 1984 - March 1994, Monthly
Style Portfolio

(IJK: I = Size, J = E/P, K = B/M, each one either Low or High)

| | LLL | LLH | LHL | LHH | HLL | HLH | HHL | HHH |
|---|---|---|---|---|---|---|---|---|
| | | | | Intercept | | | | |
| $\alpha$ | -0.7268 | -0.4085 | 0.2425 | 0.5687 | -0.4093 | -0.2700 | -0.2840 | 0.1102 |
| | (-3.938) | (-3.801) | (1.593) | (6.065) | (-3.524) | (-1.669) | (-2.588) | (1.194) |
| | | | | APT Risks | | | | |
| $\beta_1$ | 1.0348 | 0.8738 | 1.0053 | 0.8536 | 0.8921 | 0.8168 | 0.8623 | 0.7865 |
| | (29.53) | (42.82) | (34.79) | (47.95) | (40.45) | (26.60) | (41.38) | (44.88) |
| $\beta_2$ | 0.2554 | 0.2634 | 0.2703 | 0.2100 | -0.0451 | 0.0518 | -0.0723 | -0.1458 |
| | (7.290) | (12.91) | (9.354) | (11.80) | (-2.047) | (1.685) | (-3.469) | (-8.322) |
| $\beta_3$ | 0.1293 | 0.0605 | 0.1837 | 0.1361 | -0.1065 | -0.2034 | -0.0944 | -0.0669 |
| | (3.693) | (2.965) | (6.359) | (7.650) | (-4.831) | (-6.627) | (-4.531) | (-3.821) |
| $\beta_4$ | 0.0852 | 0.1935 | 0.0711 | 0.1666 | -0.1750 | 0.0625 | -0.1161 | 0.0297 |
| | (2.433) | (9.486) | (2.460) | (9.364) | (-7.938) | (2.037) | (-5.573) | (1.694) |
| $\beta_5$ | -0.0418 | -0.0832 | -0.0775 | -0.0297 | -0.0486 | -0.0243 | -0.0247 | 0.0904 |
| | (-1.194) | (-4.078) | (-2.684) | (-1.670) | (-2.203) | (-0.791) | (-1.187) | (5.163) |
| | | | | Explained Variation | | | | |
| $R^2$ | 0.8890 | 0.9473 | 0.9196 | 0.9564 | 0.9349 | 0.8645 | 0.9364 | 0.9462 |

Sample Size: 120 Months

t-statistics are in parentheses.

The results are tabulated in Exhibit 10 and the coefficients plotted in Exhibit 11. An "*" in Exhibit 11 signifies a coefficient that is statistically different from zero at the 1% level. The risk coefficients on the first factor have much more than this level of significance for all eight style portfolios; the smallest t-statistic is 27. Most of the higher-order risk factors also have significant coefficients. The extra-risk returns of five style portfolios, LLL, LLH, LHH, HLL, and HHL, differ from zero at the 1% level.

Comparing the SUR results in Exhibit 11 with the simpler pooled time series/cross-section results in Exhibit 9, we see that there is little material difference. The patterns among the risk coefficients are virtually identical, although there is some minor variability in the higher-order coefficients for large-cap portfolios.

# Exhibit 11: Estimates from Seemingly Unrelated Regressions

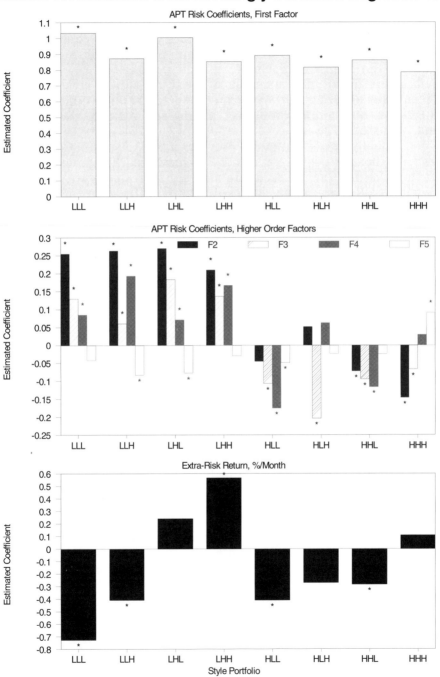

The extra-risk returns estimates, however, do differ between the two econometric methods in an interesting way: estimates from SUR display a wider disparity across styles among the four portfolios of small-cap stocks but less of a disparity for large-cap stocks. By accommodating cross-sectional dependence, the SUR method produces estimates that appear to be even more intuitively consistent with an inefficient markets explanation: If investment styles really do account for differing *extra-risk* expected returns, one would anticipate the effect to be more pronounced among smaller and thus less well-analyzed stocks.

Finally, the SUR method provides a convenient method of testing hypotheses across equations. We are particularly interested here in testing whether the intercepts in all eight regressions with the eight style portfolios are *jointly* and significantly different from zero.[27] Of course, from Exhibit 10, we can already observe that five of the eight intercept coefficients have t-statistics in excess of levels usually considered significant, so a joint test is likely to provide a similar inference. It does. The joint test of the hypothesis that all eight intercepts are really zero produces a Chi-square statistic of 123.1 with 8 degrees of freedom. If the hypothesis were true, the probability of observing such a value is zero to more than five significant digits!

## Non-Stationarity in Extra-Risk Return

One of the most puzzling empirical results in this paper, at least to the author, concerns the estimated relative importance of the three style dimensions, particularly with respect to estimated extra-risk return. In every test, the earnings per share/price (E/P) dimension is the most important. Although book equity/market equity (B/M) does finally appear as a significant style dimension after accounting for multi-factor risk with the APT, it has a smaller impact than E/P. Market capitalization has no significant effect in any of the tests.

These findings are puzzling because they seem to conflict with earlier results. Size, for example, is perhaps the earliest style dimension documented by rigorous research to yield extra-risk return (relative to a single risk factor).[28] The more recent Fama/French article also presents evidence that Size is inversely cross-sectionally related to average return, although its influence was somewhat larger before 1977.[29] Fama/French conclude that E/P is not an important explanatory variable for average return after controlling for Size and B/M.

---

[27] A similar procedure is developed for tests of the CAPM in Michael R. Gibbons, "Multivariate Tests of Financial Models: A New Approach," *Journal of Financial Economics* (March 1982), pp.3-27.

[28] See Rolf W. Banz, "The Relationship Between Return and Market Value of Common Stocks," *Journal of Financial Economics* (March 1981), pp.779-794.

The data samples in previous research are of course drawn from an earlier period, and the empirical methods differ to some extent. It does not seem likely, however, that empirical methods could cause the differential results. In the sample decade of this paper, high E/P stocks performed better, whether or not returns are adjusted for risk. It is hard to believe that an alternative empirical method would make any difference.

If the results are chiefly sample period-specific, they represent just another level of the investment enigma: style may matter, and style investing may produce extra-risk return, but which particular style is most important *now*? If styles change rapidly, the practical investor may derive little benefit from knowing that styles even exist. If they change more slowly, there is hope that they can be tracked and exploited with appropriate analytics.

In a preliminary foray along this path, the simplest type of intertemporal model, a deterministic time trend, was appended to the intercept terms, and then Seemingly-Unrelated Regressions (SUR) were recomputed for the eight style portfolios. The idea was to estimate whether the extra-risk returns of any of the eight style portfolios, as measured by their intercepts, had a reliably different value at the beginning and the end of the sample period. The amended SUR regression for style portfolio j is

$$R_{j,t}\text{-}R_{f,t} = \alpha_{j,0} + \alpha_{j,time}\tau + \sum_{k} [\beta_{j,k}F_{k,t}] + \varepsilon_{j,t} \text{ (6)} \tag{6}$$

where $\tau$ is a linear time index.[30] Given the base intercept, $\alpha_{j,0}$, and the slope coefficient on time, $\alpha_{j,time}$, an estimate of the extra-risk return for portfolio j at any time $\tau$ is simply $\alpha_{j,0} + \alpha_{j,time}\tau$. Exhibit 12 presents values of the extra-risk returns for each of the eight style portfolios at three different points during the sample period, the beginning, middle, and end, from the SUR regressions.

The middle bars, those for April 1, 1989, are almost identical to the average extra-risk returns reported in Exhibits 10 and 11. But among the four small market capitalization style portfolios, on the left side of Exhibit 12, there is a substantial reduction in extra-risk return during the sample period. For each of the four small Size style portfolios, the estimated extra-risk return was closer to zero at the end than at the beginning of the decade. There is not such a clear pattern among the large Size portfolios.

---

[29] Black, op. cit., argues that the size effect was originally uncovered by data-mining. He notes: "In the period since the Banz study (1981-1990), they [Fama/French] find no size effect at all, whether or not they control for beta [single factor risk]....Lack of theory [about why there *should* be a relation between size and return] is a tip-off; watch out for data mining!" (p. 9, bracketed phrases added for clarification).
[30] For convenience, $\tau = t/120$ for the $t^{th}$ month of the sample period.

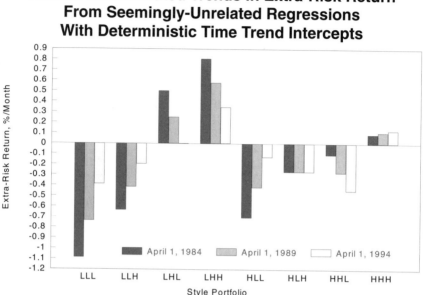

**Exhibit 12: Estimated Trends in Extra-Risk Return From Seemingly-Unrelated Regressions With Deterministic Time Trend Intercepts**

However, the statistical significance of this nonstationarity is questionable. None of the t-statistics associated with $\alpha_{j,time}$ is large for any j; the largest in absolute value is only 1.46. A joint test that they are *all* zero produces a Chi-square statistic of 14.8 with 8 degrees of freedom. This implies a significance level of about 6%. The ex post odds are almost 20-to-1 that at least some of the eight coefficients are nonzero, but no particular coefficient can be singled out as responsible.

Thus, there is marginally significant evidence that style-specific returns are nonstationary. A model more sophisticated than a simple deterministic time trend may provide interesting details about the extent and form of the nonstationarity.

## A Caveat About Risk Adjustment and Pricing Efficiency

*Any* risk adjustment model that employs factor portfolios is subject to a technical problem: If the risk factors cannot be combined linearly to produce an *ex ante* mean-variance efficient portfolio, expected returns *cannot* be expressed as linear combinations of risk coefficients.[31] This implies that the intercept terms in our

---

[31] This result was emphasized about previous single-factor CAPM tests in Richard Roll, "A Critique of the Asset Pricing Theory's Tests," *Journal of Financial Economics* (March 1977), pp.129-176.

regressions could differ significantly across style portfolios without necessarily implying pricing inefficiency. In the context of a single-factor model, Roll and Ross show that even minor departures of the index from mean-variance efficiency can allow room for considerable cross-sectional variation in what appears to be "extra-risk" return.[32]

As a consequence, the evidence that risk models do not eliminate significant investment performance variation across styles is consistent not only with pricing inefficiency but also with a technical failure of the risk factors to be mean-variance efficient portfolios. From a practical investment viewpoint, however, this has virtually no operational relevance. If an investor had structured a portfolio during the past decade to have larger investments in high E/P and B/M stocks while holding risk at the same level as either the S&P 500 or at the same multiple levels as every one of five APT factors, the performance results would have been splendid. The portfolio would have outperformed benchmarks with equivalent single-factor or multiple-factor risk profiles without displaying any greater total volatility. Whether this result was induced by market inefficiency or simply because the structured portfolio was closer to the true efficient frontier might be an interesting issue for the scholar; but the investor enjoying surplus wealth could probably care less!

## SUMMARY

Using U.S. domestic equity returns over the past decade, from early 1984 through early 1994, stocks were classified by three indicia of investment style: market capitalization (Size), earnings per share/price (E/P), and book equity/market equity (B/M). At the beginning of each sample month, all listed and OTC stocks in the upper and lower halves of these variables were assigned to separate groups, thereby creating eight style portfolios. The subsequent monthly return was then observed for each portfolio.

Style portfolios had dramatically different performance over the decade. The best portfolio (LHH, for low Size, high E/P, and high B/M) outperformed the worst portfolio, LLL, by more than 15% *annually*. Using pooled time series/cross-section regressions with dummy variables for investment style, the raw return differences were found to be statistically significant.

---

[32] Richard Roll and Stephen A. Ross, "On the Cross-Sectional Relation Between Expected Return and Betas," *Journal of Finance* (March 1994), pp.101-121.

Both the single-factor CAPM (with the S&P 500 as the factor) and the multi-factor APT (with five factors) were employed in an effort to determine whether style performance could be attributed to risk. Style portfolios *do* differ markedly in their risk profiles. There is substantial statistical evidence that all three style dimensions are associated with diverse sensitivities to various risk factors, a broad market factor *and* higher-order factors.

Yet, the risk models used here do not fully explain style performance. There is statistically significant evidence in this empirical sample that style is associated with extra-risk return. Specifically, a high E/P portfolio returned more than 60 basis points *per month* in extra performance over the decade, holding constant both multi-factor APT risks and other dimensions of style. The estimated t-statistic for this effect was 6.3. Similarly, a high B/M portfolio returned about 30 basis points per month in extra performance with a t-statistic of 3.0. Size is the style exception; it was associated with no significant difference in returns.

Various specification tests were conducted to assure that econometric difficulties were not responsible for the results. The Seemingly-Unrelated Regressions method was employed to ascertain the impact, if any, of cross-sectional dependence in the pooled time series/cross-section model. Although there is evidence of minor cross-sectional dependence, correcting it with SUR actually strengthens the conclusions about extra-risk return to E/P and B/M, particularly in the small size group of style portfolios.

The three style dimensions are ranked differently here from previously published research, a fact that raises the specter of nonstationarity. A cursory empirical investigation was initiated into whether style returns change substantially over time. Using a very simple model, a deterministic time trend in extra-risk returns, there is marginally significant evidence that styles have changed in comparative importance over the decade. In general, extra-risk return appeared to diminish among smaller firms. A more sophisticated intertemporal model might well produce more meaningful and significant nonstationary effects and better investment performance.

# CHAPTER 6

## TACTICAL STYLE MANAGEMENT

JOHN L. DORIAN
MANAGING DIRECTOR
FIRST QUADRANT CORPORATION

ROBERT D. ARNOTT
PRESIDENT AND CHIEF EXECUTIVE OFFICER
FIRST QUADRANT CORPORATION

### INTRODUCTION

The investing world has been moving away from the generalists toward specialists for at least three decades. We have migrated from a world of balanced managers in the 1960s to a world of stock managers and bond managers in the 1970s to a world in which each niche in the investing world has its own specialists. We have index managers, tilted indexes, large-cap managers, small-cap managers, growth and value managers, micro-cap managers, small-cap growth specialists, and so forth.

This migration toward specialists did not happen by accident. The catalyst is performance measurement, which did not even exist in any serious way before the 1970s. Measurement of performance revealed that the average balanced manager did a poor job in each of the asset management specialties. Typically, stock selection, bond selection, and allocation between the two were each a source of shortfall, so that the combination was quite poor.

But the migration toward specialists is not without drawbacks. As one moves from balanced management to stock and bond managers, the mix between the two is no longer managed (see Exhibit 1).

# Exhibit 1: Crisis of Complexity — The 1990s

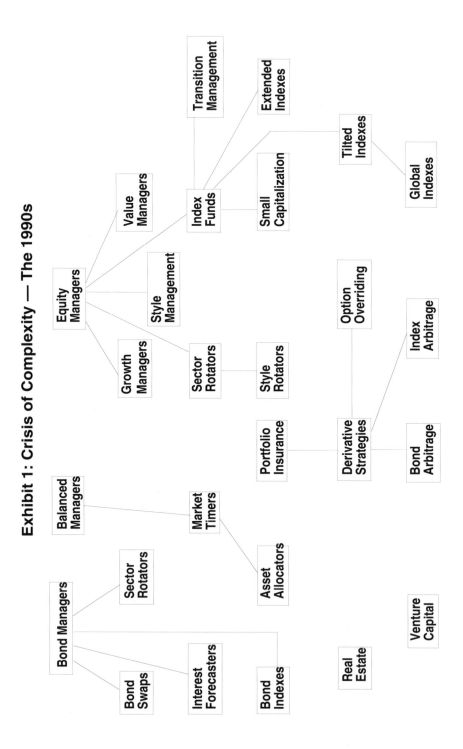

## Exhibit 2: Style Shift

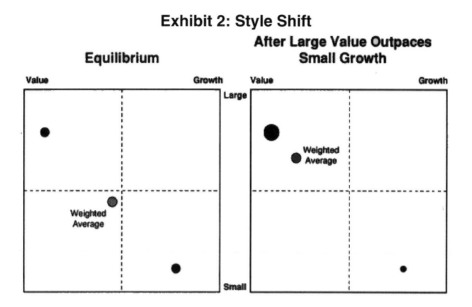

| Equilibrium | After Large Value Outpaces Small Growth |

As most balanced managers proved unsuccessful in this decision (hence the widespread view that "you can't time the markets"), this is not an entirely bad development, but the fund is without a rudder to steer the asset mix. This opened the door for the emergence of tactical asset allocation as an important element in the management of institutional assets — it restored the rudder and, during the 1980s was a distinctly successful source of profits for the funds.

Today, we see similar developments at work in the equity markets. We have index management and index-like core management, but other equity assets are often managed by specialists who have a special expertise in large or small stocks, growth or value stocks, or subspecialities within these categories. The equity portfolio is running "without a rudder." When growth outpaces value, it attains dominant weighting in the equity portfolio, just before its performance heads south; then value dominates the portfolio just as the relative performance of value is cresting.

Just as asset mix drift creates a need for tactical asset allocation (or rebalancing for those who reject active asset allocation) in many funds, style drift creates a need for style management (or passive or core management for those who reject active management of portfolio style). (See Exhibit 2.)

Indeed, the problem of style drift is not the only threat faced in today's world of equity specialists. As with asset allocation, one finds that active management of style typically occurs at the sponsor level.

Here, it is more reactive than active, and is usually characterized by moving assets away from recently unsuccessful styles. Not surprisingly, these shifts are often in the wrong direction at the wrong time.

A tactical framework for style management has two principal merits. First, this kind of process can impart a certain discipline to the allocation among equity investment styles, and likely improve portfolio returns at the same time.

The second benefit is more subtle but no less important: The use of a rigorous discipline for style management can serve to dissuade an investment committee from the ad hoc style shifts that are so tempting and so devastating after a particular style has been unrewarding for a few years. Often, this is when a style management process can increase the allocations to that very style.

## THE NEED FOR STYLE MANAGEMENT

In the long-term transition from generalist managers to specialty managers, something has been overlooked. The overall *style* of the equity portion of institutional pension funds, however diversified, is either unmanaged or mismanaged, resulting in overweighting on the style that has the best recent performance.

Most funds now diversify among a variety of management styles: large-cap, small-cap, growth, value, and so forth. The growth managers will not buy low P/E stocks. The value managers will not buy high-growth stocks. The large-cap managers will not buy small opportunistic companies, and the small-cap managers will not buy large companies.

Should managers deviate by buying stocks outside their normal style domain, they are often fired by the sponsor and stricken from the approved list by consultants. Therefore, the only time a manager risks changing style is when results have been dreadful, a demonstrably poor strategy.

The result is that the active management of style in today's world of specialists occurs only at the sponsor level, more often than not in the wrong direction at the wrong time. Sponsors were giving up on large-cap managers in 1983 and 1984, on growth managers in 1986 to 1988, and on small-stock and value managers in 1990, only to see superior results in the very style they had just abandoned. At best it is structurally difficult (in many organizations, impossible) to persuade a pension committee to boost exposure to a style or manager that has recently been unsuccessful.

By shifting money *away from* recently unsuccessful styles in a reactive fashion, the institutional investing community itself creates inefficiencies. Whichever style has recently been most successful tends to be overweighted in the equity portfolio. Absent an effective discipline for deliberately managed shifts in style, this pattern is likely to be exaggerated by actual hire/fire decisions of investment committees. That is, growth managers will be fired after a period of disappointments (when commitments perhaps ought to be increased), thereby assuring the kind of systematic underperformance that is so pervasive at the overall fund level.

This structural pattern of sponsor behavior actually can insure the long-term success of disciplines that shift style in the opposite direction.

## QUANTIFYING STYLE

Investment style shapes the pattern of equity returns more than any other element of the investment process. For example, we know that in a year that rewards value, almost all growth managers will suffer. Conversely, in a year that rewards growth, almost all value managers will suffer. A discipline that anticipates which style will be rewarded is a valuable tool for both portfolio management and manager selection. Just how valuable depends on the accuracy of the characterization and forecasts of sources of performance.

Exhibit 3 describes the thirteen common factors BARRA uses in its equity risk model. These factors are widely used in the investment community to quantify investment style in portfolios. They cover a wide spectrum of descriptors, from measures of volatility, size, and value to measures of corporate growth and success.

Most of these common factors are recognizable components of portfolio style. A traditional value manager, for example, will frequently have high exposure to book-to-price, earnings-to-price, and dividend yield. Also, value managers often exhibit low exposure to "growth orientation" and "variability in markets" (loosely analogous to beta). Growth managers tend to have the opposite exposures. Either class of managers may tend to favor large or small stocks, companies with or without foreign exposure, and so forth.

# Exhibit 3: Common Factors

## 13 BARRA FACTORS

**Variability in Markets** - Risk prediction, analogous to beta and sigma, based upon stock price behavior.

**Success** - Past success of the company, as measured by stock's performance and earnings growth.

**Size** - A size index based on assets and capitalization.

**Trading Activity** - Indicator of share turnover.

**Growth Orientation** - A predictive index for subsequent earnings per share growth, based upon growth in assets and IBES earnings growth.

**Earnings-to-Price** - Ratio of various measures of earnings per share to stock price.

**Book-to-Price** - Book value of common equity per share divided by market price.

**Earnings Variation** - Variability of earnings and cash flow.

**Financial Leverage** - Balance sheet leverage.

**Foreign Income** - Proportion of income identified as foreign.

**Labor Intensity** - Ratio of labor cost to capital cost.

**Dividend Yield** - Predicted common stock dividend yield.

**LOCAP** - Dummy variable for small capitalization.

## PROPRIETARY FACTORS

**Earnings Revision** - The change in IBES earnings estimates and the earnings surprise.

**Residual Reversal** - The tendency for stock prices to reverse over the short term.

The 13 BARRA common factors are supplemented by other proprietary stock selection factors. Although these proprietary factors are not components of portfolio style, they are most beneficial at the stock selection level due to their persistent pattern of returns. For example, more than any other single factor, changes in consensus expectations drive individual stock prices. Consequently, it may always be profitable to have a high exposure to the "earnings revision" factor, regardless of style bias.

## THE FOURTH GENERATION

Until recently, there have been three generations of quantitative investment management methodologies:

1. The *first generation* approach sought to predict returns based on the average historical reward to a univariate model. The "low P/E" or "yield tilt" managers exemplify this first generation.

2. In the *second generation* approach, investment decisions were based on the average historical reward to the factors in a multivariate model. Examples include some of the "active core" strategies offered in the early 1980s.

3. The innovation of the *third generation* approach was to apply an optimizer to the second generation model in order to minimize tracking area and control risk. Most of the "index tilt" managers use this approach.

This work establishes a viable *fourth generation* methodology. With the fourth generation, the *variability* in rewards is predicted for factors in a multivariate model. An optimizer is then used to tilt toward the most favorable factors while neutralizing unintended "bets" and minimizing tracking error. The innovation of the fourth generation model is that it recognizes the current market environment in determining each factor's weight, rather than relying on average historical effectiveness.

As Exhibit 4 illustrates, the different sources of style have varying degrees of importance. Traditionally, investors have focused upon the return to each factor, betting on persistent sources of return and riding out the times when those factors do not work. The variance in factor returns has been viewed as a problem that requires control. The higher the variance in the factors they emphasize, the more volatile their "alphas" (and their client retention).

## Exhibit 4: Common Factor Returns (1/73 - 12/93)

| BARRA Factor | Monthly Factor Returns (%) | |
| --- | --- | --- |
| | Mean | Standard Deviation |
| Variability in Markets | -0.05 | 1.40 |
| Success | 0.23 | 1.14 |
| Size | -0.12 | 0.80 |
| Trading Activity | -0.07 | 0.73 |
| Growth Exposure | 0.08 | 1.09 |
| Earnings/Price | 0.27 | 0.75 |
| Book/Price | 0.25 | 0.69 |
| Earnings Variation | -0.01 | 0.66 |
| Financial Leverage | -0.02 | 0.47 |
| Foreign Income | -0.03 | 0.36 |
| Labor Intensity | 0.04 | 0.58 |
| Dividend Yield | 0.07 | 0.78 |
| LOCAP | -0.18 | 1.24 |
| | | |
| Other Factors | | |
| Earnings Revision | 0.40 | 1.55 |
| Residual Reversal | -0.41 | 1.11 |

Rather than being resigned to periods of weak or perverse returns that can last a year or more, the fourth generation approach seeks to profit from volatility. By forecasting the rewards to factors (styles), profitable shifts can be made between them. Moreover, the fourth generation approach recognizes that highly volatile factors, previously used primarily for controlling risk, themselves offer rewards. If we *understand* risk, we can benefit from it.

In summary, money can be made in factor return modeling by correctly predicting the persistence of returns associated with factors such as earnings revision, which exhibit persistent returns with tolerable volatility. Alternatively, a return forecasting discipline can add value by predicting the ups and downs of factors with no persistent pattern of reward, but with a good deal of volatility, such as variability in markets.

In either case, money can be made by building a portfolio with exposure to the factors that are likely to be rewarded near term. The advantage of this methodology is that the returns can be higher and, particularly important, more consistent than returns from traditional quantitative methods.

# STYLE FORECASTING

A rigorous modeling framework and a large collection of potential predictive variables are not enough for a credible historical evaluation. The variables themselves must make sense in terms of explaining the factor returns, and they must be lagged in accordance with the timeliness of their availability.

Our investigation into factor return modeling concentrates on three primary areas: macromarket predictors — stock market volatility, equity risk premium; macroeconomic predictors — producer price inflation, leading indicators; and calendar relationships.

Equity risk premium, stock market volatility, and recent changes in Treasury bill yields all show statistical significance as predictors of factor returns (see Exhibit 5). Not surprisingly, when equity risk premium is high, risky stocks do well, as they are often oversold during the "flight to quality" that frequently occurs in volatile markets. As expected, these same "risky" stocks and other interest rate sensitive issues do poorly if Treasury bill yields are up.

Producer price inflation and the leading indicators also exhibit statistically significant relationships with future factor returns (see Exhibit 6). Accelerating inflation torpedoes the high-dividend yield issues. Rising inflation also hurts companies dependent on foreign income. This is because rising inflation tends to push interest rates higher, which attracts foreign capital, and thereby depresses foreign currencies and foreign-denominated earnings. Improved economic prospects, as suggested by a rise in leading economic indicators, are most helpful to companies characterized by low P/E ratios or foreign income. Conversely, a softening economy hurts these issues first.

We observe significant calendar effects for many attributes of stock price performance (see Exhibit 7). In fact, the well-known small-stock effect in January is actually one of the weaker January effects; low price-to-book value has three times its magnitude. High earnings variability, disappointing recent performance ("unsuccess" in BARRA parlance), illiquid issues, and high-yield issues also exhibit significant January effects. Strong October effects relating to the book-to-price ratio and size, and *opposite to* the January effects, are also found. We believe these effects result from the year-end stimuli of tax trading, window dressing, and copious information at the company level.

In summary, market, economic, and calendar influences do affect the future performance of various investment styles, in ways that can be predicted. Multivariate models are constructed for each factor using these indicators and focusing on consistency of performance and reasonable turnover, while emphasizing value added.

## Exhibit 5: Sensitivity of Factor Returns to Macromarket Predictors

| Factor Return | Equity Risk Premium Correlation | Stock Market Variability Correlation | Cash Yield Change Correlation |
|---|---|---|---|
| Variability in Markets | 0.32 | 0.16 | -0.17 |
| Success | -0.19 | -0.16 | 0.16 |
| Size | -0.12 | -0.12 | 0.18 |
| Growth Exposure | 0.23 | 0.15 | -0.16 |
| Earnings Variation | 0.16 | 0.12 | -0.15 |
| Financial Leverage | 0.19 | 0.13 | -0.21 |

## Exhibit 6: Sensitivity of Factor Returns to Macroeconomic Predictors

| Factor Return | Inflation Correlation | The Economy Correlation |
|---|---|---|
| Earnings/Price | | 0.21 |
| Labor Intensity | | 0.14 |
| Foreign Income | -0.26 | 0.20 |
| Dividend Yield | -0.19 | |

## Exhibit 7: Sensitivity of Factor Returns to Calendar Effects

| Factor Return | Significant January Effects Correlation | Other Significant Calendar Effects Correlation |
|---|---|---|
| Variability in Markets | 0.22 | |
| Success | -0.29 | |
| Size | | October: 0.16 |
| Book/Price | 0.20 | |
| Earnings Variation | 0.22 | |
| Dividend Yield | 0.21 | |
| LOCAP | 0.20 | |

## Exhibit 8: Simulated Returns (1/80 - 12/93)
## Net of Transaction Costs

|  | Long Style Returns | | |
|---|---|---|---|
|  | S&P 500 | Long Style | Value Added |
| Annualized Returns | 15.5 | 33.5 | 18.0 |
| Annual Standard Deviation | 15.5 | 16.9 | 4.4 |
| Annual Reward/Risk | 1.0 | 2.0 | 4.1 |
| | | | |
| Consistency of Value Added: | | | |
| Monthly | | | 85% |
| Quarterly | | | 95% |

The forecasts are generated under a rigorous *ex ante* framework, where the only information used for each forecast is that available prior to the period being forecast. Data available from January 1973 to December 1979 are used to construct a regression model for predicting each of the factor returns. This model is then applied to predict January 1980 factor returns.

Data available from January 1973 to January 1980 are then used to develop a model applied in turn to predict February 1980 factor returns. This process is repeated through December 1993 resulting in 14 years' worth of monthly forecasts for each of the factor returns. The predictive power of these *ex ante* forecasts is significant at the 1% level.

## BACKTEST RESULTS

The *ex ante* forecasts are then used as input to BARRA's portfolio optimizer. The S&P 500 is used as the benchmark portfolio and industries are constrained to deviate no more than 4% above or below their representation in the S&P 500. Each month the optimizer constructs an efficient "index-tracking" portfolio of about 100 stocks ($R^2$ averaging 0.95). The benefit of active management over the 14-year test period is then evaluated using BARRA's performance analysis software. These results are summarized in Exhibit 8.

## REAL-TIME RESULTS

The real proof of any investment strategy is its real-time performance. The disciplines described in this chapter have been applied to real assets since June of 1990.

## Exhibit 9: Real-Time Returns

| | | Core Style Returns (%) | | |
| | | S&P 500 | Core Style | Value Added |
|---|---|---|---|---|
| 1990 | June | -0.7 | -0.0 | 0.7 |
| | Q-3 | -13.8 | -11.1 | 2.7 |
| | Q-4 | 9.0 | 12.8 | 3.8 |
| 1991 | Q-1 | 14.6 | 15.6 | 1.0 |
| | Q-2 | -0.2 | 0.9 | 1.1 |
| | June | | | |
| | Q-3 | 5.4 | 8.9 | 3.5 |
| | Q-4 | 8.4 | 9.8 | 1.4 |
| 1992 | Q-1 | -2.6 | 0.6 | 3.1 |
| | Q-2 | 2.0 | 0.7 | -1.3 |
| | Q-3 | 3.1 | 1.0 | -2.1 |
| | Q-4 | 5.1 | 5.6 | 0.5 |
| 1993 | Q-1 | 4.3 | 5.7 | 1.5 |
| | Q-2 | 0.5 | 2.0 | 1.5 |
| | Q-3 | 2.6 | 5.8 | 3.3 |
| | Q-4 | 2.3 | -1.9 | -4.2 |
| 1994 | Q-1 | -3.8 | -3.7 | 0.1 |
| | Q-2 (to 4/30) | 1.3 | 3.7 | 2.4 |
| Compound Return | | 40.6 | 68.7 | 28.1 |
| Annualized Return | | 9.1 | 14.3 | 5.2 |
| Annualized Standard Deviation | | 11.9 | 11.4 | 4.0 |
| Annualized Reward/Risk | | 0.8 | 1.3 | 1.3 |
| Consistency of Value Added: | | | | |
| Monthly | | | | 64 |
| Quarterly | | | | 78 |

Exhibit 9 shows the real-time results for this style management strategy. It is important to note that the value added with live assets is only 30% of the value added in the simulation. This is mostly due to the problem of nonstationarity (the future is never identical to the past). It has been our experience that you can rarely capture more than half of a simulated alpha with live implementation.

## APPLICATIONS

An approach that changes the actual style of an investment portfolio according to shifting market conditions fills an array of needs in the institutional portfolio. Perhaps the most obvious application is as the "swing portfolio" between a fixed allocation to growth managers. Without it, the style of the portfolio is "rudderless." Alternatively, fund sponsors can shift assets and/or direct cash flow among managers to control style. A disciplined process, which is responsive to style mispricing, can give an investment committee the confidence to stay the course with styles that have fallen out of step.

A second natural application for this kind of approach is in a long/short portfolio. Our research suggests that the capital markets may be less efficient in identifying "overpriced" stocks than "underpriced." Virtually all investors are looking for "cheap" stocks. Far less diligence is applied to isolating sale candidates.

A tactical style discipline may be profitably applied to precisely this kind of arbitrage. This long/short application is a zero-beta hedged portfolio with essentially no market risk (of course, market risk could be reintroduced through futures).

A closely related application is a long/short strategy overlaid on an index fund. If a sponsor has $500 million invested in an index fund, there are likely to be $100 million worth of investments in issues that are particularly vulnerable. The long/short strategy can be used to eliminate the least attractive portion of an index fund, replacing those issues with unusually attractive alternatives. The advantage of an index overlay is that no short position is required, since the unattractive stocks are simply sold out of the fund and replaced with more attractive issues.

## CONCLUSION

A portfolio that shifts style offers not just excellent added value, but also highly consistent value added in both up and down markets, and especially during volatile periods.

The real-time forecasts for value versus growth and small versus large stocks can enhance returns at the fund level, as well as at the portfolio level.

Style management is an entirely new approach to equity management. As a new market inefficiency is first exploited, those organizations that strike first are frequently rewarded with the greatest successes. The inefficiency in the area of style management (neglected by most institutions) represents just such an opportunity.

Style management may represent the most intriguing advance in quantitative equity management of the 1990s. There is good reason to believe that the strategy should succeed, because there are natural pressures in the capital markets that create precisely the inefficiencies that style management exploits.

# CHAPTER 7

## VALUE-GROWTH BETAS

*KEITH QUINTON, CFA*
*VICE PRESIDENT*
*FALCONWOOD SECURITIES CORPORATION*

The author thanks Garry Allen and John Dorian for their insights in this area
and the DAIS Group, Inc. for their data and computational support.

## INTRODUCTION

Style investing and style benchmarks are a natural evolution from the
concepts of assets and asset benchmarks. The most critical decision in
any investment process is the asset allocation: how much to put in
stocks and bonds, in a two-asset world, for example. Once the asset
allocation decision is made, performance can now be measured not in
absolute returns, but in returns relative to the benchmarks that define
the assets: say, the S&P 500 for stocks and the 20-year Treasury bond
for bonds. The investor is now focused on the critical variable (asset
allocation) and has a measuring rod (returns relative to the benchmark).

Style investing is the next level of detail down from asset allocation. Rather than lump all stocks together, we split them up into
"sub" asset classes: value and growth, for example. Then we focus on
allocating across these groups, and measure performance relative to
the representative benchmark. Once again the investor is focused on
the bigger picture, and also has a way to measure manager or portfolio
performance.

## WHY STYLE?

There is some debate as to whether style classifications represent different asset classes. Clearly, value and growth stocks are not as different as stocks and bonds, but there appear to be meaningful

143

differences in returns on a monthly basis; and allocation across growth and value can add to an asset allocation process, since the returns are not perfectly correlated. Chapter 1 covers this issue in more detail.

There are different views on whether benchmarking managers to a style index is fair from a performance perspective, as the sponsor may now have raised the bar that the manager must jump to exhibit skill in investing. Conversely, some sponsors may feel that the manager has a lower bar to exceed during prolonged periods of weak style performance. Appropriately selected, style benchmarks are *fairer* comparison standards, not better or worse, easier or harder. They eliminate the systematic return bias in a style portfolio, allowing a manager's stock-picking ability to be revealed.

In addition to its role in asset allocation and performance evaluation, style investing can also be a tool for performance attribution in a stock portfolio that is not indexed to a specific style. Does a portfolios return come from a higher or lower than market exposure to value or growth? Is the style consistent over time? How much of the portfolios return comes from stock selection skills versus systematic bets?

Finally, style investing can also be a source of excess return, either by identifying a style category that *regularly* experiences excess return, or by developing a methodology that identifies (episodically) when a style is going to outperform. In summary, there is an important role for style in a modern investment process at many levels in a variety of ways.

## STYLE DEFINED

Most current style benchmarks identify a starting universe of stocks of interest and then develop criteria that classify these stocks into style categories. (See Chapter 2.) Several problems with this process surface as soon as we use its results to analyze other portfolios or managers. First of all, what do we do with outsiders; i.e., stocks that are not a part of the original universe? One commonly used set of value and growth benchmarks, developed by BARRA and Standard & Poor's, begins with the 500 stocks that make up the S&P 500. How do we classify a stock outside the S&P?

A second problem results from weaknesses in the underlying data for any given stock. Conventional style benchmarks use book-to-price ratios to differentiate between growth and value; a high B/P ratio indicates a value stock, a low B/P ratio indicates a growth stock. Some companies may have distorted book values because of acquisitions, restructurings, and changes in accounting rules, and the book-to-price ratio may not capture the true essence of the company. By implication, if there are problems at the stock level, style measurement at the portfolio or manager level may also be suspect. What is needed is a clean, intuitively and theoretically appealing method of classifying any stock and a portfolio of stocks according to style.

## VALUE-GROWTH BETAS

The stock market is filled with uncertainty and unclear data: future prospects for companies, accounting treatments of income statement and balance sheet items, and so forth. Some of the cleanest stock data available concern end-of-day prices and actual dividends paid. Both are widely reported and usually undisputed. A methodology that classifies stocks on the basis of their price data would be subject to little question or dispute.

Methodologies that classify stocks according to some accounting-based measure — book-to-price, for example — may be suspect at the stock level, but acceptable in aggregate. For example, S&P/BARRAs book/price methodology may misclassify an individual stock, but their aggregated Value and Growth Indexes may be acceptable, as the large number of stocks in each index tends to cancel out individual problems, preserving the overall style effect.

Developing a measure of a stock's price change relative to an aggregate index by regressing monthly stock returns against the index returns combines these two acceptable data sources to generate value-growth betas. Just as a market beta identifies a stock's sensitivity to market moves, a value-growth beta identifies a stock's sensitivity to value or growth. This approach eliminates the problem of outsiders; any stock that trades can be classified according to its value or growth sensitivity. It is intuitively appealing in that it is price-driven; identifying which stocks act like growth stocks and which stocks act like value stocks, regardless of their accounting-based measures of growth and value. Essentially, we should judge a stock's style by the company it keeps.

## THE MATHEMATICS

The approach I suggest is as follows. Take 60 observations of monthly total return for any given stock for a contiguous time period, and regress them against the monthly market and style index total returns for the same time period to generate value-growth betas. These betas measure a stock's systematic sensitivity or exposure to value and growth. Equation 1 shows one potential approach:

$$R_{stock} = \alpha + \beta_{market}(R_{market}) + \beta_{value}(R_{value}) + \beta_{growth}(R_{growth}) \quad (1)$$

Where:

$R_{stock}$ = the monthly return of a given stock,

$\alpha$ = the unexplained or stock specific return,

$\beta_{market}$ = the sensitivity of a given stocks return to the overall market,

$R_{market}$ = the monthly return on the market (S&P 500),

$\beta_{value}$ = the sensitivity of a given stocks return to the Value Index (S&P/BARRA),

$R_{value}$ = the monthly return of the Value Index (S&P/BARRA),

$\beta_{growth}$ = the sensitivity of a given stocks return to the Growth Index (S&P/BARRA), and

$R_{growth}$ = the monthly return of the Growth Index (S&P/BARRA).

Solving for the alpha and betas would result in individual stock sensitivities to both value and growth. Unfortunately, regression analysis leads to very unstable coefficients when the independent variables are highly correlated. For January 1981 through December 1993, growth and value had a correlation of monthly returns of 0.91, value correlated with the market at 0.97, growth at 0.98. This correlation of the independent variables is too high to be acceptable in a multiple regression environment.

Equation 2 shows a needed modification:

$$R_{stock} = \alpha + \beta_{market}(R_{market}) + \beta_{value-growth}(R_{value-growth}) \quad (2)$$

Where:

$\beta_{value-growth}$ = the sensitivity of a given stocks return to the spread between the Value Index and the Growth Index (S&P/BARRA), and

$R_{value-growth}$ = the monthly return of the Value Index minus the Growth Index (S&P/BARRA).

The cross-correlation problem is mitigated by using the spread in return between the growth and the value indexes. The spread and the market are negatively correlated, but significantly less than the indexes themselves. Solving for the alpha and betas here results in a truer, more stable measure of a stock's value-growth sensitivity. Exhibit 1 shows a detailed example of this approach for a hypothetical company.

## Exhibit 1: Sample Calculation of Value-Growth Beta

| Date | S&P | Value | Growth | V-G | XYZ |
|------|------|--------|--------|--------|--------|
| 8101 | -4.38% | -2.03% | -6.70% | 4.67% | -5.16% |
| 8102 | 2.08% | 1.39% | 2.73% | -1.34% | 1.14% |
| 8103 | 3.80% | 4.33% | 3.29% | 1.04% | -2.92% |
| 8104 | -2.13% | -0.10% | -4.12% | 4.02% | -6.01% |
| 8105 | 0.62% | 0.92% | 0.23% | 0.69% | 1.68% |
| 8106 | -0.80% | -0.17% | -1.54% | 1.37% | -1.49% |
| 8107 | 0.07% | -1.37% | 1.68% | -3.05% | -3.02% |
| 8108 | -5.54% | -4.56% | -6.35% | 1.79% | -0.25% |
| 8109 | -5.02% | -3.91% | -6.14% | 2.23% | -1.81% |
| 8110 | 5.28% | 3.85% | 6.70% | -2.85% | -4.85% |
| 8111 | 4.41% | 4.78% | 3.92% | 0.86% | 7.50% |
| 8112 | -2.65% | -2.57% | -2.85% | 0.28% | 4.36% |
| 8201 | -1.63% | -1.87% | -1.36% | -0.51% | 11.87% |
| 8202 | -5.12% | -3.45% | -6.71% | 3.26% | -1.40% |
| 8203 | -0.60% | 0.29% | -1.57% | 1.86% | -3.43% |
| 8204 | 4.14% | 2.82% | 5.50% | -2.68% | 7.53% |
| 8205 | -2.88% | -2.45% | -3.04% | 0.59% | -2.94% |
| 8206 | -1.74% | -1.78% | -1.66% | -0.12% | -1.42% |
| 8207 | -2.15% | -2.97% | -1.15% | -1.82% | 8.25% |
| 8208 | 12.67% | 13.62% | 11.47% | 2.15% | 8.74% |
| 8209 | 1.10% | 0.50% | 1.64% | -1.14% | 4.08% |
| 8210 | 11.26% | 11.21% | 11.35% | -0.14% | 8.86% |
| 8211 | 4.38% | 3.55% | 5.29% | -1.74% | 9.37% |
| 8212 | 1.73% | 1.34% | 2.00% | -0.66% | 11.27% |
| 8301 | 3.48% | 4.69% | 2.26% | 2.43% | 2.73% |
| 8302 | 2.60% | 2.16% | 2.92% | -0.76% | 1.00% |
| 8303 | 3.65% | 3.91% | 3.34% | 0.57% | 2.78% |
| 8304 | 7.58% | 8.29% | 6.79% | 1.50% | 14.99% |
| 8305 | -0.52% | 0.02% | -1.15% | 1.17% | -4.10% |
| 8306 | 3.82% | 1.94% | 5.72% | -3.78% | 8.09% |
| 8307 | -3.13% | -1.65% | -4.48% | 2.83% | 0.10% |
| 8308 | 1.70% | 3.87% | -0.46% | 4.33% | 0.06% |
| 8309 | 1.36% | 0.85% | 1.83% | -0.98% | 6.17% |
| 8310 | -1.34% | -0.58% | -2.10% | 1.52% | -0.10% |
| 8311 | 2.33% | 2.63% | 2.02% | 0.61% | -6.65% |
| 8312 | -0.61% | -0.08% | -0.97% | 0.89% | 3.94% |
| 8401 | -0.65% | 2.21% | -3.26% | 5.47% | -6.45% |
| 8402 | -3.28% | -2.37% | -4.20% | 1.83% | -2.56% |

## Exhibit 1 (Concluded)

| Date | S&P | Value | Growth | V-G | XYZ |
|------|------|--------|---------|--------|--------|
| 8403 | 1.71% | 1.28% | 2.11% | -0.83% | 3.40% |
| 8404 | 0.69% | 0.75% | 0.61% | 0.14% | -0.22% |
| 8405 | -5.34% | -5.41% | -5.10% | -0.31% | -4.44% |
| 8406 | 2.21% | 1.25% | 3.06% | -1.81% | -1.86% |
| 8407 | -1.43% | -2.31% | -0.63% | -1.68% | 4.73% |
| 8408 | 11.25% | 12.29% | 10.22% | 2.07% | 12.73% |
| 8409 | 0.02% | 1.60% | -1.46% | 3.06% | 0.40% |
| 8410 | 0.26% | -0.46% | 1.04% | -1.50% | 1.19% |
| 8411 | -1.01% | -0.26% | -1.75% | 1.49% | -2.31% |
| 8412 | 2.53% | 2.42% | 2.57% | -0.15% | 1.13% |
| 8501 | 7.68% | 7.31% | 7.97% | -0.66% | 10.76% |
| 8502 | 1.37% | 1.29% | 1.51% | -0.22% | -0.93% |
| 8503 | 0.18% | 0.34% | -0.24% | 0.58% | -5.22% |
| 8504 | -0.32% | 0.94% | -1.49% | 2.43% | -0.39% |
| 8505 | 6.15% | 5.49% | 6.41% | -0.92% | 2.55% |
| 8506 | 1.59% | 1.16% | 1.90% | -0.74% | -3.79% |
| 8507 | -0.26% | -0.23% | -0.38% | 0.15% | 6.16% |
| 8508 | -0.61% | -0.09% | -1.23% | 1.14% | -2.78% |
| 8509 | -3.21% | -2.84% | -3.66% | 0.82% | -2.17% |
| 8510 | 4.47% | 4.81% | 4.19% | 0.62% | 4.84% |
| 8511 | 7.16% | 5.36% | 8.90% | -3.54% | 8.45% |
| 8512 | 4.67% | 3.21% | 6.13% | -2.92% | 11.27% |

Regression Results:
Alpha                                    1.27

|  | Regression Coefficient | T-stat |
|------|------|------|
| $Beta_{Market}$ | 0.70 | 4.72 |
| $Beta_{V-G}$ | -0.61 | -2.05 |

The value-growth beta that comes out of this regression is a measure of the sensitivity of a given stock to the relative performance of value versus growth. Stocks with positive value-growth betas are value stocks; they have done well when value outperformed growth. Stocks with negative value-growth betas are growth stocks; they historically have done poorly when value outperformed growth, i.e. done well when growth outperforms value.

In the Exhibit 1 example, XYZ stock has a value-growth beta of -0.61, indicating that XYZ is a growth stock. The regression equation predicts a negative relationship between the value-growth spread and XYZs return. For every 1% that value outperforms growth, XYZ is forecast to have a -0.61% return.

This approach develops Arbitrage Pricing Theory (APT)-type betas. A stocks return is a function of its market beta, value-growth beta, and some stock-specific return. Another benefit of this approach is that it quantifies a stocks exposure exactly. Value and growth are not all or nothing — shades of gray exist on the continuum of value-growth. The value-growth betas capture this range of sensitivities, allowing stocks to be extremely sensitive to the value-growth spread (either positively or negatively), somewhat sensitive, or not at all sensitive.

The interpretation of the beta is straightforward. A beta of 1.0 indicates a one-for-one exposure. If value outperforms growth by 1%, a stock with a value-growth beta of 1.0 is expected to outperform a company with a 0.0 value-growth beta by 1%.

Exhibit 2 shows some sample betas for the Dow Jones Industrial members as of year-end 1993.

## USES OF VALUE-GROWTH BETAS

### Portfolio Analysis

Now that the sensitivity of any stock to the value-growth spread is known by computing its value-growth beta, it is possible to compute a portfolio-weighted average sensitivity to the value-growth spread. Exhibit 3 shows a sample four-stock portfolio. Its weighted-average value-growth beta or sensitivity to the spread is -0.82, indicating that this portfolio is a growth portfolio. It is exposed to the relative performance of growth. In other words, its predicted return will be more positive the more growth outperforms value. Using past sensitivities to project future sensitivities, this portfolio is a growth portfolio.

### Misclassification

The value-growth betas can also be used to flush out "masqueraders"; i.e., stocks that on the basis of book-to-price ratios may be classified as value stocks, but actually have behaved like growth stocks, and vice versa. Exhibit 4 shows the ten stocks with the most negative value-growth betas in the S&P/BARRA Value Index and the ten most positive value-growth betas in the Growth Index as of December 31, 1993. (Remember that negative value-growth betas are a characteristic of growth stocks, and positive value-growth betas are indicative of value stocks.)

## Exhibit 2: Regression Results for Dow Jones 30 as of 12/93

| Symbol | Name | Alpha | Market Beta | V-G Beta |
|---|---|---|---|---|
| AA | Aluminum Co. America | -0.56 | 1.25 | 0.72 |
| ALD | Allied Signal Inc. | 0.78 | 1.14 | 0.88 |
| AXP | American Express Co. | -0.55 | 1.25 | 0.45 |
| BA | Boeing Co. | -0.02 | 1.04 | -0.02 |
| BS | Bethlehem Stl Corp. | -1.21 | 1.48 | 0.54 |
| CAT | Caterpillar Tractor Co. | -0.26 | 1.23 | 1.51 |
| CHV | Chevron Corporation | 0.92 | 0.63 | 0.64 |
| DD | Du Pont E I De Nemours & Co. | 0.00 | 1.20 | 0.86 |
| DIS | Disney Walt Productions | 0.31 | 1.34 | -0.07 |
| EK | Eastman Kodak Co. | 0.13 | 0.70 | 0.30 |
| GE | General Electric Co. | 0.33 | 1.27 | 0.04 |
| GM | General Motors Corp. | 0.15 | 1.07 | 1.88 |
| GT | Goodyear Tire & Rubber Co. | 0.39 | 1.13 | 0.45 |
| IBM | International Business Machines | -1.29 | 0.61 | 0.39 |
| IP | International Paper Co. | -0.25 | 1.16 | 0.45 |
| JPM | Morgan J P & Co. Inc. | 0.41 | 1.12 | 0.17 |
| KO | Coca Cola Co. | 1.36 | 0.96 | -0.99 |
| MCD | McDonald's Corp. | 0.45 | 1.04 | -0.13 |
| MMM | Minnesota Mng. & Mfg. Co. | 0.38 | 0.80 | 0.12 |
| MO | Philip Morris Cos., Inc. | 0.64 | 0.85 | -1.69 |
| MRK | Merck & Co., Inc. | 0.15 | 0.88 | -1.18 |
| PG | Procter & Gamble Co. | 0.87 | 0.87 | -0.81 |
| S | Sears Roebuck & Co. | -0.24 | 1.13 | 0.61 |
| T | AT&T Corp. | 0.31 | 0.96 | 0.11 |
| TX | Texaco Inc. | 0.54 | 0.58 | 0.46 |
| UK | Union Carbide Corp. | -0.24 | 0.92 | 1.25 |
| UTX | United Technologies Corp. | -0.20 | 1.12 | -0.21 |
| WX | Westinghouse Electric Corp. | -1.51 | 0.95 | 0.16 |
| XON | Exxon Corp. | 0.47 | 0.52 | 0.22 |
| Z | Woolworth Corp. | -0.86 | 1.16 | 0.00 |

## Exhibit 3: Sample Portfolio

| Symbol | Name | Alpha | Market Beta | V-G Beta | Shares Held | 12/31/93 Price | Portfolio Weight (%) |
|---|---|---|---|---|---|---|---|
| DEC | Digital Equipment Corp. | -2.68 | 1.39 | 1.11 | 10000 | $34 | 20.70 |
| MO | Philip Morris Cos., Inc. | 0.64 | 0.85 | -1.69 | 10000 | $56 | 33.70 |
| MRK | Merck & Co, Inc. | 0.15 | 0.88 | -1.18 | 10000 | $34 | 20.80 |
| PEP | PEPSICO Inc. | 0.95 | 0.96 | -0.94 | 10000 | $41 | 24.80 |
| | Portfolio Average | -0.07 | 1.00 | -0.82 | | | |

## Exhibit 4: Masqueraders

The 10 Most Negative Value-Growth Betas in the Value Index

| (As of 12/31/93) | Alpha | Market Beta | V-G Beta |
|---|---|---|---|
| United States Surgical Corp. | 1.40 | 0.80 | -2.30 |
| Apple Computer Inc. | -1.00 | 0.90 | -2.00 |
| Northern Telecom Ltd. | 0.70 | 0.50 | -1.40 |
| Liz Clairborne Inc. | -0.70 | 1.30 | -1.40 |
| Jostens Inc. | -0.90 | 1.20 | -1.20 |
| Nike Inc. | 1.00 | 1.40 | -1.20 |
| Coors Adolph Co. | 0.00 | 0.10 | -1.00 |
| Rite Aid Corp. | -0.50 | 0.60 | -1.00 |
| Archer Daniels Midland Co. | 0.20 | 1.00 | -1.00 |
| Alberto Culver Co. | -0.40 | 0.90 | -0.90 |

(63 negative overall)

The 10 Most Positive Value-Growth Betas in the Growth Index

| (As of 12/31/93) | Alpha | Market Beta | V-G Beta |
|---|---|---|---|
| Unisys Corp. | -1.70 | 2.40 | 2.70 |
| Varity Corp. | 0.50 | 1.40 | 2.40 |
| Tenneco Inc. New | -0.40 | 1.20 | 2.00 |
| Owens-Corning. | -1.00 | 2.80 | 1.80 |
| Oracle Systems Corp. | 2.00 | 2.20 | 1.70 |
| NL INDS INC. | -2.90 | 1.50 | 1.60 |
| McCaw Cellular Communication | -1.20 | 2.70 | 1.60 |
| Cincinnati Milacron Inc. | -0.90 | 1.80 | 1.40 |
| DSC Communications Corp. | 4.20 | 1.00 | 1.40 |
| TEXAS Instrs Inc. | -0.60 | 1.90 | 1.40 |

(79 positive overall)

These are examples of stocks that may be misclassified — they have behaved like one style, but show up in another style index based on accounting data. Overall there are 63 stocks in the Value Index with negative value-growth betas and 79 stocks in the Growth Index with positive value-growth betas. Each index contains approximately one-half of the 500 stocks that constitute the S&P 500. Some of the betas may not be statistically significant, but the large number of cross-members indicates the potential for misclassification and the importance of value-growth betas.

## Exhibit 5: Value-Growth Beta Evolution
### IBM 12/85 - 12/93

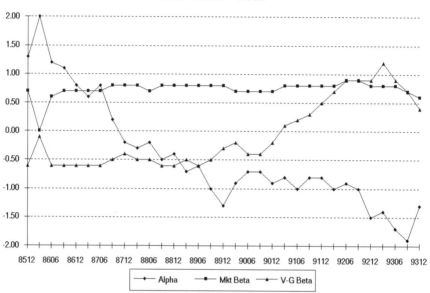

## Company Evolution

Value-growth betas can also be used to study the evolution of companies; i.e., how a company's style changes over time. Exhibit 5 shows the evolution of IBM's value-growth beta from December 1985 to December 1993. IBM's stock clearly has undergone a style shift. It has changed from acting like a growth stock to acting like a value stock over an eight-year period. This type of style shift allows some insight into a company's fundamentals, and the value-growth betas can help highlight these changes by identifying companies and industries that are evolving.

## Pairs Identification

Traditional pairs analysis and trading begins with the identification of pairs of stocks that are essentially equivalent from a systematic risk perspective. Once pairs are identified, their short-term performance is tracked. In the absence of any stock-specific information that would predict performance, the presumption behind pairs trading is that any short-term relative performance will be reversed, as a pair of stocks have the same exposures to the broad forces that drive performance in the stock market.

Pairs trading can be implemented as a pure arbitrage strategy, where the expensive half of the pair is sold short, and the cheap half purchased. In a more traditional long-only portfolio, pairs trading can be used to switch out of the expensive half of the pair if it is held in the portfolio, and purchase the cheap half, keeping the overall systematic exposure of the portfolio to the market and the value-growth spread the same, while potentially picking up some short-term relative performance. Value-growth betas can be used in this pairs definition process to identify pairs of stocks that have similar market and style betas.

## Research Focus

It is also possible to find many stocks with essentially zero market and style betas. These are stocks that tend to move solely on the basis of stock-specific events — they have little or no systematic exposure. Their return is primarily driven by fundamental happenings at the company level; hence they are independent of the broad forces that drive most stocks. These stocks are therefore good candidates for in-depth analyst research and are also good for diversifying holdings in a portfolio.

## Excess Return

Finally, value-growth betas are a potential source of excess return. Book-to-price is one of the most commonly used tilts in portfolio construction. Historically, high book-to-price stocks have outperformed low book-to-price stocks. Positive value-growth betas correspond to high book-to-price companies, but in a purer form. Hence, they can potentially identify cheap stocks.

Additionally, the alpha that comes out of Equation 2 can be thought of as the residual return: the Y intercept of the regression, or the excess return after removing market and style effects. Research has shown that a stock's subsequent performance tends to be negatively correlated with its trailing excess return. This is the so-called residual reversal effect. The alpha that comes out of the value-growth regressions is one measure of residual return, and residual reversal practitioners could use it as a potential source of alpha.

## CONCLUSION

There are many more dimensions to style than the value-growth dimension presented here. Clearly it makes sense to use the same regression methodology against the spread in performance between other style groups. Large-small immediately comes to mind. Clearly there is a role for style in the investment process, given the inherent weaknesses in accounting-based classification methodologies. Value-growth betas serve as a price-based method of classification that can provide insight into individual stocks, portfolios, and managers by giving a clearer picture of the value-growth dimension of style.

# CHAPTER 8

## THE ROLE OF COMPLETION FUNDS IN EQUITY STYLE MANAGEMENT

CHRISTOPHER J. CAMPISANO, CFA
MANAGER
ASSET ALLOCATION AND ECONOMIC RESEARCH
AMERITECH CORPORATION

MAARTEN NEDERLOF
MANAGING DIRECTOR
RESEARCH AND PORTFOLIO MANAGEMENT
TSA CAPITAL MANAGEMENT

## INTRODUCTION

Most pension fund sponsors allocate assets to domestic equities through a multi-manager approach that involves attempting to replicate the stock market as a whole by piecing together representative portfolios of differing specialties, such as growth- or value-oriented managers, as well as large- and small-capitalization managers. This mosaic of managers is designed so that its return and risk characteristics match the market that drives the original asset allocation assumptions. If the manager mix is not perfectly balanced, however, a multi-manager structure may have a significant tilt away from the benchmark, exposing the fund to unintended risks.

One way to avoid these risks is to use a *dynamic completion fund*. A completion fund is a portfolio that is adaptive in nature and explicitly changes its risk characteristics to compensate for unintentional tilts caused by the "building block" nature of the manager selection process. In this chapter, we discuss the dynamic completion fund concept and its relationship to equity style investing.

## Exhibit 1: Risk Structure Layers

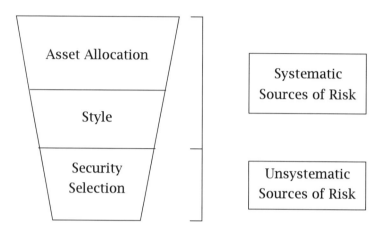

# INVESTMENT RISK STRUCTURE

The risk structure of institutional investments can be broken into several sources, or layers, for better understanding. Exhibit 1 is a schematic representation of the steps. The asset allocation decision remains the dominant determinant of return and risk. Large and complex funds, however, often find it necessary to hire several investment managers to represent the assets chosen at the asset allocation level. The type of investment managers, or the approach they use to building asset portfolios, can have a significant impact on fund performance.

The systematic effect of manager style is most profound in domestic equity portfolios, although the effect is similar in fixed-income management. The immunization (or neutralization of sensitivity to interest rate changes) of bond portfolios is commonplace in fixed-income management, eliminating the most important risk to the bond investor. Convexity, credit, and sovereign risk are also commonly managed risks that could be categorized as systematic.

The most prevalent equity risk factors chosen by the institutional community have to do with capitalization (small versus large) and more recently "style," such as growth versus value. The impact of these risk factors on a fund's performance can be enormous as evidenced by the considerable volatility in the returns of BARRA's style indexes that we see in Exhibit 2.

## Exhibit 2: Style Index Returns

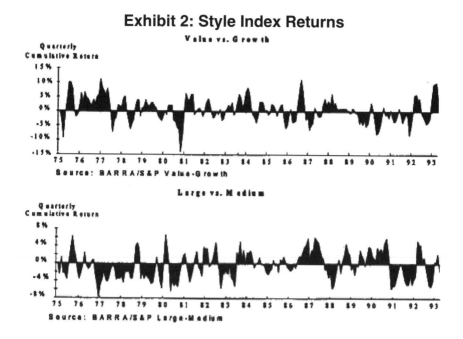

Value vs. Growth

Quarterly Cumulative Return

Source: BARRA/S&P Value-Growth

Large vs. Medium

Quarterly Cumulative Return

Source: BARRA/S&P Large-Medium

Managers matching these representative style indexes are likely to have the same volatility in performance, thus forming a second layer of return versus risk. The more extreme a manager is on either the capitalization or the growth-value continuum, the greater the return swings attributable to "style" effects. If an institution selects a group of managers who are biased toward a particular systematic style risk, the fund will tend to have volatility in performance due to that bias. This tilt can have a significant impact on return that is often unintended, since managers are usually selected for their ability to generate excess returns (alpha) as opposed to their style of management. The accurate assessment of style bias requires a thorough understanding of the manager's normal style.

The final risk structure layer is the security selection layer. The risk that derives from security selection is called several names, among them the unsystematic, diversifiable "alpha," and stock-specific risk. If a manager passively replicates a benchmark, there is no security selection risk, and no prospect for return enhancement over the benchmark. The selection of superior securities for return enhancement purposes will necessarily lead to deviations in performance from the benchmark (the sponsor hopes these are positive deviations). The volatility of deviations is measured as tracking error, or the standard deviation of the difference in returns between the actively managed portfolio and its benchmark.

## METHODS OF STYLE DETERMINATION

To get an accurate assessment of the second risk layer, it is necessary to assess the normal style of each manager by a process known as custom benchmarking. Comparing managers against a custom benchmark or normal portfolio that represents the way they invest allows the separation of performance data into that attributable to manager "style," or asset class exposure of the manager, and manager skill within that particular individual style.

The basic concept behind developing a normal or benchmark portfolio is to capture all of the manager's systematic biases to produce the portfolio that would result from naively implementing the systematic biases in the manager's investment process. In theory, if this is perfectly accomplished, it would be a simple matter to identify manager styles that benefit from manager skill, and manager styles that should be represented through passive investments.

While normal or benchmark portfolios serve the dual role of identifying manager style and evaluating individual manager performance, it is the former that is key in implementing a completion portfolio. Regardless of the particular benchmarking methodology chosen, the first step toward managing aggregate portfolio tracking error versus a target benchmark is to identify the asset class (style) exposure that exists through passively implementing the systematic biases in all of the underlying managers' investment processes.

It is understood that there are three broad approaches to establishing custom benchmarks: index-based, factor-based, and asset-based benchmarking. We describe them only briefly here. Index-based benchmarking was first described by William Sharpe in 1992 in his survey of mutual fund performance, shown in Exhibit 3. This approach regresses the historic returns of a portfolio against a series of common benchmarks. In Exhibit 3, the benchmarks are the BARRA Large Value, Large Growth, Medium Capitalization and Small indexes.

Performance attribution, as it is also known, describes the contribution to performance of a series of benchmarks. Note that in his study of mutual funds Sharpe estimates that 97% of Fidelity's Magellan Fund's performance is attributable to the concurrent return on a passive portfolio constituted as described in Exhibit 3.[1] The choice of benchmarks is arbitrary, but is usually based on metrics like capitalization and style.

---

[1]  William F. Sharpe, "Asset Allocation: Management Style and Performance Measurement," *Journal of Portfolio Management* (Winter 1992), pp. 12-13.

## Exhibit 3: Sharpe's Analysis of Mutual Funds
### Results of Style Analysis of Mutual Funds
### (1985 - 1989) As Percentages

| Funds | Approximate Exposures to Styles | | | | | Average Performance Explained by | |
|---|---|---|---|---|---|---|---|
| | Value | Growth | Medium | Small | Other | Style | Selection |
| 161 Growth Equity | 12 | 41 | 15 | 20 | 12 | 90 | 10 |
| 118 Growth and Income | 28 | 29 | 14 | 10 | 19 | 91 | 9 |
| 4 Utility Funds | 44 | Negligible | Negligible | Negligible | 56 | 59 | 41 |
| 5 Convertible Bonds | 13 | 14 | 11 | 17 | 45 | 89 | 11 |
| Vanguard's Trustees Commingled | 70 | Negligible | Negligible | 30 | 0 | 92 | 8 |
| Fidelity's Magellan | Negligible | 45 | 30 | 18 | 7 | 97 | 3 |

Source: Summarized from William Sharpe, "Asset Allocation: Management Style and Performance Measurement," Journal of Portfolio Management, Winter 1992, pp. 11-15.

Factor-based benchmarking involves the comparison of risk factors common to the manager portfolios and a particular style. This depends on being able to detect certain management styles by their risk factor "fingerprints." We give an example of a style's fingerprint in our analysis of the outperformance of Large Value by Large Growth, and the returns attributable to seven key risk characteristics as defined by BARRA. Exhibit 4 graphs the correlations between the performance value-growth differential and the returns to each risk factor.

Note that book-to-price (the factor used to differentiate between growth and value in the benchmark construction) and dividend yield are rewarded when value investors are rewarded. Also, earnings growth, success (relative strength), size (capitalization), and variability in markets are all associated with the outperformance of growth versus value. Knowing these characteristics allows any manager's portfolio to be assigned to either growth, value, or some mix between the two. This same analysis can also be performed using macroeconomic, industry-based, or statistically derived factor models, as long as there is a high degree of confidence that the styles can be fingerprinted accurately.

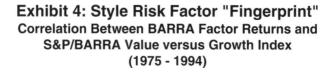

**Exhibit 4: Style Risk Factor "Fingerprint"**
Correlation Between BARRA Factor Returns and
S&P/BARRA Value versus Growth Index
(1975 - 1994)

Individual Correlation

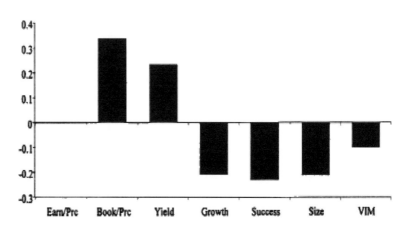

There are several different methods of asset-based benchmarking, but all attempt to get a more accurate benchmark by specifying a "normal" portfolio or benchmark portfolio as opposed to a parametric approach (a "style mix" of indexes, or a series of factor exposures). The benchmark construction process often involves studying the individual holdings of a manager's active portfolio over a sufficient period, drawing conclusions as to which issues are always present (i.e., identifying the systematic biases), and creating a proxy portfolio (benchmark or normal) by naive execution of the manager's selection criteria. This process requires manager interaction feedback, since the manager must approve the benchmark as investable (it must be attainable), and as a good representation of his or her approach.

Quantitative analysis alone cannot differentiate between systematic biases in the manager's investment process and strategic bets that will ultimately mature. For example, assume a quantitative review of a manager's historical portfolio reveals no exposure to utility stocks. If the manager purposely excludes utilities, this should be reflected by excluding utilities from the benchmark. If discussion with the manager reveals that the absence of utilities is a strategic, long-term active bet, utilities should be included in the benchmark so as to evaluate the strategic bet.

## Exhibit 5: Two-Dimensional View of Risk Structure

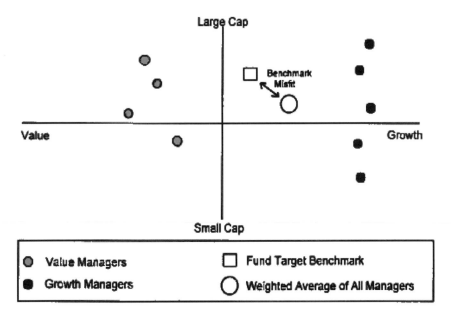

## A VIEW OF EQUITY FUND RISK STRUCTURE

Once each manager is being compared against an appropriate bench-mark, it is possible to view the risk structure of the fund along several dimensions. Exhibit 5 is a two-dimensional plot that shows the location of each manager's benchmark on a scale of growth to value and small- to large-capitalization. The risk factors considered here can be combined linearly, meaning that it is possible to calculate the location on this "map" of the weighted average of the managers represented (the large empty circle). This represents the location of the portfolio that would result from all managers investing in their special benchmark portfolios passively (i.e., an aggregate of all the manager benchmarks).

If this portfolio is not in the same location as the fund's target benchmark (represented by the square), the fund has not accurately represented the desired target, and it is bearing an unintended risk. In this example, if small growth managers underperform other styles of investing, this fund will underperform the target, possibly threatening the incremental returns gained by active management because the aggregate benchmark is smaller and more growth-oriented than the target benchmark.

The distance between the aggregated benchmarks and the fund's target benchmark is called the *misfit*, and is usually quoted in tracking error terms. A misfit risk of 200 basis points refers to the annualized standard deviation of the difference in performance between the aggregated benchmarks and the target benchmark. This can then be translated into crude probability terms. For example, assuming a normal distribution, a tracking error of 200 basis points would imply that the portfolio return should fall within ±400 basis points of the benchmark about 95% of the time.

## ANALYZING THE MISFIT

Misfit can have many sources. It is rarely due to a "simple tilt toward growth," for example. We often find that a particular industry (e.g., oil stocks) or type of stock (e.g., high-yield stocks) is purposely avoided by a particular manager. Our approach involves using a factor fingerprint to analyze the misfit. The misfit is generated by differences in both systematic and nonsystematic characteristics of the fund. There are typically differences in the style layer shown in Exhibit 1 as well as in the security selection process that describes each manager's benchmark.

Subtracting the aggregate of the managers' benchmarks from the target benchmark yields a long/short portfolio that, if transacted, would convert the aggregate of the managers' benchmarks to the target benchmark. The long/short approach is the most efficient method of constructing a completion fund. It is the membership in this long/short portfolio that exactly characterizes the misfit risk:

(Target Benchmark – Aggregate of Managers´ Benchmarks) = Misfit Long/Short Portfolio

(shown in Exhibit 6).

Note that the long misfit portfolio includes those stocks that need to be bought, and the short portfolio includes those stocks that need to be sold in order to bring the manager benchmarks in line with the target benchmark. Factor fingerprinting of this long/short portfolio will yield the sources of misfit. It may be necessary to use several different factor models to capture an accurate picture of the sources of risk, since some dimensions may not be visible from a single perspective. While it is convenient to analyze or locate portfolios visually in two-factor space (Small-Large, Value-Growth), this is usually insufficient to fully analyze and manage misfit. BARRA factors, industry composition, and macroeconomic APT models are all useful to give descriptions of the misfit.

## Exhibit 6: Derivation of the Misfit Long/Short Portfolio

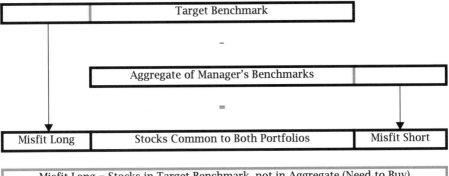

## APPROACHES TO PENSION FUND STYLE MANAGEMENT

Once the misfit is understood, a solution can be devised. Simple alternatives range from shifting physical assets between managers (to return the aggregate mix to the target benchmark) to doing nothing and hoping that the misfit risk will go your way. A more deterministic approach would be to build a dynamic completion portfolio that is updated periodically. This is a portfolio that approximates the characteristics of the misfit long/short portfolio. It contains issues that specifically counter the biases detected with the intent of controlling the misfit risk.

### The Role of Completion Funds

A completion fund is a portfolio that is specifically designed with the objective of controlling or managing the misfit risk. If the completion portfolio were exactly the misfit long/short portfolio described earlier, all the misfit risk would be eliminated, and the only deviation away from the target benchmark would be from the active bets by the individual managers. That portfolio may not be investable, however, and needs to be represented in an investable manner. Additionally, many funds do not want to short stocks (or cannot), making it difficult to replicate the short portion of the completion portfolio.

The long portfolio is made up of under-represented issues, and is straightforward to replicate. The short portfolio consists of issues that are overweighted in the fund benchmarks. These are not easily dealt with when shorting is not allowed. The only way to replicate the short position is to throw more assets into all of the other industries, dwarfing the overweighted groups. While it is possible, and in fact done in practice, increasing industry exposures is not as efficient a use of assets as using the long/short approach.

Passive replication of the misfit portfolio, while straightforward, is not as effective, since the periodic rebalancing process and its transactions costs tend to cause a performance drag. Some active stock selection, applied with the restriction that the systematic goal of the completion fund must be maintained, can be used to offset transactions costs. Turnover is created by the passage of time and its impact on the portfolio mix. The manager and target benchmarks shift because of changes in pricing or the method of management. No rebalancing of manager portfolios is required, however, because the completion portfolio adapts to the new risk structure and is dynamically maintained in a risk-reducing position.

## Implementing a Completion Fund

Once it is decided whether to use a long/short or long-only fund, and once an investable portfolio is constructed, transition from the existing structure to the new structure of active managers and a completion fund can occur. The choice of securities for a completion fund can be made while taking into account their risk "fingerprint" as well as their potential for positive stock selection return. In order to reduce costs, the portfolio construction process can weigh the benefits of stock appreciation potential versus transaction costs; those stocks already in the portfolio that meet the risk and return requirements are preferable to those that would need to be bought.

*Transactions Cost Savings:* Significant savings in transactions costs are possible if the completion fund acts as the transition portfolio for any major changes in allocations to equity managers. For example, if a growth manager is terminated in a multi-manager structure, the response by the fund as a whole would typically be a tilt to value. The completion fund would then have to become more growth-like to compensate. This shift would make the completion fund the natural buyer of some of the growth stocks that would otherwise need to be traded, assuming the risk characteristics of those stocks satisfy the other requirements for inclusion.

*Retention of Best Value-added Managers:* The dynamic nature of the completion portfolio obviates the need to shift assets between managers. Should a group of growth managers be performing particularly well (whether because of systematic outperformance of the growth style of management, or skilled stock selection by that subset of managers), that outperformance would require rebalancing periodically. A completion fund can compensate for the tilt to growth, preventing the need to take assets away from the most successful managers.

*Providing the Ability to Add Value:* The completion portfolio does not have to be passively implemented. Periodic rebalancing costs can be offset by application of some active security selection within the completion portfolio, which at a minimum should recover the costs of running the fund. The trade-off that should be considered is the amount of tracking error between the invested portfolio and the completion benchmark. A long-only completion portfolio with about 150 basis points of tracking error should be able to recover all transactions costs in the long run. A more aggressive active management mandate can also be applied in order to provide more opportunity to add value to a greater portion of the overall fund's assets.

## Managing the Misfit Risk
We believe the most significant issue in the management of a multi-manager equity fund is the explicit management of the misfit risk. Misfit risk is the difference in performance between the fund's target benchmark and the collection of managers' benchmarks chosen to represent it. Unless the fund's target is replicated passively, there will be some misfit. Periodic physical rebalancing of managers can keep the misfit low, but this is a costly and unpopular strategy (taking assets from the best-performing managers). The completion fund can centralize the misfit management process and approach it in a more cost-effective manner.

The dynamic completion fund can also be a valuable tool in the process of changing allocations to equity managers (through restructuring or termination) in a multi-manager structure. As a result, some plan sponsors find the completion fund concept an effective way to manage misfit risk in multi-manager porfolios. For examples, see Chapters 11 and 12.

# CHAPTER 9

## IMPLICATIONS OF STYLE IN FOREIGN STOCK INVESTING

*PAUL M. BAGNOLI*
*SENIOR PORTFOLIO MANAGER*
*DIRECTOR OF INTERNATIONAL PRODUCT DEVELOPMENT*
*SANFORD C. BERNSTEIN AND COMPANY, INC.*

## INTRODUCTION

In 1988, foreign stocks accounted for $45 billion of U.S. pension-plan assets, using the universe as defined by Greenwich Associates (Exhibit 1). The amount estimated for 1994 is close to $200 billion. (Throughout this chapter, the phrase "foreign stocks" refers to non-U.S. stocks.) This really isn't surprising, since foreign stocks represent an opportunity to invest in some of the best-run companies in the world — which just happen to be domiciled outside the U.S. Equally important, foreign stocks are a high-expected return asset that diversifies U.S. equities. Plan sponsors are aware of these facts and are globalizing their portfolios more and more.

Another way of understanding these developments is to look at the amount of money that pension plans are giving to investment managers for foreign and global accounts as a percent of the total dollars placed (Exhibit 2). In the first half of 1993, that number was at 25% — up from less than 15% five years earlier. There is a cyclical component to foreign hiring, but the appetite among plan sponsors for investing abroad is clearly increasing, and will doubtless grow further.

The rationale for expanding internationally is intuitive. But as the process unfolds, it raises the question of active management style. In the U.S., management style is an integral part of the equity allocation decision, and many plan sponsors purposely diversify between the two most common styles — value and growth — to try to reap the best of both worlds. Neither style wins all the time, and in fact, in the U.S., there have been distinct cycles favoring one or the other approach. But in the long run, the value style — seeking stocks that are underpriced relative to their companies' fundamental earnings power — has outperformed the market average handily.

**Exhibit 1: U.S. Pension Plan Assets in Foreign Stocks**

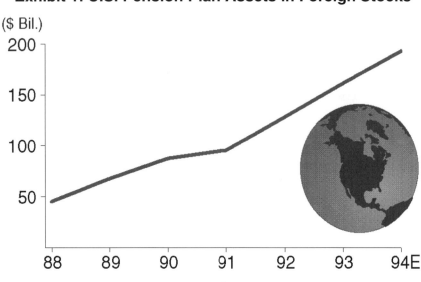

Source: Greenwich Associates.

**Exhibit 2: International and Global Accounts
as Percentage of Total Pension Dollars Placed**

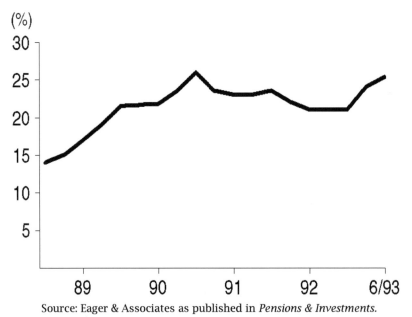

Source: Eager & Associates as published in *Pensions & Investments.*

The question is whether this applies to foreign stocks. After all, the foreign markets are a different animal.

## A LOOK AT JAPAN

Let us review the empirical evidence on this issue, and begin with Japan, a country very different from the U.S. in customs, institutions, and social mores. Although there is little academic research on the issue, it seems only logical that a country as different from the U.S. in the sociopolitical sphere would also be different in the way its investors behave.

In many important ways, this is true. If we look at compound stock returns for the last four full decades, in local terms, Japanese equities have outperformed U.S. equities consistently — by margins ranging from three percentage points a year, in the sixties, to seven points, in the seventies (Exhibit 3). And while the Japanese market has been somewhat off its stride in the early nineties, it seems to be coming back very strong.

If you look at valuation, the story is equally extreme. The top of Exhibit 4 shows the price-to-book ratios of the Japanese and U.S. markets from 1975 through the middle of 1989, when the "bubble" in Japan was at its peak. These are the years that helped form our mindset on Japan, and gave credence to the notion that Japan is truly a domain apart. The gap between the two markets is impressive; it kept widening until Japanese stocks hit a high of five times book value. Even after the Japanese market collapse in 1990, the price-to-book ratio remained very high.

We see the same pattern in P/Es (bottom of Exhibit 5), which went as high as 64. It's not easy to find a major U.S. company that trades at that multiple, let alone a market average. (The recent P/E statistics in Japan are even higher, since earnings have been so poor in the current recession.) Valuation levels in Japan have been simply stratospheric.

Exhibit 6 presents another way of understanding how lofty Japanese valuation levels can become, especially when combined with the enormous size that Japanese companies can reach. The capitalization of the two biggest banks in Japan, Mitsubishi and the Industrial Bank of Japan, totals approximately $155 billion, as of the middle of 1993. For that money an investor could effectively have bought all the banks in the S&P 500: all the money-centers, all the big regionals, and everybody else.

## Exhibit 3: U.S. Versus Japan Stock Performance Annualized Total Returns (in Local Currency)

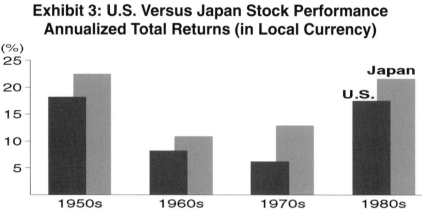

Source: Ibbotson Associates, Morgan Stanley Capital International, Goldman Sachs and Company, and Bernstein estimates.

## Exhibit 4: Historical Price/Book Ratios (1/75 - 6/89)

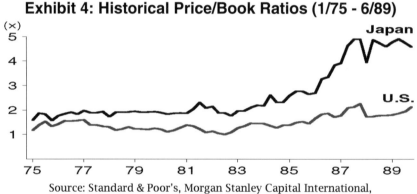

Source: Standard & Poor's, Morgan Stanley Capital International, and Bernstein estimates.

## Exhibit 5: Historical Price/Earnings Ratios (1/75 - 6/89)
### Using trailing 12-month earnings.

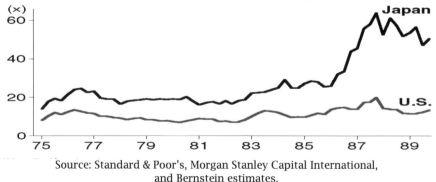

Source: Standard & Poor's, Morgan Stanley Capital International, and Bernstein estimates.

## Exhibit 6: Japanese Capitalization (Banks)

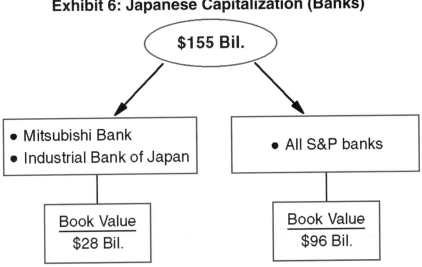

Source: World Scope, Standard & Poor's, and Bernstein estimates.

But an investor is not getting nearly as much value in Japan. The $155 billion spent for the two huge Japanese banks would buy $28 billion in book value, which is a far cry from the $96 billion available in the U.S. bank composite. In Japan, an investor paying five times book to own two banks; an investor could buy virtually the entire U.S. banking system for about one times book. Meanwhile, the combined earnings of the two Japanese banks over the past 12 months were $710 million; for the S&P bank universe it was $11 billion, as of the middle of 1993.

The same kind of phenomenon is at work if an investor looks at the capitalization of the largest company in Japan as of the middle of 1993, Nippon Telephone & Telegraph, which is a huge $180 billion (Exhibit 7). For the money spent to buy this one Japanese company, an investor could buy a big chunk of the whole S&P 500: in fact, its 150 smallest companies. And once again, the disparity in book value is tremendous: $39 billion for Nippon Telephone, versus double that amount for the S&P companies.

If there is a different frame of reference at work in the Japanese stock market, there is also a different trading mentality. Over the ten years ending 1992, trading volume in Japan has averaged about 700 million shares a day, against 135 million for the U.S. (Exhibit 8). Annual turnover in Japan has been as high as 127%. There is more buying and selling, a more speculative bent, among Japanese investors.

**Exhibit 7: Japanese Capitalization (Nippon Telephone)**

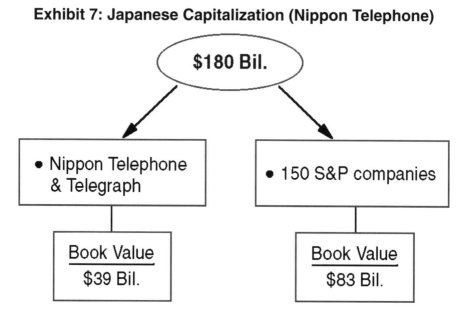

Source: World Scope, Standard & Poor's, and Bernstein estimates.

**Exhibit 8: U.S. Versus Japan Trading Volume
Daily Shares Traded: 10-Year Average**

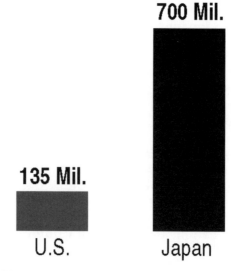

Source: Goldman Sachs and Company, Yamaichi Research Institute, and Bernstein estimates.

## Exhibit 9: Ratio of Short-term to Long-term Analyst Forecasts

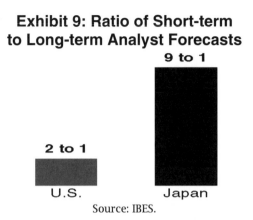

Source: IBES.

This bias toward speculation in the Japanese market is reflected in the kind of research coverage that Japanese companies get. Institutional research statistics show that the ratio of short-term to long-term earnings forecasts for S&P 500 companies is, on average, about two-to-one (Exhibit 9). To be specific, the average S&P company is followed by 20 analysts who do short-term forecasting and 11 who make long-term forecasts, which means about five years out. For Japanese companies, the ratio is nine to one. Not many analysts are bothering to take a long-term perspective on Japanese stocks — which follows logically from investors' trading patterns.

## A Closer Look

These observations do not bode well for the importance of investment style in Japan—and certainly not for the value approach. But as Ross Perot says, sometimes you have to look under the hood. When we did that, because we weren't ready to give up on value based on just the way things appeared, the results turned out to be extremely provocative.

Our research methodology (Exhibit 10) follows models established in the U.S. We went back to 1975, the earliest year for which reliable data are available, and, on a quarterly basis, we ranked the stocks in the Japanese market by their price-to-book ratios. We thought of the highest 20% of the market on this price-to-book measure as a proxy for growth stocks, and the lowest 20% as value stocks. We then built portfolios of growth stocks and of value stocks, and measured their performance in local-currency terms going forward. (We applied the same methodology consistently across nine other major foreign markets in assessing worldwide value performance.)

**Exhibit 10: Bernstein Research Methodology**

➤ Universe = key foreign markets.

➤ Rank stocks by price-to-book ratios.

➤ Highest 20% = Growth; Lowest 20% = Value.

➤ Construct value and growth portfolios.

➤ Measure performance (in local currency) going forward.

Note: Morgan Stanley International coverage universe for each country.

Exhibit 11 shows the characteristics of the two subgroups of stocks: the top and bottom 20% of the Japanese market on this price-to-book basis from 1975 through 1993. The most expensive stocks show quite a pattern: their price-to-book averaged 6.6, and peaked at a phenomenal 22 times book.

It's no surprise that numbers like these color people's perceptions about the Japanese market. But in fact, they apply only to its growth subset. These stocks may represent a good chunk of the market on a capitalization basis, but they're only a small part of the total universe of opportunity in Japan. The bubble of the late eighties, for example, was led by three industries: banking, insurance, and real estate.

We can draw three conclusions about that least expensive 20% of Japanese stocks. First, there has always been such a group— a "value" universe—in Japan. Second, its characteristics have been remarkably stable; price-to-book ratio in this group has never risen much higher than 2.0, even when things were at their craziest in Japan, and it has stayed pretty consistently around its average of 1.4—which would be attractive even by Western standards. Finally, the gap between what's cheap in Japan and what's expensive is remarkable.

We see the same kind of picture in P/E ratios (Exhibit 12). P/Es on expensive stocks have averaged 71 and reached an outlandish 186— versus a fairly consistent 25–50 for the value universe, which may not sound cheap but is quite attractive when the market is at 70.

## World's Best Market For Value

The question remains: Do investors get paid for going with cheap stocks in Japan? The answer is, handsomely so. When performance by style is examined, there is a light and a dark side of the moon, but completely reversed.

### Exhibit 11: Japanese Price/Book Ratios (1975 - 1993)

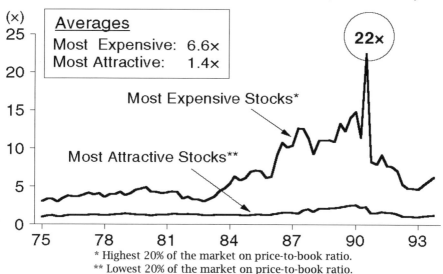

* Highest 20% of the market on price-to-book ratio.
** Lowest 20% of the market on price-to-book ratio.
Source: Morgan Stanley Capital International and Bernstein estimates.

### Exhibit 12: Japanese Price/Earnings Ratios (1975 - 1993)
#### Using trailing 12-month earnings

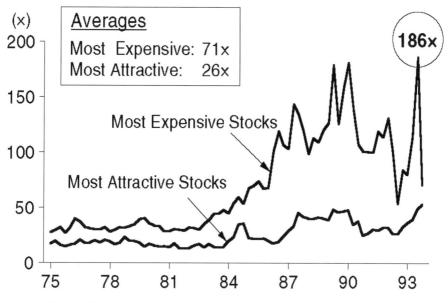

Source: Morgan Stanley Capital International and Bernstein estimates.

## Exhibit 13: Growth of ¥1 (1975 - 1993)

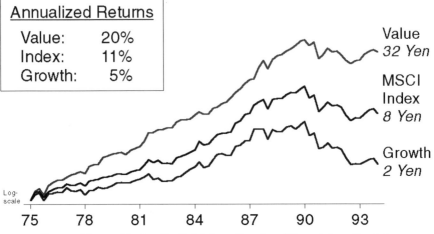

Source: Morgan Stanley Capital International and Bernstein estimates.

Between 1975 and 1993, Japanese value stocks compounded at 20% a year in yen terms, versus 11% for the market average, and 5% for growth stocks (Exhibit 13). Looked at another way, it means that a yen invested in Japanese value stocks would have grown over 30-fold over the period, versus sevenfold for the benchmark, and two for growth stocks. Ironically enough, considering how unfriendly the Japanese environment looks for value, Japan has been the best market in the world for this approach. And value has achieved this outperformance with less volatility than growth stocks.

## Extremes Create The Performance Edge

This level of performance has been fueled by the same extremes that at first glance appear so daunting. If a group of stocks is selling for 70 times earnings, it suggests that price is no object: owning them becomes almost a civil right, something done without thinking. Other stocks — the ones facing short-term disappointments, or where earnings growth has been a little duller — just get crowded out. Few investors are paying attention; few have the patience to let cycles play out. With the discrepancy in Japan between the attention paid to expensive and cheap stocks, the value approach has flourished.

To put it another way, if an investor believes that a company is under a temporary cloud, and it is selling at a P/E of 35 when the market is at 70, an investor is likely to win big if right and the cloud lifts. Conversely, if an investor is looking at a fast-growing company that he bets is going to be able to sustain its growth, and the stock is trading at 185 times earnings, he had better be right.

### Exhibit 14: Composition of Returns (Japan)
#### Annualized 1975 - 1993

| | Batting Average (Frequency) | | Slugging Percentage (Magnitude) | |
|---|---|---|---|---|
| | Winning | Losing | Win | Lose |
| Value | 57% | 43% | 16 points | -9 points |
| Growth | 39% | 61% | 8 points | -12 points |

Source: Morgan Stanley Capital International and Bernstein estimates.

## "Batting And Slugging" Averages

You can see the performance dynamic at work through one of our models that explains why value is efficacious: the so-called batting average and slugging percentage. The batting average is the frequency of results: the percentage of the time that a group of stocks outperformed the market, versus the percentage of the time that it underperformed. The slugging percentage reflects the magnitude of outperformance when a style wins, or underperformance when it loses. Both have been very favorable for value in Japan (Exhibit 14).

Between 1975 and 1993, Japanese value stocks, on average, outperformed the market 57% of the time, compared to 39% for the growth stocks. While that 57% figure clearly beats growth, it may not sound too impressive; that is, value stocks still underperformed 43% of the time. But here's where the slugging percentage comes in, because when value stocks won, they won by a lot — 16 percentage points over the market on average, versus eight for growth. And when they lost, it was by less. The combination of respectable batting and superior slugging has proved powerful for the value style in Japan.

There's a Biblical precept that says, don't hide your candle under a bushel. That's what's happened with value in Japan. The "candle" of value tends to get lost under the bushel of 180 P/Es. As a result, many investors don't even look for it. Historically, that has been a sizable mistake.

## CAN STYLE WORK IN BRITAIN?

Now, let's examine another country, where, for very different reasons, the environment would appear unreceptive to a value style: the U.K. If Japan is perceived as the world's "superstar," Britain is its "has-been." Once it was said that the sun never sets on the British empire, but we all know what happened. There's some reality behind the perceptions.

Over the years, the U.K. has accounted for less and less of the world's economy, and its share of the global stock market has followed suit (Exhibit 15). A quarter century ago, British stocks represented almost a third of all the stock capitalized in the world; the figure is down to 10% today. Still, we view the U.K. as a declining annuity; it may be worth less with the passage of time, but it still pays off.

## Exhibit 15: U.K. — A Declining Annuity
### U.K.% of World Stock Market Capitalization

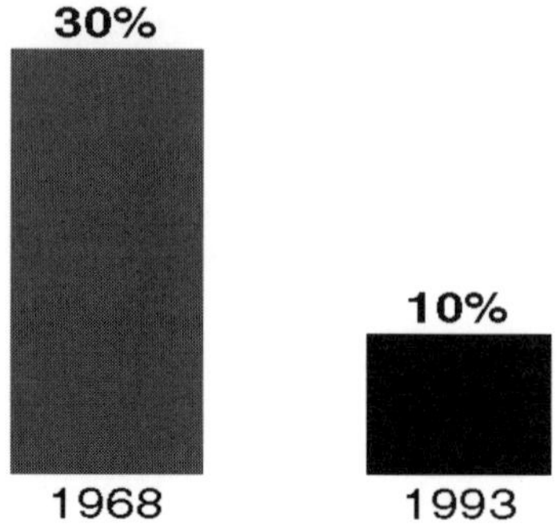

Source: Morgan Stanley Capital International and Bernstein estimates.

## British Market Stronger Than U.S.

The sun may have set on the British empire, but it's still shining on its capital markets. In fact, in five of the seven full decades since the 1920s, stocks in the U.K. have done as well as or better than their U.S. counterparts (Exhibit 16). And when the U.S. did have the edge, it wasn't recently, as might be expected, but in the 1920s and the 1940s.

In the seventies, British stocks compounded at 11%, versus 6% for the U.S. — in local currency terms. And in the eighties, which was an unusually robust ten years for the U.S., British stocks did even better, growing at an extraordinary 24% a year. In total, over the seven decades, the U.K. has beaten the U.S. by two percentage points annually. This is hardly a deteriorating market.

## Value Wins Again

As in Japan, there's a distinct value subset in the British equity market (Exhibit 17). While the most expensive 20% of the market had an average price-to-book of more than four over the 1975-1993 period, the cheapest 20% — our value universe — has sold for less than its book value. And dividend yields on the value stocks have been significantly higher.

Once again, these characteristics have been associated with outperformance (Exhibit 18). Between 1975 and 1993, British value stocks outpaced the market benchmark by two percentage points a year in pounds sterling, and beat growth stocks by three points — results that are not as extreme as what we saw in Japan, but meaningful over time. A pound sterling invested in value stocks would have grown to 90 pounds, which was 27 pounds more than the market and 37 pounds more than growth stocks achieved.

## Exhibit 16: U.K. Versus U.S. Stock Market Returns
### Annualized Total Returns (%)

|          | U.K. | U.S. |
|----------|------|------|
| 1920s    | 10   | 13   |
| 1930s    | 6    | -0.3 |
| 1940s    | 7    | 10   |
| 1950s    | 18   | 18   |
| 1960s    | 8    | 8    |
| 1970s    | 11   | 6    |
| 1980s    | 24   | 18   |
| Compound | 12   | 10   |

Source: Barclays de Zoete Wedd Research

## Exhibit 17: U.K. Stocks (Valuation Characteristics)
### 1975 - 1993 Average

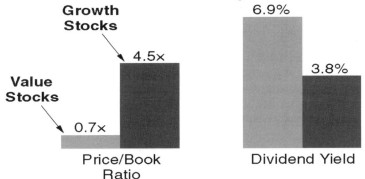

Source: Morgan Stanley Capital International and Bernstein estimates.

## Exhibit 18: Growth of £1 (1975 - 1993)

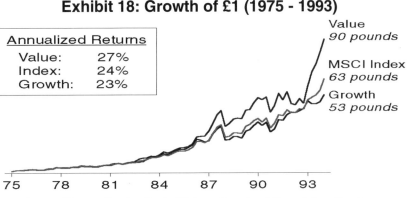

Annualized Returns
Value:   27%
Index:   24%
Growth:  23%

Value
90 pounds

MSCI Index
63 pounds

Growth
53 pounds

Source: Morgan Stanley Capital International and Bernstein estimates.

### Exhibit 19: Composition of Returns (U.K.)
**Annualized 1975 - 1993**

|  | Batting Average (Frequency) | | Slugging Percentage (Magnitude) | |
|---|---|---|---|---|
|  | Winning | Losing | Win | Lose |
| Value | 52% | 48% | 6 points | -3 points |
| Growth | 48% | 52% | 5 points | -5 points |

Source: Morgan Stanley Capital International and Bernstein estimates.

The market-like performance of growth stocks in Britain was far better than growth's track record in Japan, which makes sense, since in the less-polarized British market, the penalty for being wrong on growth stocks has been less severe. Behind value's superior performance in the U.K. are batting and slugging averages that are favorable rather than stellar (Exhibit 19). Value outperformed slightly more of the time than growth, and when it succeeded, it won by a little more. When it lost, it was by less. The combination is enough to create a long-run premium.

## GLOBAL OUTPERFORMANCE — WITHOUT EXTRA RISK

Value also outperforms globally. The style has worked to varying degrees, of course, in the different countries, and it has not worked in every country every year. But, as shown in Exhibit 20, it has produced a meaningful long-term premium in key markets, with truly stand-out performance in Japan, where the style has extreme market characteristics in its favor.

The absolute performance numbers behind these premiums are given in the left two columns of Exhibit 21. Risk, however, is just as important a consideration for plan sponsors, since excellent performance can mask unacceptable levels of volatility. It turns out that the risk of value investing is generally comparable to or lower than the risk for growth. Where value is modestly more risky — France is the example here — returns tend to be outsized.

### An Additional Advantage
One reason the value style works so well is that at any time the efficacy of the approach tends to be different country-to-country. For example, when the value style is achieving sizable outperformance in the U.K., it may be outperforming only modestly — or even underperforming — in Japan. So when an investor puts value portfolios from the U.K. and Japan — or any other two countries — together, there is the benefit of an additional layer of risk reduction.

## Exhibit 20: Value Premium to Growth
### Annualized 1975 - 1993

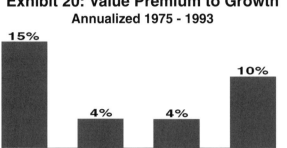

Source: Morgan Stanley Capital International and Bernstein estimates.

## Exhibit 21: Value Versus Growth (Risk/Reward Profile%)
### Annualized 1975 - 1993

|  | Return | | Volatility | |
|---|---|---|---|---|
|  | Value | Growth | Value | Growth |
| Japan | 20 | 5 | 20 | 22 |
| U.K. | 27 | 23 | 23 | 23 |
| Germany | 16 | 12 | 19 | 20 |
| France | 25 | 15 | 26 | 23 |

Source: Morgan Stanley Capital International and Bernstein estimates.

## Exhibit 22: Value as a Diversifier
### Correlations of Value-Stock Relative Returns

| U.K./Japan | 0.12 |
|---|---|
| Japan/Germany | 0.02 |
| U.K./France | 0.38 |
| France/Italy | 0.08 |
| U.K./Germany | 0.19 |

Source: Morgan Stanley Capital International and Bernstein estimates.

## Exhibit 23: Most Underpriced Industries

|  | Japan | U.K. | Germany | France |
|---|---|---|---|---|
| ❶ | Appliances | Steel | Industria Components | Textiles & Apparel |
| ❷ | Autos | Data Processing | Aerospace & Defense | Autos |
| ❸ | Data Processing | Real Estate | Chemicals | Steel |
| ❹ | Electrical & Electronics | Aerospace & Defense | Airlines | Banking |
| ❺ | Publishing | Leisure & Tourism | Forest & Paper | Non-Ferrous Metals |

Source: Morgan Stanley Capital International and Bernstein estimates.

This can be quantified by showing the statistical correlations in relative performance between value stocks in several representative markets as shown in Exhibit 22. Performance hardly moves in lockstep; in fact, the correlations have been extremely weak. The highest on the list, between the U.K. and France, is only 0.4 out of a possible 1.0, and in some pairings the relationship is essentially random (a zero correlation).

In other words, how the value stocks of one country are doing relative to the market at any given time tells you very little about how the value stocks of another country are performing. The result is that the sharp ups and downs of short-term performance tend to be smoothed out when a systematic value approach is employed in each country. An investor gets a less bumpy ride year to year.

## Style Is Inherently Diversifying

This greater stability is associated with significant diversification in individual stocks, because industries that are cheap in one country are not necessarily cheap in others at the same time. Exhibit 23 lists the five cheapest industries in four markets as of the end of 1993, and while there are some duplications — steel makes the list in both the U.K. and France, for instance, and autos in both Japan and France — basically this is impressive diversity.

The most underpriced industry at that moment in Japan was appliances; in Germany it was industrial components; in France it was textiles. With weak correlations country-to-country, and a high degree of portfolio diversification, the result is more return per unit of risk.

## More Efficient Portfolios

To sum it up, Exhibit 24 compares returns and volatility for value stocks and the market benchmarks in the same four key countries since 1975. In Japan, value stocks have outperformed by nine percentage points a year on average, with an annualized volatility of 20% compared with a benchmark volatility of 21%. The pattern is similar for all the other countries: a meaningful performance premium with comparable — often modestly less — risk in most cases. This is a strong picture.

The composite numbers are more provocative. Because the diversification effect smooths the edges of country-by-country volatility, foreign value stocks in the aggregate compound at two points higher than the composite benchmark without any incremental risk. This is a classic case of moving up on the efficient frontier.

### Exhibit 24: Value Versus Market (Risk and Reward%)
#### Annualized 1975 - 1993

|  | Return | | Volatility | |
|---|---|---|---|---|
|  | Value | Market | Value | Market |
| Japan | 20 | 11 | 20 | 21 |
| U.K. | 27 | 24 | 23 | 24 |
| Germany | 16 | 13 | 19 | 20 |
| France | 25 | 19 | 26 | 23 |
| Composite | 17 | 15 | 18 | 19 |

Source: Morgan Stanley Capital International, Datastream, and Bernstein estimates.

## CONCLUSIONS

The conclusions are clear. First, despite the many differences between the U.S. and foreign markets, investment style is as key to performance abroad as it is here. Second, value investing confers long-term benefits in all the key foreign markets. And third, when systematically employed on a global basis, value investing adds a further dimension of risk-reducing diversification. As plan sponsors become more involved in the foreign markets, we believe they should pay careful attention to these concepts.

# CHAPTER 10

## EVOLUTIONARY IDEAS IN INTERNATIONAL STYLE MANAGEMENT

*DAVID J. LEINWEBER, PH.D.*
*DIRECTOR*
*FIRST QUADRANT CORPORATION*

*DAVID KRIDER*
*ASSOCIATE*
*FIRST QUADRANT CORPORATION*

*PETER SWANK, PH.D.*
*ASSOCIATE*
*FIRST QUADRANT CORPORATION*

The author gratefully acknowledges H. Russell Fogler for attentive editing.

## INTRODUCTION

In Chapter 6, "Tactical Style Management," Arnott and Dorian explain the motivation and methodology for a U.S. equity style management investment process, which has been very successfully used for both long and long/short portfolios.[1] This chapter covers two topics: internationalization of the U.S. process, and use of the genetic algorithm (a machine-learning method based on natural selection) to improve upon it. Conservative estimates indicate that the genetic algorithm has the potential to improve returns by over 370 basis points annually.

---

[1] Or market-neutral. The terms are interchangeable in this context.

We first review quantitative evidence showing that international style shifts can add value as the basis of an active management strategy. We base our implementations of these strategies on the use of multiple-factor models of equity risk and return. We forecast the returns to these factors, and use an optimizer to construct investable portfolios to capture these returns. With this level of understanding of the process, we demonstrate how the genetic algorithm is an evolutionary step toward a better international style management process.

J. Robert Oppenheimer, the physicist who led the development of the atomic bomb at Los Alamos in the 1940s, maintained that the scientist who could not explain a course of action to a six year-old child was a charlatan. This standard should apply equivalently to quantitative investment managers. Mathematical techniques that express the ideas behind quantitative strategies should be explicable without invoking the Greek alphabet. For the readers who feel cheated if they do not see equations, we include exactly two.

## QUANTITATIVE MOTIVATION
## FOR INTERNATIONAL STYLE MANAGEMENT

Value and growth have been central concepts in the U.S. perspective on equity investing for some time. The classification of managers by style, the growing popularity of managed style, the publication of scholarly quantitative analyses of investing style, and the appearance of books like this reflect this trend. Style management is now widely accepted in the U.S. As investors diversify internationally, it is reasonable to ask the question: Can we make money by managing style internationally?

Carlo Capaul, Ian Rowley, and William Sharpe addressed this question.[2] They use the simplest definition of value and growth: Start with a broad index, sort all the stocks by price-to-book ratios (P/B), and divide the ordered list of stocks into two equally capitalized halves. The low price-to-book half are the value stocks; the others are growth stocks.[3]

There are more elaborate definitions based on accounting data other than book value and price, but the simple approach is better

---

[2] Carlo Capaul, Ian Rowley, and William Sharpe, "International Value and Growth Stock Returns," *Financial Analysts Journal*, (January/February 1993), pp. 27-36
[3] The construction method used for the S&P/Barra Value and Growth indices.

when considering international stocks, where international accounting standards present problems. Even the simple P/B approach is not as simple as it appears. There is general agreement on the meaning of "price," but the definition of "book" is more problematical across international borders. Nevertheless, P/B provides the best means for analyzing the returns of value and growth stocks consistently in different world equity markets.

Having settled on a value/growth definition that travels well across borders, examine patterns of returns to value and growth stocks. There are two questions to consider. The simple question is just to look at the returns to each style over time, and see which is superior. The next, more significant, question is to look at the month-to-month variation in returns to the two styles, and see if there is an opportunity to add value over a "buy a style and hold it" strategy by making tactical style shifts.

Plotting the cumulative returns to value minus growth (V-G) demonstrates this graphically. In a month when value outperforms growth, the line slopes up; when growth outperforms value, the slope is negative. The endpoints of the V-G plot indicate the long-term performance of the two styles. The high variability in the slope of V-G is indicative of the potential value of style management.

The pair of hypothetical V-G plots seen in Exhibit 1 illustrates this possibility. In this exhibit, value outperforms growth over the full period. Yet, the smooth slopes with little monthly variation in slope seen in the left graph mean there is little value to add by frequent tactical switches from value to growth. Note that there are only two months shown where the slope of the line changes sign: January 1984 and January 1988. This contrasts sharply with the situation on the right, where there is an identical outcome for V-G over the same period, but with frequent changes in the sign of the slope, indicating frequent opportunities to add value by active style management decisions.

When Capaul, Rowley, and Sharpe constructed V-G charts to look at cumulative returns to the V-G spread in the U.S., they found that value has outperformed growth over this period, and there was ample opportunity to add value by active style management on a monthly time scale. What do the value minus growth returns show us outside the U.S.?

Once again, we can refer to the Capaul, Rowley, and Sharpe study. They found that the cumulative returns to V-G in the U.K., France, Japan, Germany, and Canada exhibit a remarkably consistent pattern: Value outperforms growth over long periods, and there is an opportunity to add value by active style management in every market examined. In the words of Capaul et al.:

## Exhibit 1: Hypothetical Value/Growth Plots

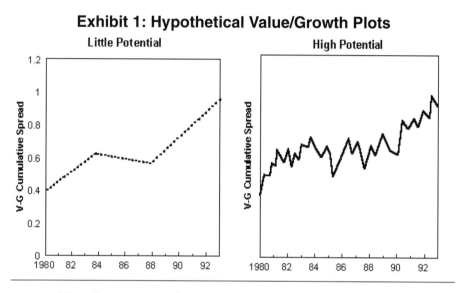

"Results suggest the existence of a significant value-growth factor' in each country. The returns on portfolios formed according to the value-growth factor differ far more from month to month than would be expected if the securities had been selected randomly."

# IMPLEMENTING STYLE MANAGEMENT

## A Simple but Costly Method

The most straightforward way to implement style management is to switch all assets from a value index portfolio to a growth index portfolio according to a tactical indication of which style is expected to outperform each month (or other forecast period). At any particular moment, the portfolio is invested entirely in growth stocks or value stocks.

If there were no transactions costs, this method might be practicable. In reality, the cost of transacting would overwhelm most, if not all, of the value added by this strategy. If value and growth each outperform in roughly half the months (which is the case), the entire portfolio would turn over six times a year on average. Even with a low round-trip transactions cost of only 1%, the annual performance drag would average 6%, and could be as high as 12% in the worst case.

This simple strategy is viable only when costs for implementing the style transitions are very low. A liquid futures market for U.S. value and growth indexes would make this approach feasible. At present there are no plans for international value and growth futures, and the transactions costs in these stocks are typically higher than in the U.S. In a country with 2% round-trip transactions costs, the performance drag would average 12%. Clearly the cost of this rough approach to style management is prohibitive. We need something more refined.

## Reducing Turnover with Factor Models

Factor models of equity risk and return are perhaps the most well-established tool in the field of quantitative equity management. The simplest factor model is, of course, the Capital Asset Pricing Model, which explains equity returns using a single market factor, known as beta ($\beta_m$):

$$R_s - R_{rf} = \beta_m (R_m - R_{rf}) + \tilde{\varepsilon}$$

where $R_s$ is the return to the security, $R_{rf}$ is the risk-free rate of return, $R_m$ is the return to the market, and $\varepsilon$ is the residual error.

Intuition and analysis tell us that additional factors will also affect equity returns in a systematic way. The stock of companies with heavy debt will respond differently to changes in interest rates than less levered firms. Stock in firms with substantial foreign income will be more sensitive to exchange rates than those with only domestic sales. Industry classifications are well-known factors that explain some of the patterns observed in equity returns. Oil stocks, for example, respond differently as a group to economic and market events than transportation stocks.

Price/book (i.e., value and growth) and earnings/price are also important factors in models of equity risk and return.[4] Factor models based on considerations such as these, which have the general flavor of fundamental analysis, are known as fundamental factor models.[5] These multi-factor models generalize the CAPM equation:

$$R_s - R_{rf} = \sum_f \beta_f (R_f - R_{rf}) + \tilde{\varepsilon}$$

where $\beta_f$ are factor exposures, and $R_f$ are the factor returns.

[4] Eugene F. Fama and Kenneth R. French "Permanent and Temporary Components of Stock Prices," *Journal of Political Economy*, Volume 96, Issue 2 (1988), pp.246-273.
[5] It is also possible to derive purely statistical factor models, where the factors are not clearly associated with company characteristics, but simply extracted numerically from a historical database of equity returns.

## Exhibit 2: The BARRA Factors for U.S., U.K., Japan, and Canada

|  | USA | UK | Japan | Canada |
|---|---|---|---|---|
| Variability in Markets | ✓ | ✓ | ✓ | ✓ |
| Success | ✓ | ✓ | ✓ | ✓ |
| Size | ✓ | ✓ | ✓ | ✓ |
| Growth | ✓ | ✓ | ✓ | ✓ |
| Book to Price | ✓ | ✓ |  | ✓ |
| Earnings to Price | ✓ | ✓ | ✓ | ✓ |
| Earnings Variability | ✓ | ✓ |  |  |
| Financial Leverage | ✓ | ✓ | ✓ | ✓ |
| Foreign Exposure | ✓ | ✓ | ✓ |  |
| Labor Intensity | ✓ | ✓ |  |  |
| Trading Activity | ✓ | ✓ | ✓ | ✓ |
| Yield | ✓ | ✓ | ✓ | ✓ |
| Low Capitalization | ✓ | ✓ | ✓ | ✓ |
| Specific Variability |  |  | ✓ |  |
| Profitability |  |  |  | ✓ |
| US Sensitivity |  |  |  | ✓ |
| Industry Factors | 55 | 35 | 40 | 40 |

The factor exposures are calculated from information about the firm and its stock. The stock returns are market data, so the factor returns can be determined by linear regression.

Barr Rosenberg did much of the seminal work on fundamental factor models in the 1970s.[6] The company he founded, BARRA, is in the business of supplying, maintaining, and refining factor models based on these ideas. BARRAs models in each country are based on a very similar set of common factors and on a more diverse set of industry groups. The slight differences in common factors arise from different information reported for companies in different countries. The differences in industry groupings are due to the use of local classifications. In the U.S., the industry groups correspond to S&P industry groups; in the U.K., they are set by the Financial Times, in Japan by the Tokyo Stock Exchange. Exhibit 2 lists the BARRA factors for the U.S., U.K., Japan, and Canada.

---

[6] Barr Rosenberg and Andrew Rudd. Factor Related and Specific Returns of Common Stocks: Serial Correlation and Market Efficiency, *Journal of Finance*, Volume 37, Issue 2 (1982), pp. 543-554.

## Exhibit 3: U.S. Factor Returns and Standard Deviations

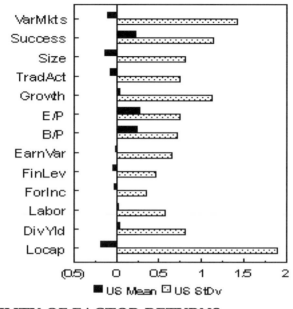

■ US Mean  ▫ US StDv

# VARIABILITY OF FACTOR RETURNS —
# A LEVER FOR ACTIVE MANAGEMENT

In Chapter 6, Arnott and Dorian point out that the variations in U.S. factor returns are large relative to their means. Exhibit 3 is a bar chart of the same U.S. factor return data they show in tabular format. The large standard deviations relative to the means indicate that there is an opportunity to add value by active management decisions that adjust exposure to these factors.

Is this variability in factor returns with the same potential value added observed outside the U.S.? A group of figures show the corresponding comparisons of factor return means and standard deviations for the U.K. (Exhibit 4), Canada (Exhibit 5), and Japan (Exhibit 6). In each country, there is the same clear pattern of standard deviations much larger than the mean returns. The same opportunities for active management decisions are present. A similar pattern is observed in the monthly returns to industry factors.

Note that presentation of evidence of variability in bar graph form is a compact way of showing the same information seen in the charts of cumulative returns to V-G (value minus growth) earlier in the chapter. Value and growth also appear as factors in each of the countries shown here.

## Exhibit 4: U.K. Factor Returns and Standard Deviations

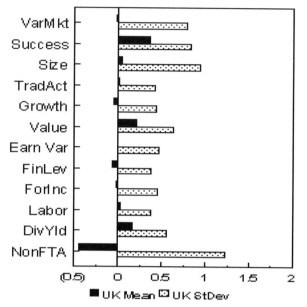

## Exhibit 5: Canadian Factor Returns and Standard Deviations

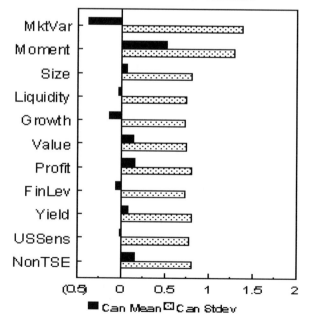

## Exhibit 6: Japanese Factor Returns and Standard Deviations

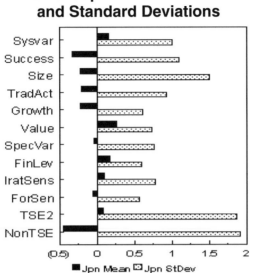

## Exhibit 7: Sensitivities of BARRA Factors to Lagged Predictors Across Countries
### (Empty entries indicate no significant relationship exists.)

| | Change in Price/Earnings Ratio | Percent Change in Market Index | Long-Term Government Bond Yield | Unemployment Rate |
|---|---|---|---|---|
| Financial Leverage | | | | |
| US | 0.153 | 0.200 | -0.227 | |
| UK | | 0.222 | -0.244 | 0.278 |
| Japan | | | | 0.182 |
| Canada | 0.256 | 0.295 | -0.281 | |
| Size | | | | |
| US | -0.172 | -0.202 | | -0.130 |
| UK | -0.396 | -0.429 | 0.164 | |
| Japan | | | | |
| Canada | -0.239 | -0.200 | 0.246 | |
| Market Variability | | | | |
| US | | | -0.164 | |
| UK | -0.280 | -0.299 | | |
| Japan | -0.192 | -0.186 | | |
| Canada | | | | |
| Value | | | | |
| US: B/P | | 0.160 | | |
| E/P | | | | -0.138 |
| UK | 0.158 | 0.219 | -0.163 | 0.234 |
| Japan | | | | -0.175 |
| Canada | | 0.256 | | |

**Exhibit 8: Correlations of BARRA Factors
Across Countries**
**(Empty entries indicate no significant relationship exists.)**

| | U.S. | U.K. | Japan | Canada |
|---|---|---|---|---|
| Market Variability | | | | |
| U.S. | 1.000 | | | |
| U.K. | 0.244 | 1.000 | | |
| Japan | - | 0.345 | 1.000 | |
| Canada | 0.512 | 0.278 | 0.422 | 1.000 |
| Success | | | | |
| U.S. | 1.000 | | | |
| U.K. | | 1.000 | | |
| Japan | 0.240 | 0.279 | 1.000 | |
| Size | | | | |
| U.S. | 1.000 | | | |
| U.K. | 0.339 | 1.000 | | |
| Japan | 0.252 | 0.498 | 1.000 | |
| Canada | 0.313 | 0.479 | - | 1.000 |
| Growth | | | | |
| U.S. | 1.000 | | | |
| U.K. | 0.303 | 1.000 | | |
| Japan | - | 0.311 | 1.000 | |
| Canada | 0.261 | - | - | 1.000 |
| Value | | | | |
| U.S.* | | | | |
| U.K. | | 1.000 | | |
| Japan | | -0.202 | 1.000 | |
| Canada | | 0.350 | - | 1.000 |

\* The value factor in the U.S. is defined across two separate factors: book-to-price and earnings-to-price.

The multi-factor approach to style encompasses the basic considerations of value and growth and expands upon them by incorporating additional common factors and industry factors. The variability in returns to all of these factors indicates that active management decisions can add value. Now we must decide how to make these decisions.

## FORECASTING FACTOR RETURNS

We know each stocks exposure to the various factors from accounting and market data. These are revised monthly, but generally depend on data reported over periods substantially longer than a month. They tend to be fairly stable from one month to the next. There is not much to be gained by forecasting the factor exposures for next month.

As we have seen, there is substantial variability in the factor returns, and the active decisions we make are based on our forecasts of future factor returns. We know the past history of returns to the factors, and the market and economic environment at the corresponding times. The goal is to use these data to build factor return forecasting models.

The biggest part of this problem is in specification of the model, i.e., choosing the best data to be used as inputs in the forecasting model. This is where we apply the genetic algorithm. There is more on this subject in a subsequent section, but first we complete the description of the multi-factor approach to style management.

### Commonalities and Differences in Factor Return Sensitivity

Exhibit 7 demonstrates the sensitivity of several factor returns to selected lagged predictors. With minor exceptions, there is a surprising consistency in the relationship of factor returns to market and economic variables across the countries studied. Exhibit 8 also illustrates the degree to which selected factor returns behave in a common fashion across countries.

### Performance of Factor Return Forecasts

Factor return sensitivity measures the relationship between the given factor return and market or economic data. The data along with the corresponding sensitivities are combined in a multivariate equation expressing the predicted return. The information coefficient (IC), the correlation between the forecast value and the observed value the next period, measures the forecasting performance of this relation. The forecast is made using only data available at the time of the forecast.

Exhibit 9 shows the information coefficients for factor return forecasters used in style management. They range from 0.19 to 0.71. Simulations show that an IC of approximately 0.2 is needed to cover transactions costs. The combined effect of all of these factor return forecasts substantially exceeds transactions costs at the allowed turnover levels.

## FROM FORECASTS TO PORTFOLIOS

If the following statements were true:

1. Factor models are perfect predictors of equity returns.
2. Factor forecasting models are always right.
3. All stocks are infinitely liquid.

## Exhibit 9: Predictive Power of Factor Return Forecasts

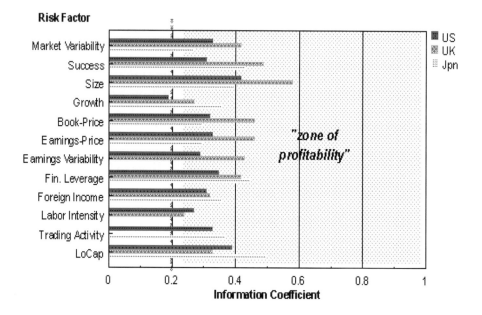

then the investment decision implied by a set of factor return fore-casts would be easy. We would just calculate the total forecast return for each stock, and use all our money to buy the stock with the highest forecasted return. If there were no short-selling constraints, then we would also short the one with the most negative forecast.

Alas, not a single one of these three conditions is true, so we are faced with the problem of constructing real investable portfolios using our forecast factor returns. We cannot call up a broker with an order to "Buy the factor 'financial leverage' and sell 'variability in markets.'" We need a way to select stocks that maximize exposure to positive forecast returns and minimize exposure to negative forecast returns, while controlling risk and turnover. This is what the portfolio optimizer does.

## Optimization and Risk Control

Risk control is an important aspect of optimization. Risk is measured by the variance of returns or by deviation (tracking error) from a benchmark portfolio, typically an index (the S&P 500 for the U.S., the FTSE 350 in the U.K., the TOPIX first section in Japan, and the TSE 100 in Canada). We control tracking error by constraining the industry weights of the managed portfolio to fall within a specified band around the industry weights of the benchmark. Similarly, weights of each stock are constrained to a region around its weight in the benchmark. Stock constraints have the effect of forcing the largest stocks in the index into the portfolio. The allowed holdings region for stocks with small weights in the index typically goes down to zero.

Risk control implemented in this manner is one of the most common applications of optimization. In style management, the same multi-factor formalism is used for risk control and producing active return. These industry and stock constraints provide the means to capture the alpha of the strategy while controlling risk relative to the benchmark.

## Long and Long/Short Portfolios

We use the optimizer to construct both long and long/short (or market-neutral) portfolios. Our comments above regarding risk control relative to a benchmark index are applicable to long portfolios. The long/short portfolios, being market-neutral, do not track an index. They are benchmarked against the equivalent of the T-bill rate in the corresponding country. Long/short portfolios can capture more of the information contained in the return forecasts than their long-only counterparts.[7]

The minimum exposure to any particular stock in a long portfolio is zero. No matter how bad it looks, the least you can do is not to hold any at all. Allowing short-selling eliminates this constraint. If desired, it is possible to restore the market exposure of long/short portfolios using futures, or for that matter, to transfer the value added to any other benchmark with a liquid futures market.[8]

## Turnover, Transactions Costs, and Liquidity

Transactions costs in international markets are typically higher than in the U.S., so it is even more important to control turnover and avoid illiquid positions in these markets. Both backtesting and the ongoing portfolio construction process explicitly incorporate transactions costs.[9]

Restriction of the stocks included in the investable universe is an important aspect of transactions cost control. Liquidity is typically lower for short positions. An example of the type of data used in selecting a liquid investable universe is seen in Exhibit 10, which shows a three-dimensional data set for the FTSE 350 stocks.

---

[7] This is provided that the long and short sides of the portfolio are sufficiently uncorrelated.

[8] Bruce I. Jacobs and Kenneth Levy, "Long/Short Equity Investing," *Journal of Portfolio Management*, (Spring 1989), pp.19-27.

[9] Andre Perold and Erik Sirri, "The Costs of International Equity Trading," Working Paper, Harvard Business School (April 1993).

**Exhibit 10: Visualizing the Liquid Universe**

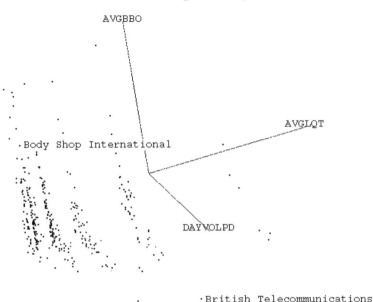

## Incorporating Stock-Specific Forecasts

So far, we have discussed how to exploit forecasted returns for attributes of stocks (the common factors) or groups of stocks (the industry groups). This optimization framework also captures stock-specific forecast returns by modeling the errors in the model specification. An important example is a returns forecast based on earnings revision and earnings surprise. The value of this information has been widely reported in the U.S., there is evidence that similar effects are observed internationally.[10]

## SUMMARY OF THE STYLE MANAGEMENT PROCESS

The quantitative process we have describe may seem complex, but it is based on a few simple ideas:

---

[10] Masako Drrough and Trevor Harris, "Do Management Forecasts of Earnings Affect Stock Prices in Japan," in W. Ziemba and Y. Hamao, editors, *Japanese Financial Market Research* (Elsevier Science 1991); and Elroy Dimson and Paul Marsh, "An Analysis of Brokers' and Analysts' Unpublished Forecasts of U.K. Stock Returns," *Journal of Finance* (December 1984), pp. 1257-1289.

1. Factors such as growth, value, interest rate sensitivity, and industry group membership explain equity returns. Returns to these broad characteristics are called factor returns. Factor returns explain equity returns.

2. Factor returns can be forecasted. We can forecast the returns to these factors by studying how they have responded in the past to various market and economic circumstances. These insights can be used to build empirical models to forecast factor returns. The models should make economic and financial sense, and be validated using data outside the period used for their development

3. Factor exposures can be bought and sold. Investable portfolios can be constructed that deliver the desired factor exposures, both positive and negative, with reasonable turnover and broad diversification for low risk. This is the role of the optimizer.

## PERFORMANCE OF INTERNATIONAL STYLE MANAGEMENT PORTFOLIOS

The method described in this chapter has been used to develop a quantitative management process for United Kingdom, Japanese, and Canadian equities. As of this writing (October 1994), there are brief performance histories (less than one year) for the UK portfolios, both long and long/short. There is a very brief (several months) history for the Japanese long portfolio. Of course, there are simulated performance histories spanning several years for all of these portfolios.

Simulations must be run using realistic assumptions and constraints, and results are to be interpreted with caution. These issues are discussed in "Behind the Smoke and Mirrors: Gauging the Integrity of Investment Simulations."[11] We must ask and answer several questions.

- "Where does the idea come from?" It is based on a U.S. investment approach that has performed very well on a large asset base for five years.

---

[11] John Freeman, "Beyond the Smoke and Mirrors," *Financial Analysts Journal* (November/December 1992), pp. 26-31.

- "How is the database constructed?" Wherever possible, contemporaneous (i.e., as reported) data are used. Economic data are much more likely to be revised than market data. You never hear that last month's S&P close was really 0.5% lower than previously reported; we often hear such comparisons in the case of unemployment, inflation, or the money supply. For this reason, market data are heavily favored over economic data in our process. Multiple sources are used, and discrepancies resolved. Outliers, once identified, are verified or corrected. Realistic lag times are used in every instance to simulate realistic reporting delays and to avoid look-ahead bias.

- "How do you determine your investable universe?" Liquidity filters are applied to the contemporaneous index constituents, so there is little survivorship bias introduced by selecting from today's index stocks to pick simulated portfolios in the past.

- "How do you select your benchmark and level of aggressiveness?" Our benchmarks in every case are the passively replicated broad indexes typically used by institutional investors: the FTSE 350 in the U.K., the TOPIX first section in Japan, and the TSE 300 in Canada. The market-neutral portfolios are benchmarked against the T-bill in each country. Results are reported in local currencies. The level of aggressiveness is set to control tracking error relative to the benchmarks to approximately 3% and to limit turnover to less than 100% annually.

- "How did you test this strategy?" We use the period from 1981 to 1986 to initialize the models, then start with simulated cash in January 1987. The simulation is then run forward, using the new data to update the models, and rebalancing one month at a time using the same models and the same optimizer used to manage live assets.[12]

- "How do you handle turnover and transactions costs?" Very conservative assumptions regarding transactions costs are used to constrain turnover to approximately 100% annu-

---

[12] Freeman points out that the use of an optimizer is a much better way to put a portfolio together than the "screen and cut" approach used in many quantitative strategies. He writes, "I think it would be only slightly unfair to liken portfolio construction with screens to carpentry with an ax!" p. 29.

ally. Transactions costs are subtracted from all reported simulation results. Actual transactions costs for the live portfolios have been substantially lower than the assumptions used in the simulations.

· "How consistent are the active returns?" Each of these strategies produces a positive alpha in each simulated year, with a single exception. Standard deviations of returns and Sharpe ratios are reported in every case.

## U.K. Style Management Simulated and Real Performance
Exhibit 11 shows the performance of simulated portfolios over the period February 1987 through December 1993. These results are also shown graphically for the long portfolio in Exhibit 12, and for the long/short in Exhibit 13. All portfolio returns are net of 2% round-trip transactions costs. The monthly added value to strategies averages 0.8% long and 2.0% long/short.[13] The average number of issues in the long portfolio is 74. On the short side there are 82.

It should be noted that shortfalls relative to the FT All Share index occur in only 12% of trailing three-month periods for the long portfolio. These shortfalls average 0.9%. Shortfalls relative to the U.K. T-Bill occur in 28% of trailing three-month periods for the long/short strategy. These shortfalls average 2.6%. The worst total return is a positive 11.7% for the 12-month period ending August 1993.

## Japanese Style Management Simulated Performance
Exhibit 14 shows the performance of simulated portfolios over the period February 1987 through December 1993. Exhibit 15 shows these results graphically for the long portfolio, and Exhibit 16 shows similar data for the long/short. The Japanese style product was developed and tested in a manner that parallels the process used for the U.K. Again, all portfolio returns are net of 2% round-trip transactions costs. The monthly value added to strategies averages 0.8% long and 2.0% long/short. The average number of issues in the long portfolio is 74; on the short side there are 82.

Shortfalls relative to the Nikkei 225 occur in only 12% of trailing three-month periods for the long portfolio. These shortfalls average 0.9%. Shortfalls relative to the Japanese T-bill occur in 28% of trailing three-month periods for the strategy; the average is 1.27%. The worst total return is a positive 11.7% for the 12-month period ended August 1993. As with other style simulations, each historical forecast is created using only information known the month prior to the month being forecast.

---

[13] Simulated results are no guarantee of future performance.

## Exhibit 11: UK Style Simulated Returns
### Net of Transactions Costs (February 1987 - December 1993)

| | Core U.K. Style Returns | | | Market-Neutral U.K. Style Returns | | |
|---|---|---|---|---|---|---|
| | FTA | Core Style | Value Added | T-Bill | Style | Value Added |
| Monthly Average | 1.2 | 1.6 | 0.4 | 0.8 | 2.1 | 1.3 |
| Annualized | 13.9 | 18.8 | 5.0 | 9.7 | 25.4 | 15.7 |
| Annual Standard Deviation | 19.8 | 7.8 | 2.2 | | 8.6 | 8.5 |
| Annual Reward/Risk | 0.7 | 2.4 | 2.1 | | 2.9 | 1.8 |
| Consistency | | | | | | |
| -Monthly | | | 74% | | | 65% |
| -Quarterly | | | 89% | | | 86% |
| Expectations: Simulated returns, less 50% "haircuts." | | | | | | |

## Exhibit 12: U.K. Style Management
### Long Portfolio Simulated Returns

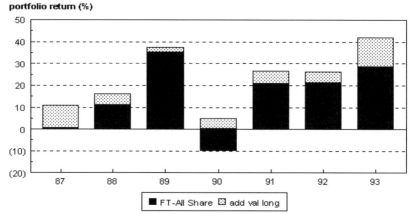

## Exhibit 13: U.K. Style Management
### Long/Short Portfolio Simulated Returns

## Exhibit 14: Japanese Style Simulated Returns
### Net of Transactions Costs (February 1987 - December 1993)

| | | Core Japan Style Returns | | | Market-Neutral Japan Style Returns | |
|---|---|---|---|---|---|---|
| | Nik 225 | Core Style | Value Added | T-Bill | Style | Value Added |
| Monthly Average | 0.05 | 0.9 | 0.8 | 0.4 | 2.4 | 2.0 |
| Annualized | 0.50 | 10.5 | 10.0 | 5.1 | 29.3 | 24.2 |
| Annual Standard Deviation | 23.70 | 25.1 | 4.8 | | 10.7 | 10.5 |
| Annual Reward/Risk | 0.02 | 0.4 | 2.1 | | 2.7 | 2.3 |
| Consistency | | | | | | |
| -Monthly | | | 68% | | | 73% |
| -Quarterly | | | 86% | | | 78% |
| Expectations: Simulated returns, less 50% "haircuts." | | | | | | |

## Exhibit 15: Japanese Style Management
### Long Portfolio Simulated Returns

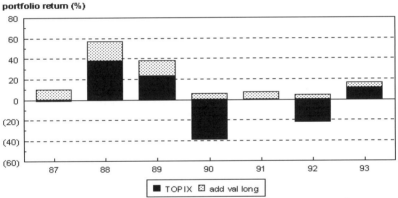

## Exhibit 16: Japanese Style Management
### Long/Short Portfolio Simulated Returns

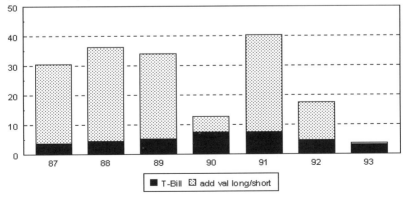

## Canadian Style Management Performance

Exhibit 17 shows performance of the Canadian simulated portfolios over the period February 1987 through December 1993. Exhibit 18 shows these results graphically for the long portfolio. The Canadian portfolios, along with those for Japan and the U.K., are generated using the same process used in constructing the U.S. portfolios. Again, all portfolio returns are net of conservative transactions costs assumptions. The monthly added value to strategies averages 1.2% monthly. The Canadian long/short style-managed portfolio is still in development as of this writing but promises results similar to those observed in other countries.

## Performance Summary

In all countries looked at, the performance of simulated portfolios is consistent with our expectations, given the simulated and actual performance in the US. All investment strategies, of course, have size limitations. At some point, transactions costs will exceed the expected active return. The U.S. long/short style is closed to new investors for this reason. The Japanese long strategy may be able to sustain performance into the multi-billion dollar range, given the roughly comparable sizes of the markets. Liquidity on the short side for Japan is notably lower than in the U.S. The maximum size of the asset base in other markets is likely proportional to market size and liquidity. The total capitalization of the U.K. market is 25% of the U.S. Canada's is 7%.

The performance numbers shown here should be interpreted conservatively. Real portfolios typically perform at 30% to 50% below simulated returns. This is consistent with the real performance we have seen in the history of these portfolios.

## THE DIVERSIFICATION VALUE OF INTERNATIONAL STYLE PORTFOLIOS

U.S. institutional investors have aggressively pursued international diversification for some time. In 1984, the average U.S. pension fund had only 3% of its equity assets in markets outside the U.S. By 1994, the percentage had risen to 7%. The reason is largely a growing acceptance of the ideas of Markowitz and Sharpe. The diversifying nature of international portfolios reduces risk and increases returns. The measure of the diversification value of an asset is its correlation with current holdings. For U.S. institutional equity portfolios, this correlation is typically measured against the S&P 500. For U.K. institutions, the standard for comparison is the FT All Share. In Japan and Canada, the benchmarks are the TOPIX and the TSE 300, respectively.

## Exhibit 17: Canadian Style Simulated Returns
### Net of Transactions Costs (February 1987 - December 1993

|  | TSE 300 | Core Style | Value Added |
|---|---|---|---|
| Monthly Average | 1.5 | 2.6 | 1.2 |
| Annualized | 18.5 | 35.6 | 17.1 |
| Annual Standard Deviation | 14.8 | 14.7 | 3.5 |
| Annual Reward/Risk | 1.3 | 2.4 | 4.9 |
| Consistency | | | |
| -Monthly | | | 77% |
| -Quarterly | | | 82% |
| Expectations: Simulated returns, less 50% "haircuts." | | | |

## Exhibit 18: Canadian Style Management
### Long Portfolio Simulated Returns

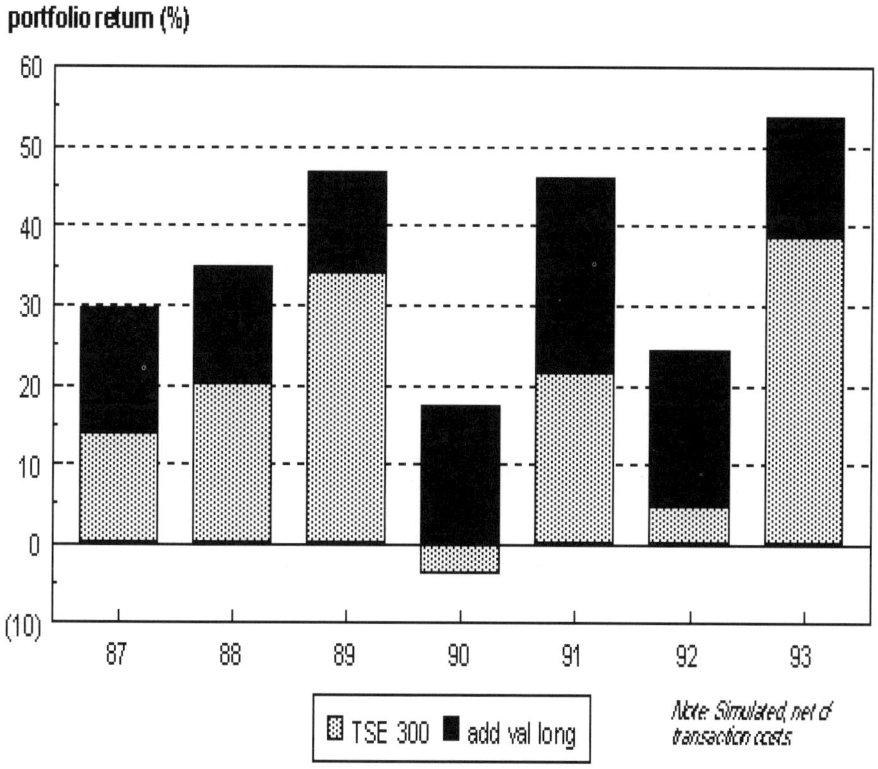

portfolio return (%)

Note: Simulated, net of transaction costs

## Exhibit 19: International Style as a Diversifying Investment
### Monthly Correlations (February 1987 - May 1993)

|  | US-L | UK-L | CAN-L | JPN-L | US-LS | UK-LS | CAN-LS | JPN-LS |
|---|---|---|---|---|---|---|---|---|
| S&P 500 | 0.97 | 0.75 | 0.34 |  | 0.20 | -0.14 | 0.05 | 0.13 |
| FT All Share | 0.75 | 0.99 | 0.65 | 0.36 | 0.23 | -0.16 | 0.03 | 0.18 |
| TSE 300 | 0.76 | 0.65 | 0.99 | 0.37 | 0.37 | -0.11 | -0.05 | 0.03 |
| Nikkei 225 | 0.32 | 0.36 | 0.39 | 0.98 | 0.05 | -0.02 | 0.19 | 0.11 |

Exhibit 19 shows the correlations of long and long/short international style portfolios with these international equity indexes. The correlations of the long portfolios with the corresponding country indexes are all close to one. This is due to the constraint on the optimizer that produces these portfolios. They are constrained to track the corresponding index on both a stock and industry scale, diverging only when significant gains may be achieved. The other numbers in the first three columns of Exhibit 19 show the diversification value of international equity investments, with correlations (to the S&P 500) ranging from 0.34 to 0.77. Comparisons to other base countries show similar correlations.

The more striking figures are seen for the long/short portfolios in the last three columns of the table. These correlations are remarkably low, essentially zero. These market-neutral portfolios bring a much greater degree of diversification than long-only international equity portfolios, whether they are actively or passively managed. A visual representation of this same information appears in Exhibits 20 through 24. These are plots of the monthly returns to various indexes and portfolios.

Exhibit 20 compares the returns of the FT All Share to the S&P 500. This is what a correlation of 0.75 looks like. Everyone would draw nearly the same line though these points. Exhibits 21 through 24 demonstrate how low the correlation for the long/short portfolios is. These plots show the monthly returns for the U.K., Japanese and Canadian, long/short portfolios with the major equity indices: the S&P 500 (Exhibit 21), the FTA (Exhibit 22), the TOPIX (Exhibit 23), and the Canadian TSE 300 (Exhibit 24). These correlations range from a low of -0.14 to a high of 0.19.

A noteworthy event visible in these graphs is seen at the left of each chart. There are three points corresponding to large negative returns to each index in October 1987. Note that all three simulated long/short portfolios had positive returns in October 1987. In Exhibit 23, the scatter plot against the TOPIX, points on the left corresponding to the worst months for the index are not October 1987, but rather several months in 1991, when Japanese equity investors looked back on October 1987 as the good old days. All three long/short portfolios, including Japan, had positive returns in these months as well.

# Exhibit 20: S&P versus FTA

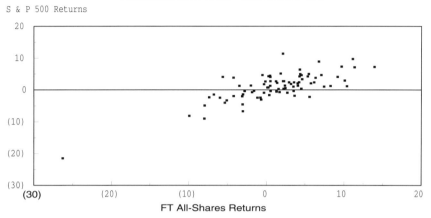

S & P 500 Returns

FT All-Shares Returns

# Exhibit 21: Long/Short Style versus S&P 500

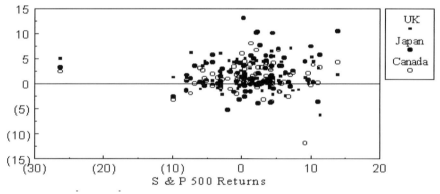

Long/Short Returns

S & P 500 Returns

UK ■  Japan ●  Canada ○

# Exhibit 22: Long/Short Style versus FTA

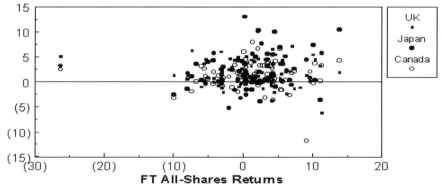

Long/Short Returns

FT All-Shares Returns

UK ■  Japan ●  Canada ○

## Exhibit 23: Long/Short Style versus TOPIX

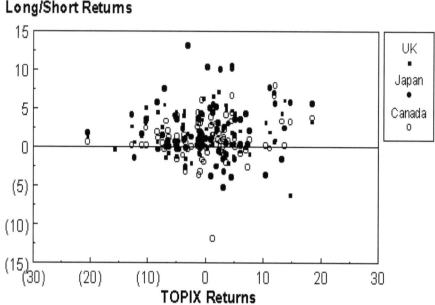

## Exhibit 24: Long/Short Style versus TSE 300

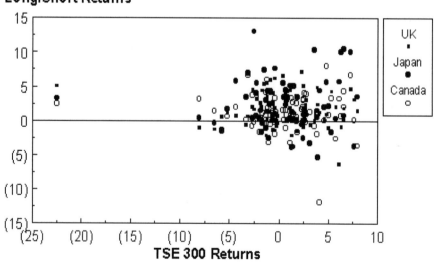

## Exhibit 25: International Style as a Diversifying Investment
### Cross-Correlations of Market Neutral Portfolios
### (February 1987 to May 1993)

|         | US-LS | UK-LS | CAN-LS | JPN-LS |
|---------|-------|-------|--------|--------|
| US-LS   | 1.00  | -0.24 | 0.03   | -0.29  |
| UK-LS   | -0.24 | 1.00  | -0.01  | -0.07  |
| CAN-LS  | 0.03  | -0.11 | 1.00   | 0.06   |
| JPN-LS  | -0.29 | -0.07 | 0.06   | 1.00   |

One further comment on the subject of diversification. While we have examined the correlations of these portfolios relative to equity indexes, it is worth asking whether they are diversifying investments with respect to each other. How much would be gained by placing assets in more than one long/short portfolio?

The answer is seen in Exhibit 25, which shows the correlations of long/short style portfolios for the U.S., U.K., Canada, and Japan, which are close to zero, with those largest in magnitude having a negative sign. These portfolios are among the most diversifying equity-based assets available to an institution today.

## GENETIC ALGORITHM OVERVIEW

The genetic algorithm (GA) is a powerful search and optimization tool that has enhanced simulated performances considerably.[14] The sort of problem solved by the GA can be viewed in a simple way in Exhibit 26. The desired solution is to find the parameters (represented by the switch settings in the figure) that maximize some payoff (represented by a dollar sign). This is simple when only a few parameters are involved: You just try all possible combinations. If the problem is "well-behaved," and corresponds to an established solution technique, then it is only slightly more difficult. It is much more difficult when there are a huge number of possible variations, and the function relating them is not well-behaved, or when the problem and its constraints do not lend themselves to traditional tools.

---

[14] See, for example, David Leinweber and Robert Arnott, "Quantitative and Computational Innovation in Investment Management," First Quadrant, 1994; John Holland, "Genetic Algorithms," *Scientific American* (July 1992), pp. 66-72; and Richard J. Bauer, *Genetic Algorithms and Investment Strategies* (New York: Wiley, 1994).

## Exhibit 26: A Simple Way to View the GA

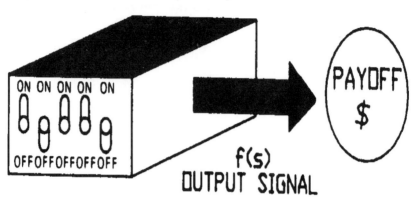

### Parallel Search and Evolving Populations

The GA solves problems by following the principle of survival of the fittest. It mimics simplified versions of biological evolutionary processes to produce successive generations of problem solutions that combine the best features of their ancestors. This use of an evolving population of solutions (rather than taking steps based on a single current best solution) creates a parallel search through a very large space of possible solutions. This is illustrated in Exhibit 27. The GA has been used successfully in many fields, ranging from jet engine design through image processing to currency trading.[15] We use it to solve the problem of constructing high-performance style management models.

### Style Management Chromosomes

The first step in applying the GA in any context is to design a "chromosome" to represent a candidate solution. A simple way of thinking about the chromosome is as a list of parameters that describe the solution. A narrowly constructed chromosome could consist of a few numerical parameters. A more elaborate chromosome includes structural parameters, which set the nature of the solution (for example, whether a bridge is suspended from cables or supported from below). There are many possibilities in designing a chromosome for style management models.

---

[15] David Goldberg, "Genetic and Evolutionary Algorithms Come of Age," in *Communications of the Association of Computing Machinery* (CACM), (March 1994), no. 3, pp. 113-119. The turbine design of the new Boeing 777 was developed using GA-based tools. Hughes Missile Systems employed a GA technique to improve the performance of a military image processing problem. The currency trading programs developed by the Prediction Company for O'Connor/Swiss Bank incorporate genetic algorithms.

## Exhibit 27: The GA in Schematic Form

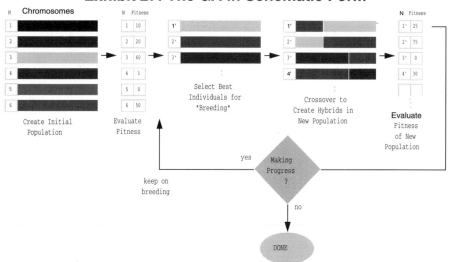

Our goal is to maximize predictability of factor returns. There are two aspects to doing this: inputs and methods.

Inputs are the data going into our forecasting models. Of the vast amount of market and macroeconomic data available in all developed countries, which indicators are most useful, and in what contexts and combinations? Are the variables useful as reported? Or do we extract more predictive power by measuring their value relative to their recent history, or by examining their changes or rates of change? Should they be considered in comparison to other variables? Will mathematical transforms, such as logs, squares, or square roots, increase their predictive value?

Techniques are the methods we use to do the forecasts. The simplest method is ordinary least squares regression. More elaborate techniques include robust regressions, kernel estimations, and neural networks. In each case, there are further structural decisions to be made regarding the type of window applied in calculating the model parameters.

The window choices are expanding, moving, or weighted, all depicted graphically in Exhibit 28. An expanding window uses all the data, but gives less weight to each new observation as time progresses. An expanding window cannot capture non-stationarity in the model data. A moving window of a fixed length does capture the effects of these changes over time, but in a coarse way. If moving windows are used, how long should they be?

## Exhibit 28: Different Ways to Window Data

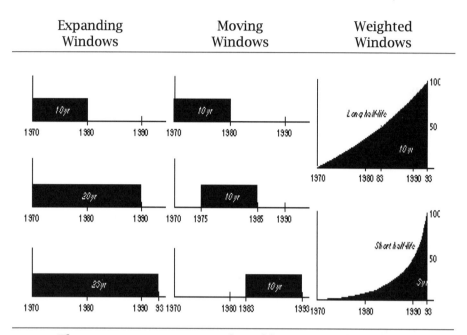

There are some conceptual problems as well. Consider a ten year moving window. If the current month is January 1995, January 1985 is included in the data used with the same weight as the current observation. However, in the next month, February 1995, the data for January 1985 have "fallen off the edge," and do not count at all. There is something unappealing about this. A more satisfying approach is to use a weighted window, which uses all the data, but reduces the weights for older observations. The issue here is how quickly the weights should fall for older observations.

## GA Model Optimization

An appropriate set of parameters is encoded on the chromosome used to represent the models for the various factor returns. An initial population is generated, which includes the conventionally developed set of models. A fitness function is designed that captures desirable features in a model: greater predictive power, improved returns, and lower volatility of returns. The fitness function determines which of the chromosomes are fit enough to survive. As expected, the fitness rises with the number of generations. By including the base model in the population, and allowing the highest-performance individual to survive across generations, we ensure a nondecreasing maximum fitness.

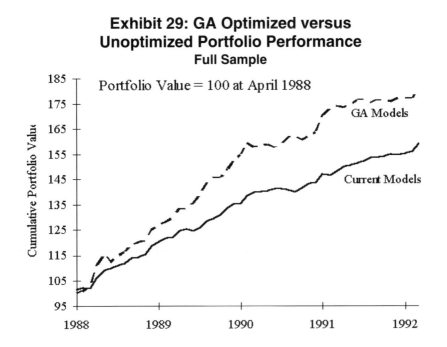

## Exhibit 29: GA Optimized versus Unoptimized Portfolio Performance
### Full Sample

## GENETIC ALGORITHM RESULTS

The value of genetic optimization is clearly seen in Exhibit 29, which shows the cumulative return to a Japanese style portfolio using the conventionally developed and GA optimized style process. In simulation the GA consistently adds about 370 bp per year over six years (in-sample performance). The more telling results are for the out-of-sample period, the data that the GA does not use in its model specification search. The performance over this period alone is shown in Exhibit 30. The GA adds over 470 bp per year during this 24-month period.

## THE GENETIC ALGORITHM WARNING LABEL

As a technology becomes more powerful, more skill is required to apply it correctly. Given enough time, many people could walk from Los Angeles to San Diego — but it is faster to drive, and it is much faster fly. In each case, more skill is required to arrive safely.  Quantitative technology is now more like an airplane than a walking shoe, so we need to understand the danger this entails.

## Exhibit 30: GA Optimized versus
## Unoptimized Portfolio Performance
### Out-of-Sample

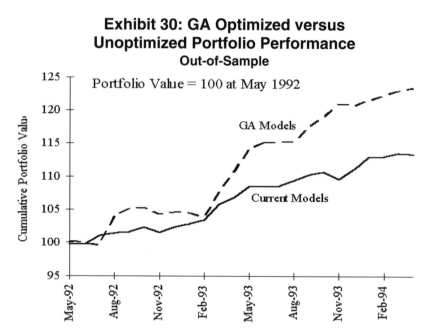

The danger in using the GA (and many other techniques) is that you may fall deep into the data mine. Recall that if you look at 100 statistical relationships that are significant at the 5% level, five of them are there only by chance. If you look at a million relationships, then 50,000 are significant only by chance. Early in our use of the GA technology, a chromosome evolved encoding for a variable based on a 15-month average lagged 7 months minus a 7-month average lagged 15 months. It had a nice symmetry to it. It had high statistical significance. It was ignominiously retired to the bit bucket.

With the GA, we know we can dig down to the deepest region of the data mine to produce models with much better statistics and even wackier variables than a predecessor. It is easy to generate models with perfect predictive power and coefficients significant at the 1% level on randomly generated data. It is important to be careful not to fool ourselves. Here are some of the ways we achieve this.

***Wetware before software:*** Wetware is the gray matter between your ears. The brain needs to be engaged before the GA is put into gear. The starting population always includes models developed using established econometric and quantitative methods. They make sense economically. Often, the result of the GA is only a slight refinement or adjustment of the initial solution.

*Immortality for the stars:* The best few solutions in each generation survive unchanged into the next. This is also called elitism. It keeps good results from being submerged by random events.

*Keep nonsensical variables out of the population from the start:* We design our own genetic code. It does not include the vocabulary for the type of nonsense variable described above, or for many other equally specious varieties.

*Good fitness functions:* Predictive ability measured by information coefficient is just one part of fitness. Total squared error, consistency and correctness of direction, and stability are also important measures of model quality that are incorporated in our fitness measures.

*Judicious use of out-of-sample periods:* To be absolutely, 100%, not guilty of any data-mining sins, each financial researcher would be allowed only one look at the out-of-sample period, and be foreclosed from reading any material on the subject. Ideally, all researchers would not have seen the *Wall Street Journal* (or each other) for the last five years. These people are hard to find, as we all have lived through the out-of-sample period. The next best thing is to be extremely careful about human looks into the out-of-sample period, and never to let the GA look it at all.

*Cross-country validations:* It is easier to have faith in similar models that produce similar results in different countries than in those that do not travel well across borders.

*Calibrate new and improved tools carefully:* If a new process can produce seemingly great results using random inputs, there is something wrong with the process. If it seems too good to be true, it is.

## SUMMARY

Style management is an idea that travels well. It works internationally for many of the same reasons it works in the US. We have described a disciplined, quantitative process for capturing the value that can be added by style management while controlling risk. The process has been applied in developing long and long/short international style portfolios in the U.K., Japan, and Canada. These portfolios offer institutional equity investors both diversification and improved performance.

These investment strategies are based on the exploitation of empirically quantifiable market inefficiencies. They must make economic and financial sense. Within this framework, there are innovative means to leverage additional performance from the same underlying concepts. This is the role of the genetic algorithm in our research. It is driven by the strong forces of an artificial evolutionary process. Like natural evolution, it can produce undesirable outcomes. We have described the multi-faceted approach we use to avoid them. The end result is a better strategy, evolved from a good strategy.

# CHAPTER 11

## EQUITY STYLE BENCHMARKS FOR FUND ANALYSIS

*MARY IDA COMPTON*
*ASSISTANT VICE PRESIDENT*
*THE COMMON FUND*

The author gratefully acknowledges H. Russell Fogler for attentive editing.

## INTRODUCTION

The investment community has become more articulate in describing investments. What was once referred to as a domestic equity may now be called a value stock or a small-cap growth stock. The securities in the universe of stocks have not changed; our categorization of those securities has merely become more technical. We slice the market primarily in two ways: by market cap, and by some measure of relative value (such as price-to-earnings, price-to-book, or price-to-cash flow) to indicate a value or growth classification.

As the classification of securities has become more precise, so has the classification of equity managers. The manager once referred to as a domestic equity manager is now more precisely described as a mid-cap growth manager, or a small-cap value manager, or possibly a style rotator. The plan sponsor community, in an attempt to diversify its portfolios, selects managers from each style group.

Evaluating manager performance requires consideration of the manager's investment style. "Good" managers outperform their benchmarks. When small-cap value stocks outperform the broad market, a small-cap value manager should also outperform the broad market. Style indexes, such as the Russell 1000 Growth Index or the BARRA/S&P Value Index, have been developed as style benchmarks for these more precisely defined markets. Consulting firms take this precision to the extreme to develop a distinct benchmark for each manager, known as a normal portfolio.

This chapter illustrates the various uses of style benchmarks for a plan sponsor. We describe different types of style benchmarks, including style indexes and normal portfolios, and discuss their appropriateness for a particular equity manager. We illustrate the way our organization develops normal portfolios for its managers and explain a low-tech alternative style analysis we use as an internal check. The chapter should provide some insight into the process of developing style benchmarks as it highlights some of the issues that can surface.

## PERFORMANCE ANALYSIS USING STYLE BENCHMARKS

There are two fundamental uses for style benchmarks in the context of performance measurement. The first is to measure manager performance. Style benchmarks "take the market out of" manager returns. They are intended to reveal the manager's ability to add value over the market, and provide a more appropriate hurdle for calculating performance-based fees. The manager's performance is decomposed as follows:

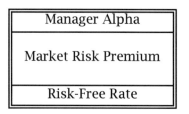

The objective of using style benchmarks is to measure a manager's ability to outperform some nonmanaged alternative, such as an index fund or normal portfolio run by consultants or banks. The appropriate style benchmark for a manager may be as broad as the Russell 3000 index or as precise as a list of specific securities. Performance comparisons of manager returns relative to the style benchmark are sometimes used to calculate compensation when a plan sponsor pays the manager. In some cases, as is true with one of our large-cap managers, the manager "owns" the normal portfolio and compensates individual portfolio managers on the basis of their performance relative to this normal.

The second use of style benchmarks is to measure the plan sponsor's performance. This is achieved by compiling the style benchmarks for all the sponsor's managers. Comparison of this aggregate style benchmark to the target benchmark of the fund exposes any "misfit" between the group of managers and the policy established by the directors. This is most easily accomplished by translating each manager's benchmark into a portfolio of securities, or "normal portfolio," and analyzing the characteristics of both the aggregate of all the managers' normal portfolios and the target policy benchmark for the fund.

The benchmark for our Growth Fund, for example, is the Russell Growth Index. This index is the target portfolio for the aggregate of the managers' normal portfolios, weighted appropriately. The misfit, or difference in risk as measured in standard deviations, between our aggregate normal and the index is 4%, which is moderate. (In terms of variance, this is 16%.) This is illustrated in Exhibit 1 for December 31, 1993.

Each bar in the graph indicates how much risk is associated with the portfolio's exposure to systematic or market risk, to common factor or "portfolio characteristic" risk, and to specific or individual security risk. The active bar represents the portfolio's actual risk exposures in excess of its normal exposures. The misfit bar represents the normal risk exposures relative to the target benchmark. The bias is the sum of the first two bars. The systematic risk is essentially zero for each bar, since market risk is roughly equal for the managed, normal, and benchmark portfolios.

The misfit of the Growth Fund comes primarily from the managers' aggressiveness in the growth area and their small-cap emphasis, as illustrated in Exhibit 2. This growth emphasis is seen in the large exposure relative to the index in successful stocks (SCS) that have strong momentum, and in stocks with high growth characteristics (GRO). The "variability in markets" (VIM) factor is highly correlated with smaller-cap stocks, and is therefore higher for our fund than it is for the index.

Conversations with our managers have led us to accept this deviation from the target as managers' attempts to add value to the benchmark by choosing stocks opportunistically from this group of high growth stocks. We can compare the performance of the aggregate normal to the benchmark to determine whether this has been a good decision.

Since the inception of this aggregate on July 1, 1993, the aggregate normal has outperformed the Russell Growth index by 3.4%. To test managers' attention to growth stocks regardless of cap size, we analyzed the portfolio relative to a target that includes a percentage of the Russell 2000 Growth Index. At 50/50 to 60/40 weightings of the 1000 and 2000 growth indexes, respectively, we reduce the misfit risk to between 1% and 2%, an excellent fit.

## Exhibit 1: Aggregate Risk Decomposition

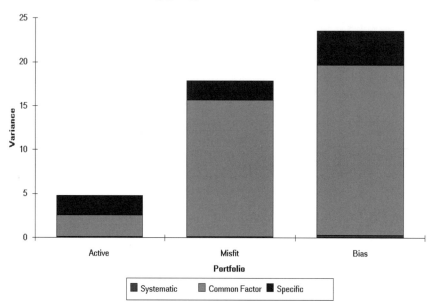

## Exhibit 2: Aggregate Risk Index Exposures

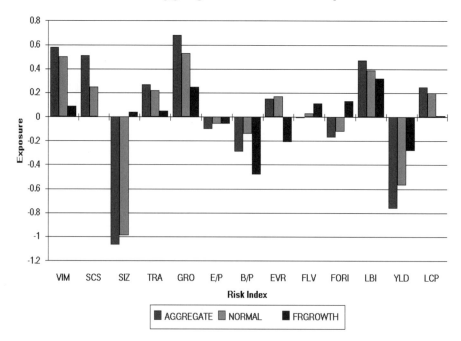

To eliminate the misfit between managers and the target index of the fund, several managers offer completeness funds. (Completeness funds are discussed in Chapter 8.) The premise behind using a completeness fund is that it allows the plan sponsor to benefit from the alpha of each of the managers and reduce the tracking error to the target benchmark. Even if each manager is adding value to his or her normal portfolio, the group in aggregate may not precisely match the index against which the fund is measured. This divergence from the target is undesirable, and the plan sponsor should bring the fund in line with its benchmark. The two alternatives are to hire a group of new managers to fill these gaps or to use a completeness fund.

The completeness fund has the mandate to invest in areas the managers are avoiding, thus exposing the fund to all areas of the market and reducing the possibility of unintended bets. It is generally felt that closely matching all other important risk factors sufficiently reduces the tracking error of the portfolio. The risk exposures of the aggregate portfolio including the completeness fund will thus be very close to those of the target index.

The misfit of the normals to the target index in terms of market cap is the most difficult to correct, as the fund is usually considerably lower in market cap than a cap-weighted index because managers are equal weighting the securities in a portfolio. To correct this would require a large overexposure in the largest market cap securities at the expense of closely matching several other important risk factors. Thus, any misfit not eradicated through the use of a completeness fund manager is a deliberate bet by the sponsor, and this performance can be measured.

The logistics of using a completeness fund are straightforward. The plan sponsor (or consultant) provides the manager of the completeness fund with the normal portfolios of the managers in the fund. This information is updated semiannually, as the normal portfolios are rebalanced. This manager creates a "difference portfolio" of securities and possibly derivatives that aligns the risk exposures of the entire fund with the target index. This is typically done using 10% of the assets of the fund.

## TYPES OF STYLE BENCHMARKS

Style benchmarks come in various forms. Different types are appropriate for different types of managers. The process of developing normal portfolios is tedious and time consuming, and requires regular attention. For some plan sponsors, this is reason enough to employ another form of style benchmark. Style benchmarks have a variety of applications beyond performance measurement.

Three basic types of style benchmark are commonly used. The first is a basket of stocks, or normal portfolio, which represents the universe of securities a particular manager would consider reasonable for inclusion in the portfolio. These securities are weighted in some appropriate way to reflect the manager's style, resulting in a portfolio whose traditional characteristics match those of the manager's invested portfolio. The screens used to determine the securities in this basket should fairly closely imitate the manager's investment process, with no significant sector bets in the normal that the manager would not consider making. The normal should include more names than the actual portfolio, usually more than 300 stocks, and the overlap with the manager's stocks should be high, at least 80%. Normals with less than 70% coverage of the active portfolio are considered inadequate. Normals are typically rebalanced semiannually.

The second type of style benchmark is a style index or weighted average of a selection of style indexes. These style benchmarks are easy to create, maintain, and understand. For example, a value manager who concentrates in small-cap value stocks but occasionally strays into larger-cap stocks may have a style benchmark composed of 75% Russell 2000 Value and 25% Russell 1000 Value indexes. A special case of a style index could be an industry index, a reasonable choice for the manager who focuses his investments in one industry or sector, such as technology.

Using an index as a portfolio benchmark is also useful for the "farm team" of managers. In two of our domestic equity funds, we use a constantly changing group of small managers selected by a consultant. These managers individually may not have the history or the assets to warrant being weighted in the fund to the magnitude of the other managers. The investment style of this group of managers is relatively consistent over time, and that style is best captured as a weighted average of indexes.

A third type of style benchmark is a style universe mean or median. The Frank Russell Company and other consultants track enough managers to categorize them by investment style, such as growth managers, or market-oriented managers with a value tilt. Relative performance of a sponsor's manager is clear and quantifiable using risk/return scatters and quartile charts, as seen in Exhibits 3 and 4. The rationale for using such a style benchmark is to compare managers to their peers.

# Exhibit 3: Universe of Equity Funds (US$)
## 10 Years Ending March 31, 1994

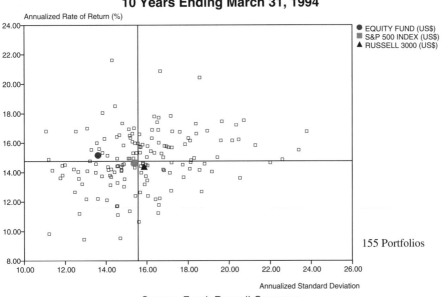

155 Portfolios

Annualized Standard Deviation

Source: Frank Russell Company

# Exhibit 4: Universe of Equity Funds (US$)
## Ending March 31, 1994

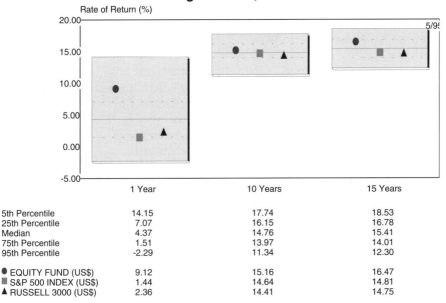

|  | 1 Year | 10 Years | 15 Years |
|---|---|---|---|
| 5th Percentile | 14.15 | 17.74 | 18.53 |
| 25th Percentile | 7.07 | 16.15 | 16.78 |
| Median | 4.37 | 14.76 | 15.41 |
| 75th Percentile | 1.51 | 13.97 | 14.01 |
| 95th Percentile | -2.29 | 11.34 | 12.30 |
| ● EQUITY FUND (US$) | 9.12 | 15.16 | 16.47 |
| ▨ S&P 500 INDEX (US$) | 1.44 | 14.64 | 14.81 |
| ▲ RUSSELL 3000 (US$) | 2.36 | 14.41 | 14.75 |

Source: Frank Russell Company

One aspect to keep in mind, which the manager may point out, is the strong survivorship bias that exists when universe results are created. The analyst is looking back in time to see how a manager performed relative to a peer group. The median manager from this universe is actually above the median of the group of managers in existence on day one, X years ago, because some of those managers have gone out of business during the X years. The plan sponsor may argue that it would not have chosen one of the since-vanished managers X years ago, so such a universe is indeed valid for comparative purposes.

## THE APPROPRIATE STYLE BENCHMARK

In a diversified fund, no single type of analysis will give equally precise information about each manager. To gain the most information on each manager, the plan sponsor must realize that different types of benchmarks are required for different managers. The objective is to imitate the manager's portfolio over time as closely as possible in terms of performance pattern without using a subjective stock selection process.

The easiest managers to measure using style benchmarks are likely to be both the quantitative managers who use linear models and the traditional stock-pickers who use a rigorous selection process based only on security characteristics. These managers often begin the selection process using a computer-generated stock screening model, which is easy to replicate given the appropriate database and software. For these managers, the most accurate style benchmark is the normal portfolio of securities selected through successive screens of the universe of stocks. This is not simply a mechanical process, however, because some of the managers' screens may use custom statistics, such as free cash flow calculated from individual companies' financial statements.

The portfolios of opportunistic managers are more difficult to model using normal portfolios. This difficulty stems from the changing style of these managers. As different styles (growth or value), industries, or market cap ranges appear to be attractive, these managers attempt to take advantage of their potential profits. Thus, the basket of securities an opportunistic manager would consider for investment purposes is the entire universe of securities. These managers require a broader benchmark, such as the Russell 3000.

Some managers are asked to outperform the better of two indexes. I have seen this in practice only in the international area, where a manager is asked to outperform the international market, as well as the domestic alternative (in order to justify investing internationally). For contrarian growth/value managers who sway with opportunity, the analogous request would be to outperform the greater of the Russell Growth and Value indexes. In practice, however, these managers prefer to be measured against the broad market, generally the S&P 500.

The most difficult manager to model may be the hedge manager. Some hedge managers hold a high percentage of derivative and international securities, which are not captured well by either a basket of securities or an index. Yet most equity managers can be compared to some universe of managers, and the hedge fund manager is no exception.

Universes exist for large- or small-cap growth or value managers, yield-driven managers, broad market managers with or without style tilt, and more recently for hedge fund, risk arbitrage, and market-neutral managers. Using universe percentiles is less labor-intensive than creating custom normal portfolios for the managers, but it has its drawbacks as well. In some cases, the data are available only quarterly. To see how well a manager is tracking a benchmark, more frequent data are desirable.

Another possible drawback is that some of the participants of these universes do not belong in their universe. This is a serious problem and common in the industry. Many data compilers take managers literally when they claim to be "value" managers, but who would claim to buy overpriced stocks? Thus, the participants in a particular universe should be reviewed before using it for comparative purposes. Also, as discussed above, there is the problem of survivorship bias.

We use universe comparisons internally with some caution. Universe data are most helpful when looking at risk/return scatter diagrams. We do not currently use universe medians for individual manager benchmarks, as we prefer normal portfolios where appropriate, and for our other managers, the universe comparisons lack sufficient history.

## DEVELOPING NORMAL PORTFOLIOS

We work with a consultant to create, update, and maintain manager normal portfolios. In some cases, the manager already has a working relationship with some consultant, and has previously constructed and is maintaining his or her normal portfolio. Through this relationship, the manager truly understands a particular investment style as well as the implications of any performance attribution results that are produced by these systems. This interest in and attention to normal portfolios tells us (and a plan sponsor) something about the manager's sophistication.

Creating a normal portfolio for a manager is a time-consuming process that requires attention at least annually, preferably semiannually. It also requires extensive computer resources and databases, which are becoming easier to obtain. At least three years of monthly portfolios are needed for construction of a meaningful normal. Unless the plan sponsor has the human resources necessary, which is unlikely, the best route is to hire a consultant for the initial task and ongoing maintenance. This creates a three-party arrangement, which can sometimes result in circular arguments.

Managers have a variety of reactions to having a normal portfolio created. Some managers are eager to find a benchmark that closely mirrors their style and performance results. These managers become actively involved in communications with the consultant, and in some cases, also engage their own consultant to verify or argue the nuances of the normal construction.

In our reevaluation process, we have seen a variety of responses to the normals presented to the managers. One of our value managers, for example, argued that the industry weights that fell out of the screening process were inappropriate. Usually, industry adjustments are not made in the normal portfolio unless it is a defined element of the manager's stock selection process, which it was in this case. The normal was altered to reflect this investment restriction.

One of our high-yield equity managers argued that the primary screen employed in his normal (yield > market) was not strong enough to capture his style. His yield was consistently higher than the yield of the normal portfolio, but the yield of the normal was much closer to the yield of his portfolio than to that of the market. The problem with using a more restrictive universe is that not enough names appear to result in a diversified normal. The normal needs to be large enough that its performance is not impacted by the performance of any single stock in it.

A third manager provided us with normal portfolios for two of his strategies that our consultant found unacceptable. One normal had several risk exposure values that were significantly different from his managed portfolio. The most extreme difference was in the exposure to the size factor, where the normal differed from the actual portfolio by 0.77 standard deviations. Size is the most easily captured variable, and 0.10 standard deviations is the maximum difference our consultant tolerates.

The other normal portfolio had a problem with coverage of the actual investments. The normal contained 746 securities, the active portfolio held 53 names, and the overlap in names was 17, or 32% of the managed portfolio. Our consultant considers a coverage of 70% to be the minimum tolerated for a meaningful normal.

Some managers feel their investment process is proprietary, and should not be revealed for construction of a normal portfolio. Others feel it is impossible to imitate their investment process with a black box. Rather than specify an exact process, a manager may decide to let the historical portfolio speak for itself. These managers may not want compensation to be based on their performance relative to a normal that they had no part in constructing. Sponsors should note that it is still important to maintain a normal on such managers for internal measurement purposes.

Once normal portfolios or weighted index benchmarks have been established for each manager, it is important to run the entire analysis through a single consultant for consistency. The resulting information should be shared with the managers. To avoid any misinterpretation because of different calculations of portfolio characteristics by different software or databases, the listing of securities in the normal should be shared with managers. Managers can then perform any analysis on this portfolio that they would perform on their own databases of stocks used in everyday security selection, and see the similarity between their invested and normal portfolios.

The ultimate decision to use some type of style benchmark rests with the plan sponsor. Some plan sponsors have refused to hire a manager who was not willing both to participate in the construction of a normal portfolio and to be compensated on the basis of performance relative to this normal. Other sponsors may analyze managers using some form of style analysis without the manager's awareness.

The concept of normal portfolios is becoming more widely accepted among equity managers, however, and many of them have BARRA'S PC product in-house. They construct their own normal portfolio, and adjust their portfolios using this system. It is optimal for a manager to own, or at least take ownership in, a benchmark. The best scenario is one in which the manager works with the sponsor or consultant to create a normal portfolio to be used for several clients, and one upon which manager compensation is based.

## INTERNAL USE OF STYLE BENCHMARKS

We use style benchmarks primarily in three ways. First, we ana-lyze the manager's past performance relative to their normal portfolios. Second, we consider the current risk exposures of the portfolios and the aggregate relative to those of our performance target. Third, we look for changes in a manager's or a fund's style by considering changes in the risk profile.

Comparison of manager performance to the performance of a normal portfolio is more precise than a similar comparison to an index. The characteristics of an index vary considerably from those of a manager's portfolio. For instance, as of December 1993, financial service and utility stocks constituted 24% and 23% of the Russell Value index, respectively. These weightings were significantly higher than the universe of value managers, and considerably higher than either our Equity-Income fund or our Value Equity fund, as seen in Exhibit 5. This means that the market's love or hate of the financial sector could cause our fund to under- or overperform. A normal portfolio will not have these extreme biases relative to the managed portfolio. We also note that we believe that significant outperformance of a normal port-folio is rare.[1]

To understand the potential for tracking error in the future, current risk exposures of the managed portfolios are compared to the risk profile of the performance target. In our Growth Equity fund, as seen above, we have a bias toward smaller-cap securities in the growth area. This is a deliberate exposure, as we have confidence in our managers and have not chosen to neutralize this bias with a completeness fund. Under-standing this bias helps us understand the strong outperfor-mance of the fund recently, as small-cap stocks were the big winners in the market.

---

[1] Measuring outperformance is a complex issue, and requires a chapter of its own. Two primary issues must be addressed. The first is that the alpha/noise ratio is usually too small to establish a statistically significant relationship. This is almost always true unless a manager's returns have an $R^2$ above 0.95 with the style benchmark, which is rare. (For the mathematics, see H. Russell Fogler, "A Modern Theory of Security Analysis," *Journal of Portfolio Management* (Spring 1993), p.11.) The second issue is that the returns from the style benchmark should be adjusted to reflect rebalancing costs, which should reflect true transac-tions costs. These costs are subject to estimation error, particularly for less liq-uid stocks.

## Exhibit 5: Universe Economic Sectors
## Price Driven Universe
### December 31, 1993

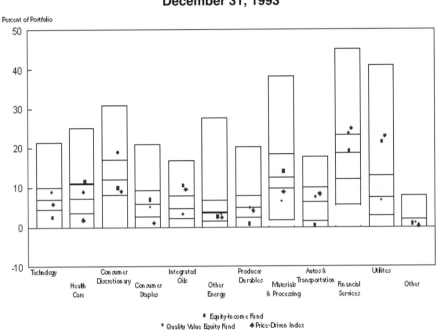

Source: Frank Russell Company

While we have not seen significant changes in any manager's style, an analysis of the risk characteristics of an aggregate normal has exposed a drift in style of a fund over time. As new managers were introduced and the weighting of existing managers in the fund changed, the market cap of the fund dropped, and "variability in markets" increased. The misfit of the fund was increasing, so we added a new manager employing a large-cap style to correct this misfit. As a result, our fund is much closer in risk profile to its target benchmark, and we are confident that the tracking error has been reduced.

# ALTERNATIVE FORMS OF STYLE ANALYSIS

Not all plan sponsors have the resources necessary to develop manager style analysis using normal portfolios. And while there is no substitute for sophisticated style analysis, there is a more user-friendly approach that we use as a check on our system and as a backup. This method is a combination of two types of analysis.

The first analysis examines the traditional portfolio character-istics of the managers, the fund, and the target index over time. These are readily available from the custodian in most cases. The plan spon-sor can look at these characteristics (such as market cap, P/E, P/B, earnings growth) to determine the deviation and growth in deviation of the managers and the fund from the index. This gives insight into the current risk exposure of the fund, the change in this exposure over time, and the potential for tracking error in the future.

The second type of analysis is based on historical performance of the fund, and is commonly referred to as "style analysis." Several consultants provide this software, which may be installed in the plan sponsor's computer or network. The program produces a two-dimen-sional map with a range of large- to small-cap on one axis, and a range of value to growth emphasis on the other. The market cap and value/growth dimensions are defined by the user according to a selection of indexes, such as the Russell 1000 and 2000 Growth and Value indexes. Then, the fund, the target index, and individual manager's return his-tories are plotted according to optimal fit along these dimensions.

This analysis gives insight into performance similarity of managers and funds to the indexes over time, and rolling time peri-ods may be used to see the migration of style over time. The style of a fund in its current composition can be seen by creating a compos-ite of the managers currently in use at their current weights, indicat-ing any adjustments made by the plan sponsor to better track the target of the fund.

These two analyses introduce the sponsor to equity style anal-ysis, and may spark an interest in using normal portfolios at some future time.

## CONCLUSION

We believe it is important to remember that most managers have an expertise in some niche of the market, and their performance should be analyzed relative to that niche. While the performance of each man-ager is important, it is vital that performance of an entire fund meet target expectations with very few negative surprises. The most rigor-ous approach to date involves the use of normal portfolios created for each manager and aggregated for each fund. The setup costs are high, but the detail of the resulting analysis makes it well worth the effort.

# CHAPTER 12

## STYLE MANAGEMENT: THE ESSENCE OF RISK CONTROL

GARRY M. ALLEN, CFA
CHIEF INVESTMENT OFFICER
VIRTUS CAPITAL MANAGEMENT

## INTRODUCTION

What would you do if the entire value-added returns of all your carefully selected active equity managers slipped through the unmanaged cracks in the structure of the pension fund? An impossibility, you believe? Actually, this is the primary condition of much of the U.S. pension fund industry in the mid-1990s. In many funds, it is the invisible disease responsible for overall underperformance, despite sufficient value added managers to achieve a fund's total return investment goal. Over time, unless the pension fund focuses on risk control, this investment malady may lay waste to all excess returns in the fund.

After a decade of investment management at the Virginia Retirement System, I believe that one of a pension manager's most important roles is controlling risk over the structure of the pension fund. The risk in the very structure of the pension fund can eventually consume all excess returns and active management fees, and negate carefully structured investment decisions if left unmanaged. This chapter sets forth the principles of total risk control management for the investment landscape unfolding in the mid-1990s and the 21st century. My comments assume familiarity with concepts developed in previous chapters.

## BENCHMARKS: THE FOUNDATION PRINCIPLE

To set the groundwork for risk control, managers must first understand the significance of benchmarks and their role in the investment management process. Benchmarks serve three primary purposes:

231

First, a benchmark serves as the home base or starting point for measuring value added capabilities. It captures where the fund would be, absent any active management positions in the portfolios. In this sense, it represents a measurement standard for returns.

Second, benchmarks serve as a quality standard for active management. Their existence creates a covenant between the plan sponsor and the money manager. In so doing, the benchmark replaces standard popular indexes, peer group comparisons, or "horse races." Thus, it customizes the risk profile of each fund's unique structure, given its set of active managers. Each fund's structure is unique because it represents a composite set of investment management decisions over time. In fact, as boards of trustees, investment committees, and staffs change over time, a specialized risk control fund represents the primary anchor for addressing subsequent money manager turnover and the uncertainty in the direction and source of returns in capital market investing.

Third, benchmarks serve as a form of due diligence. When constructed properly, benchmarks represent all the stocks about which an investment firm has an opinion. They define an investment firm's area of expertise. They turn a process of measuring generalized investment results into a process for measuring the value added skills of investment specialists. Benchmarks represent a firm's research composite, absent any active bets. In general, a firm should have a single benchmark for each investment product it offers.

Benchmarks reduce the noise inherent in the measurement of investment success or failure and thus reduce the time needed to determine the skill of a money manager. Benchmarks represent the foundation principle for risk control in a multiple-manager environment.

## THE PLAN SPONSOR DESIGNS THE COURSE

In the plan sponsor environment there is constant performance evaluation: assessing the investment trade-off between value versus growth styles of money management and large versus small size influences on the portfolio. The evaluation is complicated by the fact that the industry's traditional performance standard — the S&P 500 — is only part of the U.S. equity market. The S&P 500 represents approximately 75% of the total equity capital structure of the United States. Hidden from most evaluation standards is the fact that the S&P 500 misses the 25% of the U.S. equity market primarily devoted to medium- and small-capitalization growth and value stocks.

In reality, the S&P 500 represents two combined indexes for large value and large growth stocks. Proponents of active management should delight in this division of style. By analogy, imagine a tennis match where the S&P 500 player hits a single tennis ball to your side for play. In return, you have the choice of hitting a large value ball or a large growth ball back. In the 1990s, when returns are expected to revert to the historical norm, the distinction between large value and large growth stocks represents a powerful approach for layering and capturing excess returns. Style management represents the intellectual centerpiece for the next generation of top-tier money managers in the 1990s and beyond.

## THE PLAN SPONSOR AND THE MANY FACES OF RISK

No matter how many managers a sponsor selects, the pension manager charged with risk control for the total equity fund is the rudder that guides the pension fund through the volatile waters of uncertainty. I like to think of volatility as "the heartbeat of uncertainty." While adding numerous managers reduces risk fractionally at the margin, adding a risk control manager reduces risk geometrically at the core of the pension fund. High-quality risk control earns the pension fund incremental return by reducing risk per unit of return (i.e., it increases return per unit of risk).

Risk always wears a disguise before it strikes. It is not until after the fact that the true unmasking of risk takes place. Risk control techniques are able to reduce risk but not eliminate it totally. Market-neutral strategies may be overwhelmed by risk unless style neutrality is also achieved. Sector-neutral strategies push the risk onto stock selection as the primary determinant of excess returns. And time and time again, we see stock-specific risk escape through the safety net thrown by a large group of security analysts.

At the pension fund level, the plan sponsor has primary responsibility for the risk inherent in the structure of the pension fund. Exhibit 1 illustrates unmanaged risk. In this schematic representation we see a significant degree of overlap among active managers, where value managers are heavily loaded with growth stocks, and growth managers own significant value stock positions. The darker area represents all the unmanaged risk of the fund. It is here that additional investment risk and return opportunities exist in the U.S. capital markets, but the sponsor illustrated in Exhibit 1 has neither exploited nor neutralized its impact on the fund. It is this unmanaged darkness that overwhelms the collective skill of value added managers and absorbs the fees paid for high-expectation portfolios. It is the sponsor's most important area of risk control responsibility.

## Exhibit 1: Unmanaged Risk

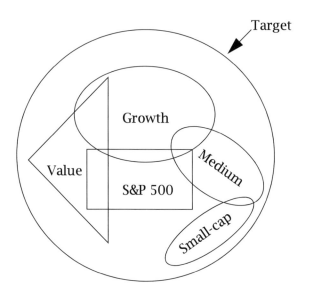

The overarching investment principle neglected in Exhibit 1 is the avoidance of uncompensated risk. Uncompensated risk is that unmanaged risk that has no expectation of return associated with it. Management of uncompensated risk is achieved by effective control of the risk structure of the pension fund.

Two primary types of risk exist at the fund structure level. First, there is manager risk. This risk is largely controllable by diversification across a number of managers. The second level of risk is style risk. This is the predominant form of risk in large U.S. pension funds. Style risk arises from too much or too little growth or value in the aggregate equity portfolio, relative to its composition in the structure of the U.S. equity market. When a pension fund moves in a significant direction toward growth or value unintentionally, an unannounced bet has entered the portfolio structure absent an invitation. The resulting unbalanced style position is the genesis of unmanaged or uncompensated risk.

I often say that "diversification is our friend." At the same time, a close correspondence to the U.S. equity markets is desirable, absent an intended style-tilted strategy. A graphic of style-managed risk appears in Exhibit 2. Notice that the problem of manager overlap in Exhibit 1 has been eliminated.

## Exhibit 2: Style-Managed Risk

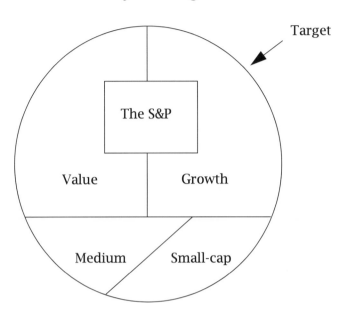

# THE TOTAL RETURN PRINCIPLE: IDENTIFY THE WEALTH BUILDERS

In general, it is appropriate to think of the plan sponsor as the risk controller and the active money manager as the wealth builder or wealth maximizer. It is here that the focus on risk shifts to the individual money manager level. The goal is to make the best decision possible in the hiring, retention, or termination of money managers. This is best achieved by an accurate assessment of the individual manager's performance over time.

Customized manager benchmarks are an important component of the sponsor's ultimate ability to achieve significant risk control at the level of the total pension fund. Hence, the sponsor's mindset is that of managing a single aggregate portfolio aimed at total risk control. The sponsor's success in this area will determine the degree of excess return that survives the full investment process.

Remember, however, that the product of process alone is simply control over investment due diligence and compliance. The product of risk control is a higher return per unit of risk taken. Sponsors often seek one at the expense of the other, resulting in undermanagement of the pension fund's full potential.

Three primary methodologies have emerged to assist money managers and plan sponsors in their quest for risk control. All methodologies are represented by well-known consultants and add to the sponsor's ability to control risk.

First, there are indexed-based benchmarks developed by 1990 Nobel Laureate William F. Sharpe. This approach offers elegance and simplicity to a world immersed in complexity and conflicting opinion. At the heart of this methodology is the ability to separate and distinguish the skills of active money management from hidden style effects driven by the market. In this methodology, a money manager's total returns are translated into the set of asset class effects (e.g., style classes such as large growth, large value, medium growth, medium value, and small U.S. domestic stocks) that produced the manager's set of total returns. Any returns unclaimed by these style asset class impacts are attributable to the stock selection skill of the money manager. Plan sponsors like the cost effectiveness and timeliness of this approach.

Second, there are factor-based benchmarks made popular by the quantitative consulting firm BARRA. This approach focuses on risk factor descriptions. The result is a mix of stock portfolios that resemble the overall characteristics of the money manager. Factor models are labor-intensive and can be a challenge to communicate to plan sponsors.

Third, there are asset-based benchmarks pioneered by consultants Richards & Tierney. This is the most comprehensive approach to customized benchmarks because it relies upon the money manager's underlying asset portfolios and selection universes to construct very tight, passive, investable portfolios representing the manager's systematic investment process. Because maximum attention is given to individual asset holdings, the persistent trends in historical portfolios are captured. This approach is built around a focused attention to detail, and requires a significant amount of time for construction.

Common to all three types of customized benchmarks is the decomposition of returns from style versus those from the active management process. The benchmark should capture the essence of the manager's style without being invasive of the manager's value added process. This is the toughest issue to be resolved in the construction of style benchmarks. Remember, the benchmark's tightness of fit around the money manager's systematic investment process is critical for the sponsor, who will then aggregate these benchmarks to form a composite benchmark for the fund's highest level of overall risk control.

All three customized benchmark methodologies are compatible, but not interchangeable. The indexed-based approach is appropriate for the highest policy level analysis of the pension fund. It is also powerful for a first viewing of a money manager's general style and value-added return capabilities. When aligned with factor-based techniques, the combination of indexed and factor-based techniques provides great insight for a top- and medium-level view of the power of a manager's investment process. The asset-based approach is most valuable at the implementation level, and provides a useful framework for such practices as performance-based fees because of its high precision at the individual asset level.

At the heart of this process is the goal of understanding the manager's active decision process. Once inside the true active management component, the plan sponsor is positioned to discern valuable information designed to make the shortest possible *informed* leap of faith in hiring an active money manager. First, the decision-maker is empowered with a benchmark that represents a passive, investable core should the active management process fall short of expectations. Second, the removal of style effects from total returns is designed to reveal the stock selection skill of the active manager. Third, the *consistency* of excess returns apart from style is revealed. Fourth, the decision-maker can now measure the degree of active management on a spectrum from extremely active to "closet indexing." In summary, the focus is fully on the *active* skills of the manager.

## A STATEMENT OF BENEFITS

A specific statement of benefits describes the advantages each constituency gains in the value chain linking the plan sponsor and the money manager.

### Sponsor's Point of View

The plan sponsor must establish a clear declaration of investment objectives. Clarity is valued over generalization. A vague set of investment objectives starts the entire investment process down a path that compounds confusion and unrewarded risk rather than returns.

In a large, multi-manager environment, the sponsor's highest purpose is to seek control over unintended style-related risk. Style is to plan sponsors what stocks are to investment managers. It is the plan sponsor's understanding of style-related risk that allows the sponsor to identify and separate active risk (created by money managers) from unmanaged or misfit risk (created by the money management structure of the pension plan). Misfit risk is another name for uncompensated risk. It is the risk found in the unclaimed territory between the sponsor's target (e.g., the Russell 3000) and the sponsor's aggregate equity portfolio. The sponsor's mastery of style management pays significant dividends.

A variety of points summarize why it is important for plan sponsors to achieve a high level of understanding of equity style management:

1. Style (value and growth) and size (large and small) represent two of the major components of systematic risk and return in the equity market.

2. Style dominates even the most skillful manager's returns.

3. Style movements are undergirded by the business cycle.

4. The lack of sponsor implementation of style management leads to excessive manager turnover because reasons for termination are misidentified.

5. The exclusion of style in decision making minimizes the impact of manager hire/terminate/retain decisions.

6. Manager fees may be ineffectively and unproductively spent when manager returns are not related to style by plan sponsors.

7. Many skillful managers are terminated because style and skill are not separated. Conversely, managers in a timely style may be retained because style bias is not accounted for.

8. Avoiding style management ignores the plan sponsor's highest responsibility for strategic management of the structure of the total equity fund.

9. In the absence of style management, huge amounts of added value can be lost through faults in the structure of the pension fund.

10. The true level of active risk is identified when style risk and active risk are separated and accounted for.

11. Style management leads to a more sensible allocation of assets among a fund's top managers.

12. Style management positions the plan sponsor for a stronger management fee negotiation position.

13. Style management reduces the level of uncompensated risk in the plan, and thus improves the risk-reward trade off.

14. Style management identifies and captures greater rewards from truly active management.

15. Style management is among the richest sources of excess return in the marketplace.

## Money Manager's Point of View

In general, style explains 80%-90% plus of an active manager's set of investment returns. That is the major reason the subject of style cannot be ignored. Currently, style is a domain largely unexplored by plan sponsors, and largely unexploited by money managers. Consultants have long commanded this vast territory of opportunity by arbitrarily restricting a money manager's categorization, without the fundamental knowledge of style analytics. This has kept the two major styles of investment, value and growth, locked in sometimes bitter competition. The plan sponsor is almost always the real loser through heavy manager casualties, attended by costly portfolio liquidations and new searches. Greater rewards from truly active management are attainable via this twin passage through style and risk control.

In addition, the best money managers will not just survive, but may in fact be worth *performance-based fees*. This is particularly so if performance-based fees result in a "win - win" situation for the plan sponsor and money manager, in that a manager commits not to overload a liquidity-constrained methodology with excessive assets under management.

I see the following *investment megatrends* for the 21st century:

1. The two greatest investment revelations of this decade are: First, that style explains 80% to 90% of most active managers returns, and second, that the S&P 500 represents the twin indexes of large value and large growth. These are "The Laws Of Investment Relativity" for the 21st century.

2. The world of active money management is not as active as once believed. Recognition of this fact by plan sponsors empowers the sponsor to take control of the pension fund.

3. Investable style indexes and normals raise the ante for active management.

4. Investment technology has placed astute plan sponsors in a position to identify and manage risk at the highest level of the pension fund. Risk management enhances returns by reducing unrewarded risk.

5. The best money managers will survive — and be worth performance-based fees.

The upshot is that the remainder of the 1990s and beyond will focus on risk control, style management, and capital preservation as the foundation of investment returns.

# CHAPTER 13

## MEASURING AND MONITORING EQUITY INVESTMENT STYLE: IS IT WORTH THE EFFORT?

*CHARLES TRZCINKA, PH.D.*
*STATE UNIVERSITY OF NEW YORK AT BUFFALO*

### INTRODUCTION

As the previous chapters document, the style management concept has become accepted throughout the money management business. Pension fund sponsors are increasingly demanding that equity managers identify their "investment style," and consultants are designing ever more sophisticated methods of determining the "true" investment style of equity managers. Motivating these efforts appears to be a belief that measuring and monitoring style leads to better portfolios. In Chapter 5, Richard Roll shows that there seems to be an extra return per unit of risk for paying attention to style, if risk measures meet certain technical requirements.

But is it worth the cost trying to find this extra return? Forcing money managers into investment styles, or allocating money on the basis of investment style can have significant costs in terms of total performance, because adopting an investment style implies that a manager will not invest in certain securities. Constraints on the selection of securities can result in suboptimal performance, that is, lower returns or higher risk. Furthermore, even if a style manager earns extra returns on average, not all money managers will achieve the style's excess returns. This means that a sponsor must spend resources on monitoring the style of managers. Thus, before style investing is adopted, its costs and benefits must be carefully weighed.

The purpose of this chapter is to use the data and analyses developed in previous chapters to help sponsors decide whether style management is worth the effort. We outline the questions that a pension fund sponsor needs to answer to determine the costs and benefits of managing a large fund by using style management. We choose the perspective of a sponsor because sponsor demand for style management appears to be the major change in money management over the past five years. We argue that sponsors must first decide what style management is intended to achieve. Once they have a clear idea of the purpose of style management, they can estimate (guess at) the costs and benefits depending on the requirements and the measurement tools available to achieve the purpose.

We do not propose to answer the question in the title of the chapter, "Is style management worth the effort?" because there is little objective evidence to support any answer. Our discussion of the questions that sponsors should ask before they adopt a style management approach is intended to help sponsors address the issue themselves.

## WHAT IS "STYLE MANAGEMENT"?

"Style management" is widely defined as making investments in two phases. In the first phase, either the money manager or the sponsor must identify the set of securities that the manager intends to consider and the general approach to buying securities in this set. When a money manager chooses an approach and identifies a set of securities, the manager is said to adopt an "investment style." For example, a "small growth" money manager considers only growth companies with a comparatively low equity capitalization. The second phase of style management occurs when a sponsor allocates most or all of the available money primarily on the basis of investment styles offered by managers.

## THE PURPOSES OF STYLE MANAGEMENT

There are multiple motives for adopting style management, but they are all ultimately related to the bottom line: increasing the return of the total portfolio. On a basic level, a sponsor may simply want to enhance communication with its money manager. In more advanced uses, style management may facilitate performance measurement, allow better risk control and diversification, and allow the sponsor to "bet" on a style. We discuss each of these in turn.

## Communication

By identifying the investment style of a money manager, the sponsor is obtaining information about the money manager's expertise, organization, and (possibly) likely success. A "small growth" money manager probably looks very different from a "large value" money manager because their processes of gathering information are very different.[1] The "small growth" manager specializes in finding small companies with good ideas. This manager will have different contacts and different expertise from the "large value" manager who invests in large, stable companies producing comparatively constant earnings.

By identifying the investment style, the sponsor becomes more informed about the subset of stocks that the manager will consider, and the sponsor can judge whether the money manager's organization (i.e., contacts, administration, coordination of efforts) is effective for the investment style. Thus, style management can be both an efficient way of classifying and summarizing portfolio selection and a tool that the sponsor uses to evaluate the manager's "culture" and organization.

## Performance Benchmark

The second purpose of style management is to measure the manager's performance. A manager with an objectively identifiable style may earn a higher return than other managers with the same style; but the style itself may still do poorly in a particular period. In that case, if measured against broad market benchmarks, this manager will be judged a poor performer. Knowing that a manager did well all the same, relative to other managers in the style, may help in satisfying portfolio constraints and in predicting the future performance of the manager.

The sponsor may have some style objectives because of portfolio constraints. For example, political objectives may give a sponsor an incentive to allocate money to managers who specialize in small firms. The presence of this constraint makes it important to determine the best small-firm manager. Some portfolio constraints may not be as obvious, however. Perhaps a sponsor needs to justify the selection of stocks using easily understood concepts. Investing by style and measuring performance by style may serve this purpose.

Measuring performance relative to a style benchmark may also provide information about a manager's future performance. A style benchmark is simply a portfolio of stocks constructed from the subset

---

[1] See Elroy Dimson and Paul Marsh, "An Analysis of Brokers' and Analysts' Unpublished Forecasts of U.K. Stock Returns," *Journal of Finance* (December 1984), for a discussion of the differences in analyst forecasts and the evidence that some forecasts are valuable.

of securities defined by the style. It represents a passive investment strategy. If the manager can consistently beat this passive strategy, then either the passive strategy itself is a consistent poor performer, or the manager has valuable information or abilities. The style benchmark can be constructed so that the sponsor can determine the likelihood that the benchmark itself is a poor performer. If a manager consistently beats such a benchmark, this may imply that the manager will do well in the future. (Of course, there is still the possibility that the style will do poorly; but at least the sponsor has more information about the quality of the manager.)

## Diversification and Risk Control by Sponsor

Diversification calls for choosing securities for a portfolio that have low correlations. If the securities are perfectly negatively (i.e., inversely) correlated, then only two securities need to be selected. Typically, however, securities are positively correlated so that portfolio managers need many stocks to diversify fully. The key problem in diversifying is to be able to predict the *future* correlation of securities. Correlations are unstable over any period, and models of correlation do not predict correlations very well.[2]

Style management can be a useful tool in diversifying a portfolio because correlations among investment styles are much more stable than correlations among securities. For example, Exhibit 1 in Chapter 1 (by Jon Christopherson and C. Nola Williams) and Exhibits 2-5 in Chapter 5 (by Richard Roll) show that there is significant correlation over time in variables typically used to represent style. The presence of relatively stable correlations over time enables a sponsor to diversify by selecting managers with a large number of stocks in each style. This may provide better diversification than trying to diversify simply using the characteristics of stocks.

The correlation is not the only statistic that is more stable for investment styles than for securities. A consistent research finding is that standard measures of risk and return are more stable for groups of assets than for individual assets.[3] This means that a sponsor can use an objectively identifiable style for risk control. Risky styles can be eliminated or added to modify the total risk of the overall portfolio. The sponsor is more assured of the future risk of the portfolio than if only a few managers with broad market investments are selected.

---

[2] See Campbell Harvey, "Time-Varying Conditional Covariances in Tests of Asset-Pricing Models," *Journal of Financial Economics*, Volume 24, 1989, pp. 289-317, for extensive tests of the time variation of covariances.

[3] See Eugene Fama and Kenneth French, "The Cross Section of Expected Stock Returns," *Journal of Finance* (June 1992), pp. 427-465, for a discussion of this point.

Finally, if a sponsor is allocating money to a group of managers on the basis of some criterion other than investment style, and is not paying attention to the balance of styles of a fund, the fund may be overinvested in some styles and underrepresented in others. Identifying the styles of managers selected and allocating money to a fund that "completes" the fund with respect to styles is another way to diversify the portfolio. Completeness funds are discussed in Chapter 8 (by Christopher Campisano and Maarten Nederlof).

## Betting on Style

The fourth use of style management is applicable when sponsors think they have an ability to predict style. The sponsor allocates money to managers in the particular styles that are expected to do well. The strategy is similar to market timing in that a portfolio manager tries to predict the future performance of risky securities versus cash. There is little evidence that market timing is better than being fully invested in risky securities, but market timing is common among money management.[4]

To the best of our knowledge, there have been no studies on whether trying to predict a style is a successful strategy. It is worth noting, however, that style betting does not have the same costs as market timing. The most significant cost of market timing is that the investor will be in cash when prices of risky assets are increasing. If a sponsor tries to bet on styles, and the bet is wrong, though, a portfolio can still be invested in risky assets and can be well-diversified. Chapter 6 (by John Dorian and Robert Arnott) addresses the issue of style prediction at the individual manager level.

## THE REQUIREMENTS OF STYLE MANAGEMENT

A critical element in a decision on whether to adopt style management is the effectiveness of the tools used in style management. Since the requirements of style management depend on the purpose for which it is chosen, the definition of an effective tool will vary. Here we discuss each purpose's requirements, after first elaborating style management's basic elements. Following that, we discuss how effective the tools of style management are in meeting these requirements.

---

[4] For a review of over 200 studies of performance measurement see Ravi Shukla and Charles Trzcinka, "Performance Measurement of Managed Portfolios," *Financial Markets, Institutions and Instruments Series*, Volume 1, Number 4 (Cambridge, MA: Basil Blackwell Publishers, 1992).

## Basic Requirements of Any Purpose

Style management begins with the ability to define some criteria that clearly identify the set of assets that the money manager intends to buy. The criteria most often used are firm-specific characteristics that classify stocks into a "growth" or "value" category or a size category. There are several other criteria discussed in this book. The key feature of each is its relationship with expected return, risk, or potential for diversification.

The criteria must also be objectively identifiable by an observer who is independent of the manager. This is important, and controversial, because the next step in the process is to determine which criteria describe a manager. If the criteria that define a style are to be believed, they must be relatively easy to verify. The controversy, which we discuss later, relates to the means of verifying the criteria.

## Communication

If the purpose of style management is to communicate the investment strategy of the money manager, then effective criteria cause a manager to be categorized in terms of some unique subset, such as a "growth" or "value" manager. If the manager falls into more than one subset, the criteria lose their ability to communicate a strategy. It makes no sense, for example, to classify a manager as a "value-growth" manager because that classification reveals nothing about the type of stocks that the manager will buy.

A second requirement of an effective criterion is that it must reveal useful characteristics about the manager. The criteria are usually related to the securities purchased but not always. For example, a small-capitalization manager buys firms with a capitalization below some level, but what type of firms does a "quantitative" manager buy? The quantitative style classification may be useful because it describes the approach the manager uses in selecting securities, but it reveals nothing about the securities themselves.

Finally, to communicate what the manager is doing, the manager must have a stable style. This means that the manager must stay invested in the set of securities or use the approach for some time. If most managers are stable, and a few managers wander between one style or another, perhaps in some predictable manner, this pattern will still communicate information about the manager. This only works, however, if most managers are stable. If all managers wander, then there will be less information revealed about their investment choices.

## Performance Measurement

When style management is used for performance measurement, the manager is measured against a benchmark that represents a passive manager in the style. Different styles must thus result in different performance over time. It need not be the case that one style has a consistently higher return or risk than another, but each style must have a different return. Each style must have clear enough criteria so that a benchmark can be constructed that is widely believed to represent the style. This means that the performance of the style must be observable independently of observing a manager. It defeats the purpose of style management simply to compute the average of all managers who claim to use a style, because they all could underperform a simple, passive strategy that captures the style.[5] Finally, the manager must have a stable style. If the manager's style wanders, the benchmark will not represent the style of the manager.

## Diversification and Risk Control

When style management is used to diversify a fund and control risks, the manager's style must be objectively identifiable, and a manager must have a unique and stable style. The style must be clearly related to systematic risk if style management is to be used to measure and control risk. This means that the criteria should be related to either betas of securities or the responses of securities to factors. The stability of the manager's style is critical because it is impossible to control risk if manager's styles are constantly changing.

If style management uses criteria that are broad enough, then selecting managers from each style can serve to diversify the portfolio. If the criteria are narrow, such as "small-growth" or "large-value," then fund may have to use a "completeness" fund (discussed in Chapter 8) to diversify the portfolio more fully. If style management is used to diversify a fund, manager's styles need not be very stable if the tendency to change style is uncorrelated across managers. If managers change style randomly, then simply choosing a relatively large number of managers will diversify the fund. If managers are perfectly stable, then choosing a large number of styles will diversify the fund. Only if managers tend to move toward the same securities (for example, widely publicized stocks), will the change in styles reduce the ability of style management to diversify the total portfolio.

---

[5] Jeffery V. Bailey, "Are Manager Universes Acceptable Performance Benchmarks?" *Journal of Portfolio Management* (Spring 1992), uses conceptual arguments and presents empirical evidence to show that manager universes are *not* acceptable.

## Style Betting

Allocating money to styles expected to perform well in the future requires that the manager have an objectively identifiable style. The style must define a segment of the market where the prices of the assets are determined by supply and demand within the segment. This means that there must be some reasons why the supply and demand from other market segments do not act to eliminate the differences in prices.

Using style management to bet on the future performance of a sector of the market typically requires careful construction of the style benchmarks that are used to measure the performance of the manager. The sponsor who is betting on style usually wants to determine whether the manager is a top performer within a style because of chance or because of effective management. This is not logically a requirement of style betting, because the sponsor will make money with a below-average performer for the style if the sponsor guesses the style correctly. If sponsors have information about style performance, however, they do not want to use this information on poor managers and will typically demand well-constructed style benchmarks.

## THE TOOLS OF STYLE MANAGEMENT

The tools of style management are the ways to classify a manager objectively into a style. There are two general approaches, portfolio-based and return-based.

## Portfolio-Based Approach

A portfolio-based approach is (or is claimed to be) an intensive examination of the manager's portfolio and security selection procedures. The categorization of a manager can use objective criteria or subjective criteria, or both. For example, in Chapter 4, Jon Christopherson and Dennis Trittin argue that it is possible to develop an objective probability model that is based on the weights of various securities in the portfolio.

The strength of this approach is that it carefully examines the individual manager's organization and assets selected. This may lead to much better predictions of a manager's *future* style and can help refine the definition of "style" itself. The authors in this book argue that style should be a characteristic of the securities selected. Examining how managers fit securities together can reveal various subcategories of a particular style. For example, managers have recently offered "mid-cap" portfolios of stocks that are neither large nor small.

This tool is very good for communication and evaluation of a manager's selection process, and it is good for determining the diversification of the portfolio. The strength of the portfolio approach is that more information in the evaluation process will, on average, produce a more accurate guess of the manager's style, if the evaluation is unbiased and complete. The portfolio weights and selection process reveal much more about how a portfolio will be managed in the future than does examining the returns of the portfolio. This approach may also be good at judging the diversification of the portfolio because each security can be evaluated individually.

A potential weakness of this approach is that it is not easy to determine whether the evaluation has been complete and unbiased. The evaluator may have biases that cause certain information not to be evaluated or to be systematically misevaluated. To determine the biases of this approach, sponsors often use return-based analysis.

## Return-Based Approach

This tool uses a statistical relationship between the returns of the managed portfolio and some benchmark portfolio or portfolios to define the style of the managed portfolio. In Chapter 3, Steve Hardy shows that there are several important decisions in a return-based analysis. First, an appropriate benchmark (or benchmarks) must be selected. Second, the analyst must decide the time period over which the managed portfolio will be judged. Third, the analyst must determine the type of statistical model.

Probably the most critical choice is the indexes chosen to represent styles. The analyst can select some basic portfolios representing broad style categories, such as small-large and value-growth. An alternative strategy is to select indexes that represent important factors in stock prices. William Sharpe suggests a model using twelve indexes representing both domestic and international factors affecting stock prices.[6] The Sharpe factors are based on the type of securities. BARRA uses 68 stock-specific factors.[7] As Richard Roll discusses in Chapter 5, published research suggests that no more than five factors are relevant for representing security returns.

---

[6] William F. Sharpe, "Asset Allocation, Management Style and Performance Measurement," *Journal of Portfolio Management* (Winter 1992). The indexes Sharpe uses are: the Salomon Brothers 90-day Treasury bill index, the Lehman Brothers Intermediate-Term Government Bond Index, the Lehman Brothers Long-Term Government Bond Index, the Lehman Brothers Corporate Bond Index, the Lehman Brothers Mortgage-Backed Securities Index, the Sharpe/BARRA Value Stock Index, the Sharpe BARRA Growth Stock Index, the Sharpe/BARRA Medium Cap Index, the Sharpe/BARRA Small Cap Index, the Salomon Brothers Non-U.S. Government Bond Index, the FTA Euro-Pacific Ex-Japan Index, and the FTA Japan Index.

[7] See the BARRA Newsletter, Spring 1994, for a description of the factor returns and their use in performance attribution.

The choice of a time period and model are less important than the choice of indexes, but can significantly influence the results. The shorter the time period, the more likely a manager will have a stable style. But short time periods may not capture the ability of the manager to earn high returns and can be statistically unreliable. Three years is commonly used; but, for volatile styles, this period may be too short.

The typical model choice is among models that constrain the coefficients of the indexes to sum to one or leave the coefficients unconstrained. If the coefficients are unconstrained, the model can better represent the manager's style. The statistical jargon is that the model has more "degrees of freedom." If the coefficients are constrained, they can be interpreted as portfolio weights on the indexes. Constrained models must be estimated with an optimization technique, while unconstrained models can be estimated with statistical techniques that have well-known properties. Whether the choice of a model or a time period is important depends on the nature of the manager's returns, and any return-based approach needs to be tested for reliability.

The strength of a return-based approach is that it is objective, once the indexes, the time period, and the model are selected. The returns of the managed portfolio are used in a statistical model that relates them to the indexes or the factors. Any investigator with the data can replicate the results. Generally, sponsors will be more confident in results that can be replicated than with results that cannot. Replication also has the advantage of making the style easily understood.

The weakness of the return-based approach is that the statistical models are notoriously unstable.[8] Stock return data have a very low "signal-to-noise" ratio, and using such data to estimate statistical models does not produce very reliable estimates. Moreover, managers can change styles intentionally and unintentionally. The portfolio-based approach is, at least in principle, much more able to capture changing styles.

In summary, the return-based approach is better for performance evaluation where the results need to be objective. It may also be better for style betting, as it is very easy to examine the manager's performance against a broad array of sectors and style indexes. It may be less useful for communication and diversification than the portfolio-based approach because it examines less information than the portfolio-based approach.

---

[8] G. William Schwert, "Why Does Stock Volatility Change Over Time?" *Journal of Finance*, (December 1989), pp. 1115-1151, argues that very long time series such as 50 years or more are needed to estimate statistically reliable relationships. If models are estimated with 16 or 20 quarters of data, they may have very unstable parameters.

# WHAT DO WE KNOW ABOUT INVESTMENT STYLES?

Unfortunately, I believe we do not know much about investment styles. In theory, in a securities market where the prices of securities capture all relevant information, style management will not be more profitable than investing in any arbitrary subset of stocks. Further, if the sponsor does not diversify across styles, then style management will cause the sponsor's portfolio to be mean-variance *inefficient* and will earn less return per unit of risk than an efficient portfolio. Thus, evidence that style management earns a higher than expected risk-adjusted return is evidence that the security market is inefficient or that the risk adjustment model is wrong.

It is worth noting that even in an efficient market, style management may be valuable as a communication device and a diversification tool. Managers may specialize in subsets of assets simply to minimize transactions costs, and this specialization can be useful for building the total portfolio. Yet the belief persists that style managers can earn excess risk-adjusted returns. For example, Mary Ida Compton writes in Chapter 11, "We believe it is important to remember that most managers have an expertise in some niche of the market...."

Jon Christopherson and C. Nola Williams in Chapter 1 and Richard Roll in Chapter 5 provide direct evidence of the returns to style management. Christopherson and Williams show style returns relative to the Russell indexes. Roll shows that three variables that are commonly used to define equity style (size, earnings/price, and book/market) are statistically significant determinants of risk-adjusted returns. These authors conclude that there can be substantial returns to managing a portfolio by equity style. Roll, however, observes that a subtle technical problem may make style management seem more profitable than it actually is. If the indexes used to adjust for risk or to measure style are not themselves efficient portfolios, then the extra return earned by a style manager could actually be the return earned by an efficient portfolio. In short, the extra return may have nothing do with style.

Other than the studies in this book, there has been little direct evidence on investment styles as used by practitioners. Equity style management is not new, but its popularity has grown substantially over the past few years. It is likely that more direct evidence will be forthcoming.

There is indirect evidence on two aspects of style management. First, there have been numerous studies of the risk return relationship, some using variables that are commonly used in practice for defining style. Roll summarizes this evidence in Chapter 5, and uses it effectively to show the potential for style management. Second, any evidence of market inefficiency is evidence that style management can potentially earn more than a risk-adjusted return.

On this question, Fama provides a comprehensive review of the hundreds of studies on the question.[9] These studies can be quite useful for specific approaches used by money managers. Market efficiency studies often provide careful descriptions of how security prices vary and how information changes prices. As Fama observes, "Academics largely agree on the facts that emerge from the tests, even when they disagree about their implications for efficiency." He notes, however, that, logically, any test of market efficiency is both a test of the asset pricing model and market efficiency. He concludes that "it is a disappointing fact that, because of the joint-hypothesis problem, precise inferences about the degree of market efficiency are likely to remain impossible."[10]

## CHOICES AND QUESTIONS
## ABOUT STYLE MANAGEMENT

What should a sponsor do about style management? There are two possible answers. One, a sponsor can simply ignore it. Sponsors can look at the available evidence and the returns earned by style managers, and decide that the costs of being potentially undiversified and of having to monitor all the styles are not worth the benefit.

Two, a sponsor can adopt it. If so, the immediate question is how? As we discuss above, the requirements and implementation of style management depend on how it is used. If the sponsor uses style management to focus on the individual manager then style management can be used primarily for communicating and measuring performance. It can provide a description of how the manager selects securities, and it can help to differentiate a manager's performance from passive strategies. If the sponsor focuses primarily on the total portfolio, then style management can be used to diversify the portfolio and for making bets on styles.

In either case, it seems clear that, in principle, the best measurement approach is to use *both* return-based analysis and a portfolio-based approach to determining the style of a manager and the way a style fits into the sponsor's total portfolio. In prac-

---

[9] Eugene Fama, "Efficient Capital Markets II," *Journal of Finance* (December 1991), pp. 1575-1618.
[10] *Ibid.*, p. 1576.

tice, the tools used depend on their cost, and the vendors have an obligation to justify the cost.

To borrow a concept from engineering, it is worth restating that the securities markets have a very low "signal-to-noise" ratio. This means that the information in stock prices is difficult to extract. It is hard to determine whether securities are overpriced or underpriced, it is hard to judge the actual risk of a portfolio, and it is hard to determine whether a manager is adding value or is just lucky. Style management is an attempt by market participants — that is, people confronted with real choices — to make sensible decisions in a noisy, capricious market. Whether it continues to be popular depends entirely on whether it helps people make better decisions at a reasonable cost. This book is evidence that interest in providing serious answers to these questions is growing among those making the choices.

# INDEX